this is... citizenship studies

for key stage 4 and GCSE

Terry Fiehn
Julia Fiehn
Andrew Miller

Key words are defined in the list on pages 227–28.

Although every effort has been made to ensure that website addresses are correct at the time of going to press, Hodder Education cannot be held responsible for the content of any website mentioned in this book.

First published 2003
by Hodder Education, a member of the Hachette Livre UK Group,
338 Euston Road
London NW1 3BH

Reprinted 2004, 2005, 2006, 2008

Layouts by Jenny Fleet
Artwork by Countryside Illustrations, Janek Matysiak, Tony Randell, Steve Smith
Typeset in 11.5/13pt Bodoni Book by Wearset Ltd, Boldon, Tyne and Wear
Cover design by John Townson/Creation
Printed and bound in Italy

A catalogue entry for this book is available from the British Library.

ISBN: 978 0 7195 7723 9
TRB 978 0 7195 7724 6

this is... tudies

d GCSE

Contents

section 1

Citizenship in a democracy

Key words
- citizenship
- democracy
- human rights
- identity
- naturalisation

Everyone has different ideas on what it means to be a citizen in a democracy. People expect rights and freedom, but citizens also have important responsibilities towards one another. Different countries have different ideas about what citizenship involves. In this section, you will look at a variety of views and decide what you think are the most important rights and duties of citizens in a democracy like ours.

You will learn about:

- the principles of democracy
- the role of citizens in a democracy
- the legal definition of citizenship in Britain
- how this differs from other countries
- freedoms, and the threats to them
- human rights
- national identity.

You will use the following skills:

- expressing and justifying opinions about the issue of citizenship
- contributing to debates on citizenship
- imagining other people's experiences and explaining views that are not necessarily your own.

1.1 What is a democracy?

Democracy is often defined as:

'government
<u>of</u> the people,
<u>by</u> the people,
<u>for</u> the people'.

Of course, this is very difficult. With huge numbers of people in a country how do you get everybody to have a say in how to make society fairer and yet also get things done? You could spend all your time asking people for their opinion, finding there is lots of disagreement and so not actually doing anything to make things better. Nearly all changes will help some people but harm others. How do you decide whose interests to follow?

Winston Churchill once said, 'Democracy is the worst system of government, apart from all the others.' So, how do you get democracies to work? Not all working democracies around the world are the same, but they all share a belief in a set of principles, which try to give people as much say in their government as possible.

These principles can be summarised as:

A Representative and accountable government

B The rule of law and equality before the law

C Freedom of opinion, belief and association

Activity

Statements 1 to 15 below describe aspects of these three principles. Draw a table like the one below and put each statement into one of the columns. The first has been done for you.

A **Representative and accountable government**	B **The rule of law and equality before the law**	C **Freedom of opinion, belief and association**
	1 Everyone must obey the laws, including the members of the government	

1 Everyone must obey the laws, including the members of the government.
2 Everyone has the right to get together to discuss their views.
3 The press and the broadcast media (radio and TV) are free to write and broadcast what they want. The media are not controlled by the government.
4 An elected assembly (group of people) is specially set up to scrutinise (watch carefully) what the government is doing and criticise it or oppose it on behalf of the people, for example to stop corruption.
5 The laws, which everybody has to obey, are made by representatives who are elected by the people.
6 People have a right to information about their government. The government should not be allowed to keep what it does secret.
7 People who believe they have been treated unjustly by the legal system can appeal and get things put right if their appeal is upheld.
8 There should be equality before the law for everyone.
9 People should have religious freedom to worship as they choose, or not at all.

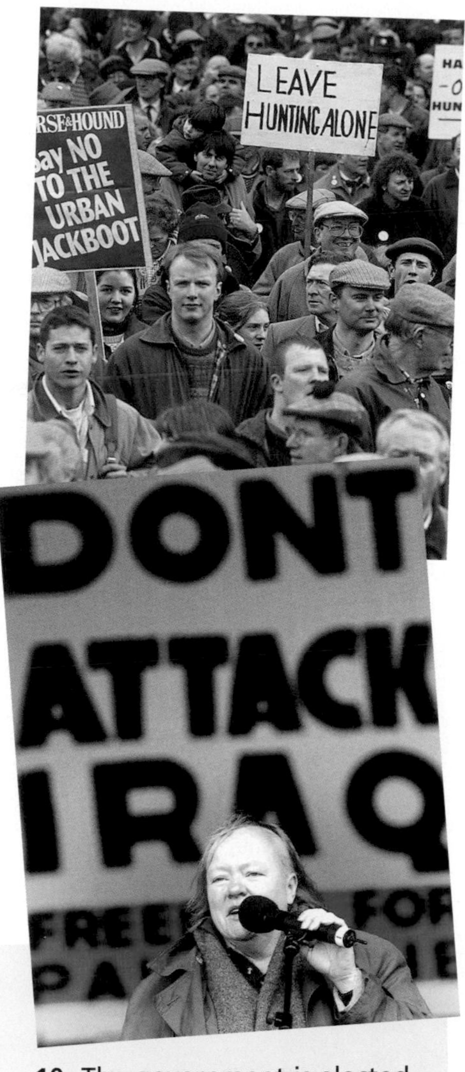

10 The government is elected for a fixed period of time so there is a regular opportunity for the people to change the government.
11 Trial is by a jury that is made up of ordinary people from every part of society.
12 Everyone has the right to join organisations like political parties and trade unions.
13 Every adult citizen has the right to vote, to join political parties and to take part in politics.
14 The system of justice is outside the direct control of the government so that it is fair.
15 There are clear and open procedures for the way the law operates.

Activity

Look at the following case studies.

1 What aspect of democracy is illustrated by each case?
2 In each case study, how did individuals help make democracy work?

Case study 1: *John Jones*

John Jones was tried for burglary. The evidence against him rested on witnesses who said they saw him at the scene. He was also found in possession of one of the items stolen from the house. He said he was somewhere else and that he had bought the item from a man in a pub. He was found guilty but was determined to prove his innocence and was given permission by the judge to appeal against the conviction. During the appeal new evidence was brought forward to prove that John Jones was not at the scene of the crime. The conviction was overturned and he was set free.

Case study 2: *The people of Risdale*

Many people in Risdale were very angry that their local hospital was closing its accident and emergency department. The nearest other A&E department was thirty kilometres away and the bus service was not regular or reliable. They were told that the cost of keeping the department open was too great. When a general election came round, one person stood for election as an independent candidate, campaigning on the single issue of keeping the department open. A majority of the voters of Risdale voted for him and he became their Member of Parliament, with a commitment to try to change the decision.

Case study 3: *The MP*

A member of the government was suspected by a journalist of taking bribes from a wealthy businessman. The businessman wanted to bring certain issues to the attention of government departments in order to help his business. The politician involved denied any wrongdoing. The journalist investigated and obtained evidence of bribes – not just money, but also trips abroad and free meals in expensive hotels. The journalist published the story in a national newspaper and, although the MP sued the paper, the evidence was upheld in court. The politician was sacked and voted out of Parliament at the next election.

1.2 What is active citizenship in a democracy?

People who live and work in a country have legal rights and duties. They are protected by the law, but also have to obey it. Active citizenship is not just about having a passport and being a citizen of a country. Many people who live in this country are citizens of other countries, especially now that Britain is a member of the European Union.

Active citizenship is also about how people behave towards one another, whether they help and support each other in their communities and work together in groups to improve things for everyone.

Active citizens are people who have opinions and want these to be heard. They use democratic processes to make things happen, in their school, college, workplace or community. This can include voting, taking part in local or national decision-making, joining community groups, helping others through voluntary work, joining a school council, and campaigning for change.

Activity

1 What sorts of things do you need to know to be an active citizen? Look at the list below. Put each sentence in order according to how important you think it is.

2 Add three things that you think it is important for an active citizen to know.

- the name of your Member of Parliament
- the services provided by your local council
- how to vote
- how to apply for social benefits
- how much tax you pay when you start work
- what the main political parties stand for
- what voluntary bodies exist to help different groups of people
- the words of the national anthem
- how to write a good protest letter
- what the law says about demonstrations
- your legal rights on arrest
- where your local council office is.

An active citizen is someone who has clear opinions about what they like about the world they live in and what they would like to change. Active citizens want to make a difference, to improve things for themselves and for others.

Learning to be an active citizen

Learning about citizenship in schools should help people learn how to discuss and debate, to form opinions, to get involved with other people to make a difference. But some people worry that citizenship lessons will simply be 'indoctrination' – teaching young people only the good things about their country.

Here is an e-mail sent to a radio programme website following a discussion about citizenship education. It is from a young woman who had been brought up in the USA.

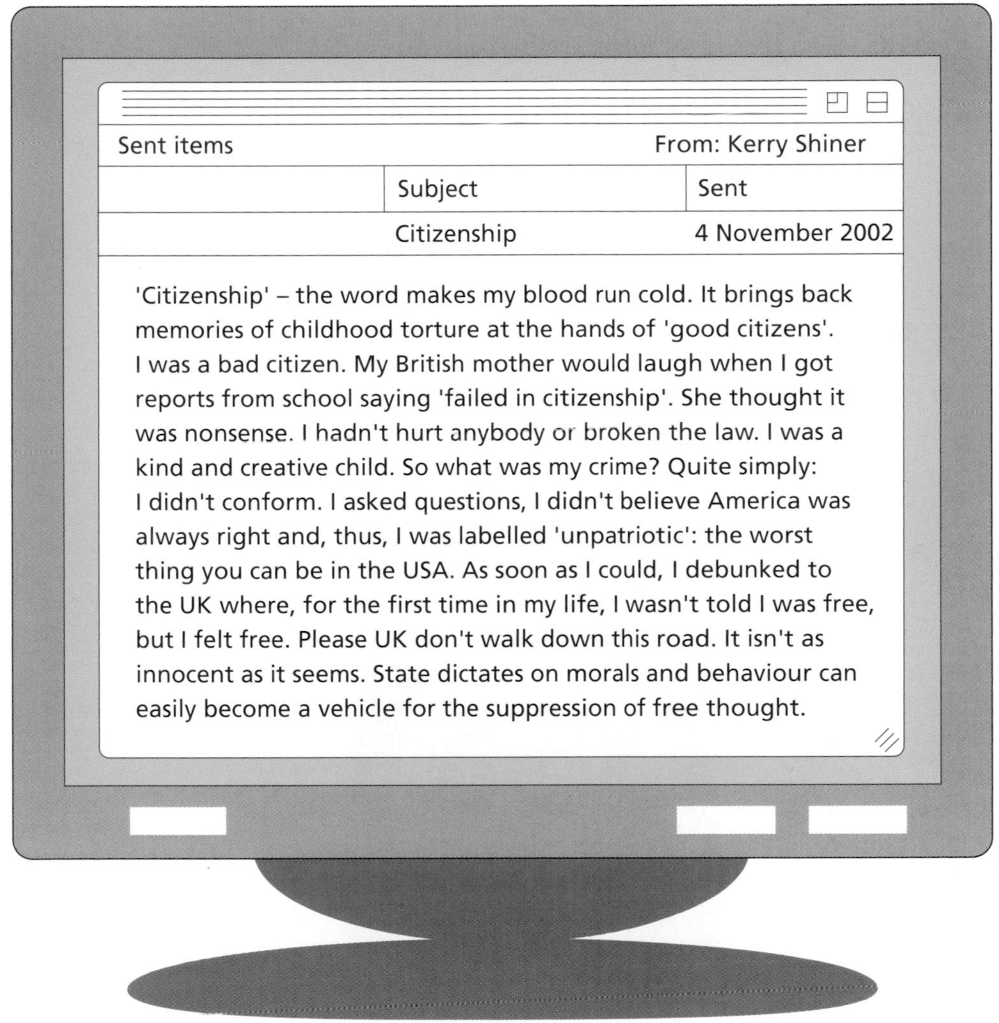

Sent items | From: Kerry Shiner

	Subject	Sent
	Citizenship	4 November 2002

'Citizenship' – the word makes my blood run cold. It brings back memories of childhood torture at the hands of 'good citizens'. I was a bad citizen. My British mother would laugh when I got reports from school saying 'failed in citizenship'. She thought it was nonsense. I hadn't hurt anybody or broken the law. I was a kind and creative child. So what was my crime? Quite simply: I didn't conform. I asked questions, I didn't believe America was always right and, thus, I was labelled 'unpatriotic': the worst thing you can be in the USA. As soon as I could, I debunked to the UK where, for the first time in my life, I wasn't told I was free, but I felt free. Please UK don't walk down this road. It isn't as innocent as it seems. State dictates on morals and behaviour can easily become a vehicle for the suppression of free thought.

Discuss

1 Why didn't Kerry like her citizenship lessons in America?
2 Do you think children should learn in school to be 'patriotic'?
3 What do you think your citizenship lessons should be like? Write a list of things you think young people should learn in school as young citizens.

1.3 What is British citizenship?

All people born in Britain are automatically British citizens. Some people also apply for citizenship. But there are many people living and working legally in the country who are not British citizens. They could be citizens of other European countries, or people who have received permission to visit, work or study here.

The ways to become a citizen

There are four main ways to become a British citizen (a citizen of the United Kingdom of Great Britain and Northern Ireland):

- by birth – if you are born in the UK and one parent is a British citizen or is settled in the UK
- by descent – if you are born abroad and have at least one British parent
- by registration – if you have a particular legal connection with the UK
- by naturalisation – a foreigner can apply to become a British citizen, but the decision is discretionary (as the authorities see fit) and depends on things like residence in the UK, good character and sufficient knowledge of the English language.

The rights of a citizen

Being a full British citizen gives you the following rights:

A passport and the right to go in and out of the UK without a visa
The right to live in the UK, called the 'right of abode'
The right to claim benefits in the UK
EUROPEAN UNION
UNITED KINGDOM OF GREAT BRITAIN AND NORTHERN IRELAND
PASSPORT
The right to work in the UK with no time limit or work permit
The right to vote in UK elections and take a full part in local and national government

There are two kinds of British citizenship:

- British citizenship (also called full British citizenship)
- British Overseas Territories citizenship, applicable for example to people from the Falkland Islands, Gibraltar and Bermuda.

The responsibilities of a citizen

A registered or naturalised citizen can lose citizenship if he or she behaves disloyally or receives a prison sentence during the first five years of citizenship. But while people who are British citizens by birth or descent have certain obligations, their citizenship cannot be revoked.

Activity

Which of the following do you think are **compulsory** for British citizens?

a) Paying taxes
b) National service
c) Voting
d) Swearing allegiance to the UK
e) Jury service
f) Obeying the law
g) Earning a living if capable
h) Carrying an identity card
i) Joining a political party
j) Completing a census form every ten years
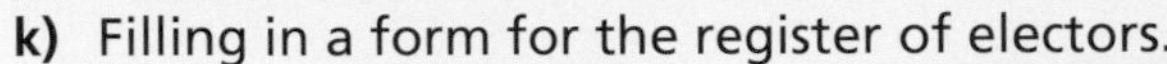
k) Filling in a form for the register of electors.

Voting is compulsory in Australia

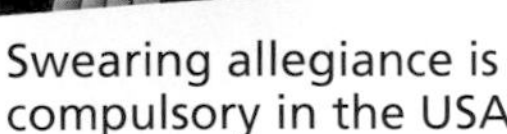

Swearing allegiance is compulsory in the USA

Doing national service is compulsory in Switzerland

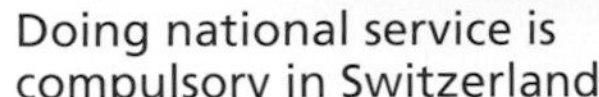

Answers: a, e, f, j, k are compulsory

Should there be tests for citizenship?

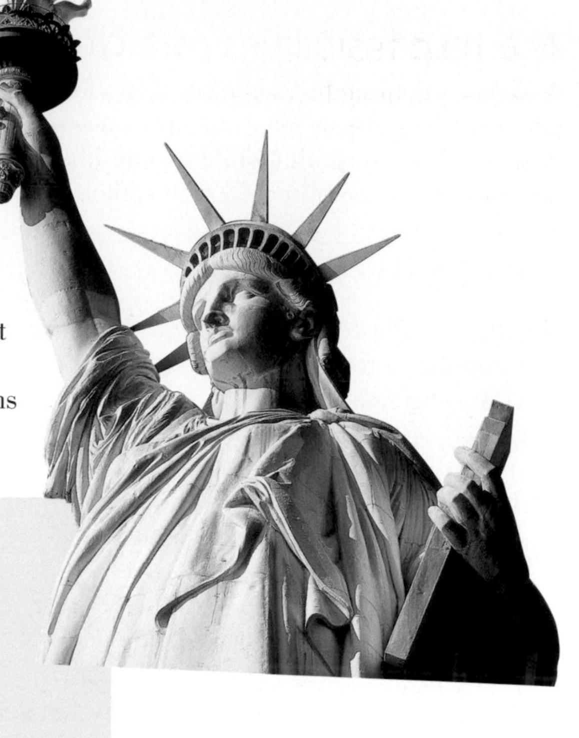

When people apply for citizenship they have to go through varying procedures to qualify for the legal rights of citizenship.

Some countries set tests to find out if the applicant knows enough about the country to qualify to be a citizen. For example in the USA, would-be citizens have to attend classes to learn about the USA and then they are tested. They have to get at least eight out of ten marks in the citizenship test to qualify.

Here is an example of an American test. How many questions would you get right?

1 How many stars are there in the US flag?

2 What color are the stripes?

3 What is the 4th of July?

4 Who was the first President of the United States?

5 Who becomes President of the United States if the President should die?

6 How many branches are there in the US government?

7 What is Congress?

8 What are the duties of the Supreme Court of the United States?

9 Which countries were US enemies during the Second World War?

10 Who was Martin Luther King Jr?

Answers: 1 50; 2 Red and white; 3 Independence Day; 4 George Washington; 5 The Vice President; 6 Three; 7 The Senate and the House of Representatives; 8 To interpret laws; 9 Germany, Italy and Japan; 10 A civil rights leader.

A British test?

Some people think there should be a British citizenship test. Others disagree.

In a radio debate on this issue, the following questions were suggested for a British citizenship test. See how you would get on.

1 On which date did all women over 21 get the right to vote?
- a) 1945 ☐
- b) 1900 ☐
- c) 1928 ☐

2 Are you a . . . ?
- a) subject of the Crown ☐
- b) citizen of the Crown ☐
- c) defender of the Crown ☐

3 Why is the Union Jack made up of its particular colours?
- a) It was chosen by Henry VIII ☐
- b) It is made up of the flags of St George of England, St Patrick of Ireland and St Andrew of Scotland ☐
- c) It is made up of the flags of the Anglo-Saxon kingdoms of Mercia and Wessex ☐

4 Is a man allowed to punish his wife physically as long as it is in his own home?
- a) Yes, although not with any recognised weapon ☐
- b) Yes, although only under provocation ☐
- c) No ☐

5 How long can a British government stay in office before a general election?
- a) 4 years ☐
- b) 6 years ☐
- c) 5 years ☐

6 Which king had his powers curbed by the Magna Carta?
- a) King Alfred ☐
- b) King Charles I ☐
- c) King John ☐

7 Which monarch broke away from the Roman Catholic Church?
- a) Charles I ☐
- b) Elizabeth I ☐
- c) Henry VIII ☐

8 Which three of the following need to agree a law before it can come into force?
- a) House of Commons, Lord Chancellor and Queen ☐
- b) House of Commons, House of Lords and Queen ☐
- c) Prime Minister, Cabinet and police ☐

9 Who was the only politician in British history to abolish Parliament?
- a) Cromwell ☐
- b) Gladstone ☐
- c) Churchill ☐

10 What did Guy Fawkes famously fail to do?
- a) Blow up Buckingham Palace ☐
- b) Blow up the Houses of Parliament ☐
- c) Blow up 10 Downing Street ☐

Discuss

1. What do you think of the citizenship tests on pages 8 and 9? Should knowing the answers qualify someone for citizenship?
2. Should people wanting to be British citizens have to pass tests in oral and written English? Give your reasons.
3. Do you think there should be a citizenship test for people who want to be British citizens? Give your reasons.

Activity

1. Work in pairs and try to write at least four test questions that you think should be included in a British test if one were going to be introduced.
2. Swap with the pair sitting next to you and try to answer their questions.

Answers: 1c, 2a, 3b, 4c, 5c, 6c, 7c, 8b, 9a, 10b.

1.4 Democracy under threat

Freedom and democracy do not exist everywhere in the world today. There are many authoritarian governments whose citizens do not get the rights and freedoms outlined on pages 2–3. Countries which were once democratic can lose their freedom, as happened in Greece in 1967 when a military coup in Athens established the regime of the 'Greek Colonels', and in Spain during the regime of Franco, 1937–75. Other countries have famously achieved democracy recently, like Eastern European countries from 1989 onwards and South Africa in 1994.

Getting the vote was so important to South Africans that they were prepared to queue for hours to make sure they could vote in the election to choose the government.

Some of us have lived in a democratic system for so long that we take our rights and freedoms for granted. Yet we might lose some of those freedoms if we are not careful.

Terrorism – a major threat to democracy?

Democratic countries allow criticism of their government. That is a good thing. But the problem is that sometimes people who criticise the government may also want to destroy it. This presents us with a difficult question: how far should we go in allowing people the freedom to say and do things that might destroy our democratic way of life?

In recent years, the most talked-about threat to democracy has been terrorism. But fighting terrorism often involves preventing people from saying and doing things that they expect to be able to say and do in a democracy. So, what should we do?

Activity

1 Read about Barat, an invented country, on page 11. Split the class into two: half will be members of the government of Barat, the other half will be members of the public. Work in small groups of either 'government' or 'members of the public'. Discuss the ten options opposite and decide:

- which of the measures you could agree with (give reasons)
- which of the measures you could never allow to happen in your democratic country (give reasons).

2 Each group of 'members of the public' should work with a group of 'the government'. Compare and discuss the two lists of measures and see how far you can agree.

3 As a class, discuss the measures and the problems they might present. See if there were any big differences between the lists made by government groups and those by the groups representing the public.

You live in Barat, a country with a democratic system of government. It is a society where people value their freedom of speech and their right to move about freely without restriction. People are generally well off. Business and commerce is well developed. Many people are employed in large companies. They travel widely within and outside Barat on business and for pleasure. Most large towns have airports. The government spends most of its money on social benefits, education and health care.

A new situation has arisen. Over the last year, there has been an increase in terrorist activities from different political groups around the world. The security services have recently received information that there could be attacks in Barat in the future. It is the government's responsibility to provide additional security for the inhabitants of Barat.

A committee has suggested ten options for the government and people of Barat to consider.

1 The introduction of identity cards, which must be carried at all times, containing data on fingerprints and iris (eye)-recognition of the card-holder.

2 The security services to have access to private bank account details of all the citizens of Barat.

3 Records of e-mails and telephone calls to be kept by internet service providers and telephone companies and given to the police if requested.

4 Closed-circuit television to be installed in all offices, airports, shops and town centres, with face-recognition capability.

5 All baggage to be scanned on both domestic and international flights, leading to longer check-in times at airports.

6 Police to be allowed to 'stop-and-search' anyone at any time.

7 New laws to be introduced to prevent speeches or newspaper articles that encourage violent action, and to allow imprisonment without trial for offenders.

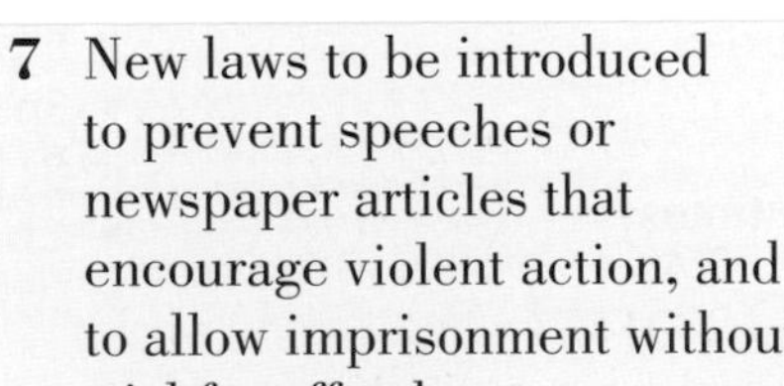

8 New laws to be introduced to allow the government to ban demonstrations or protest meetings of any group that they think is dangerous.

9 Border security to be reinforced, including thermal imaging of all vehicles. Airlines to employ armed guards at airports and on some flights.

10 People suspected of belonging to terrorist organisations to be imprisoned and held without trial.

Discuss

1. Which of the ten measures do you think should be introduced in the UK? Give your reasons.
2. Which of them would you be against? Why?

1.5 Identity cards – protection or restriction?

In many countries of the world today, people have to carry identity cards (ID cards). People can be asked to show their ID card in a variety of situations, for instance:

- when stopped by the police to prove their identity
- if they are involved in an accident
- when claiming benefits or government services
- when applying for a job.

Even in countries that do not have identity cards, people have a health and social security card, for example in Australia and the USA.

The last time that people in Britain carried identity cards was during the Second World War. But some people think it would be a good idea for everyone to have identity cards in the UK now. They believe that the advantages they bring outweigh any disadvantages. Other people think that carrying identity cards would lead to people having less freedom.

There are two big issues connected with ID cards:

1 What information should be on the card?
2 Should everybody have to carry the card at all times?

Countries that have ID cards include:

- Germany
- France
- Spain
- Belgium
- China
- Pakistan.

What could be included on an ID card?

- photograph
- fingerprint
- age
- bank details
- medical information, for example NHS number, blood type, allergies and illnesses
- driving licence
- rights to welfare benefits
- health insurance details
- criminal record, for example sex offences.

Activity

1 What do you think the four people in the illustration above might be thinking about what is happening?
2 What are your first thoughts about identity cards?
3 Which of the things listed on the left do you think should **not** be on the card? Why?

Suggested advantages of identity cards

- One card carries all necessary information
- Instant identification in a traffic or similar accident
- Medical information so that the holder gets proper treatment
- Shows that people are entitled to certain benefits
- Stops adults with a history of child abuse working with children
- Identifies illegal immigrants
- Helps prevent social security fraud, for example claiming benefits the person is not entitled to

Suggested disadvantages of identity cards

Many people are opposed to the idea of identity cards. They think that they could give the government too much control over the lives of individuals and could create a lot of problems. Look at some of their arguments below.

In this country we have always had a good relationship between the police and the public. People would not like the idea that the police would have the power to stop someone in the street and demand to see an identity card. Resentment would build up and the public would be less willing to help the police.

It will be very expensive to bring in these cards with their computer chips.

Some people in caring professions, like teachers and doctors, would be put in a difficult position as they would have to refuse services to people without cards.

As a card to catch illegal immigrants, it could lead to racial harassment as it is likely to be black and Asian people who would be stopped more often and required to show their cards. It could cause a real setback in good race relations.

An illegal trade in fake cards is bound to develop.

Suppose a government that was very authoritarian got into power in Britain, then the ID cards would be the perfect weapon to control everybody. It would be like Nazi Germany.

Activity

Hold a debate in your class on the motion: 'This house thinks that everyone should have to carry an identity card.'

Split the class into two and prepare your arguments. There is a great deal of information about identity cards on the internet.

In your debate you might want to consider:

- what you would put on the identity card
- whether an ID card could be useful even if you did not have to carry it. For example, it could 'entitle' you to certain services and make them easier to obtain.

1.6 What is it like to live without freedom?

Activity

Read the following passage from *Nineteen Eighty-Four* by George Orwell. It describes what society might be like when people have no freedoms.

1 List all the ways in which, in the extract, Winston Smith's life is different from the life of someone living in a free society.

2 What would you most dislike about living in this society? Why?

It was a bright cold day in April, and the clocks were striking thirteen. Winston Smith, his chin nuzzled into his breast in an effort to escape the vile wind, slipped quickly through the glass doors of Victory Mansions, though not quickly enough to prevent a swirl of gritty dust from entering along with him.

The hallway smelt of boiled cabbages and old rag mats. At one end of it a coloured poster, too large for indoor display, had been tacked to the wall. It depicted simply an enormous face, more than a metre wide: the face of a man of about forty-five, with a heavy black moustache and ruggedly handsome features. Winston made for the stairs. It was no use trying the lift. Even at the best of times it was seldom working, and at present the electric current was cut off during daylight hours. It was part of the economy drive in preparation for Hate Week. The flat was seven flights up, and Winston, who was thirty-nine and had a varicose ulcer above his right ankle, went slowly, resting several times on the way. On each landing, opposite the lift shaft, the poster with the enormous face gazed from the wall. It was one of those pictures which are so contrived that the eyes follow you about when you move. BIG BROTHER IS WATCHING YOU, the caption beneath it ran.

Inside the flat a fruity voice was reading out a list of figures which had something to do with the production of pig-iron. The voice came from an oblong metal plaque like a dulled mirror which formed part of the surface of the right-hand wall. Winston turned a switch and the voice sank somewhat, though the words were still distinguishable. The instrument (the telescreen, it was called) could be dimmed but there was no way of shutting it off completely. He moved over to the window: a smallish, frail figure, the meagreness of his body merely emphasised by the blue overalls which were the uniform of the Party. His hair was very fair, his face naturally sanguine, his skin roughened by coarse soap and blunt razor blades and the cold of the winter that had just ended.

Outside, even through the shut window-pane, the world looked cold ... The black-moustachio'd face gazed down from every commanding corner. There was one on the house-front immediately opposite. BIG BROTHER IS WATCHING YOU, the caption said, while the eyes looked deep into Winston's own ... In the far distance a helicopter skimmed down between the roofs, hovered for an instant like a bluebottle, and darted away again with a curving flight. It was the police patrol, snooping into people's windows. The patrols did not matter, however. Only the Thought Police mattered.

Behind Winston's back the voice from the telescreen was still babbling away about pig-iron and the overfulfilment of the Ninth Three-Year Plan. The telescreen received and transmitted simultaneously. Any sound that Winston made, above the level of a very low whisper, would be picked up by it, moreover, so long as he remained within the field of vision which the metal plaque commanded, he could be seen as well as heard. There was, of course, no way of knowing whether you were being watched at any given moment. How often, or on what system, the Thought Police plugged in on any individual wire was guesswork. It was even conceivable that they watched everybody all the time. But at any rate, they could plug in your wire whenever they wanted to. You had to live – did live, from habit that became instinct – in the assumption that every sound you made was overheard, and, except in darkness, every movement was scrutinised.

From fiction to real life

Nineteen Eighty-Four is fiction. However, some people have had to live under even worse regimes.

In Cambodia in 1975, the Khmer Rouge, an extremist movement, took over the government by force and tried to rid the country of all aspects of modern life. They forced people to leave all cities and live in the countryside. They killed people they thought were 'intellectuals' – sometimes just because they wore glasses. They abolished banking, finance and currency. They outlawed all religions, and banned private property so completely that even things like soap and toothpaste had to be shared. Everyone had to wear black, no music was to be played, everyone had to work in the countryside.

They used extreme force to make people do as they wished. The cost in human life was high. Of the total Cambodian population of some 7 to 8 million in 1975, the official tally published by the successor regime to the Khmer Rouge sets the number of dead at 3.1 million. People died from execution, disease, starvation and overwork.

Loung Ung was a child when the Khmer Rouge took over. This is an extract from an interview she gave to 'Cambodia Tales'.

Loung Ung

Activity

Work in pairs. Read Loung Ung's story below. Now read the list of human rights, A–P, on page 16. Decide which of these fundamental human rights Loung Ung and her family were denied by the Khmer Rouge.

'I had a charmed childhood. In Phnom Penh, my siblings and I had everything we could want: maids, a comfortable home, pretty clothes, toys and education. But all that was to change for ever after April 17th, 1975. I was just five years old when Pol Pot's Khmer Rouge stormed into Phnom Penh. Within hours, and clutching few possessions, my family was among the many hundreds of thousands of families forced at gunpoint to evacuate the city and made to live a new life. Over the next four genocidal years everything I knew of my old life was taken away from me. I was not allowed and did not have even the simplest of things: fresh clothes, cleaning my teeth, school, shoes, soap ... During those four years, Cambodia was like a prison, we were made to live in villages more akin to labour camps. In these camps, I had to learn to cheat, steal, fight and kill to survive. Survive I did ... though the war claimed the lives of my parents, two sisters and twenty other relatives.'

1.7 The Human Rights Act

The European Convention of Human Rights

European countries formed the Council of Europe in 1949 to make sure that a European war never happened again. Following the horrors of the Nazi regime in Germany, they agreed the European Convention on Human Rights (see below) for all European citizens.

The Council of Europe also set up a European Court of Human Rights at Strasbourg. The idea behind this was that the citizens of any of the Council's states could bring cases to the European Court if they thought that their human rights had been violated. This meant that citizens could bypass their own governments if they felt they were being mistreated. However, it was decided that it would be better if the rights in the Convention became part of the law of the countries themselves. In the UK the Convention was made part of the Human Rights Act of 1998 which came into full force in October 2000.

The Human Rights Act covers the following areas:

A Everyone has the right to life.

B No one can be tortured or given degrading punishment.

C No one can be held in slavery or forced labour.

D Everyone has the right to liberty and security.

E Everyone is entitled to a fair and public hearing in court if accused of a crime.

F No one can be punished for an action which was not a crime when it was committed.

G Everyone has the right to privacy and family life.

H Everyone has a right to freedom of opinions and religion.

I Everyone has the right to freedom of expression.

J Everyone has the right to protest peacefully and to join, or not to join, a trade union.

K Men and women of marriageable age have the right to marry and have a family.

L Everyone has the right to own and enjoy their property.

M No one can be denied the right to an education.

N There must be free elections at regular intervals, with secret voting, so that people can choose their own government.

O The death penalty is abolished.

P No one can be discriminated against, on any grounds, in getting these rights.

The Human Rights Act and democracy

The Human Rights Act applies to everyone in Britain, whether or not they are British citizens. The government must make sure they receive their rights. If someone thinks any of these human rights has been denied them, they can take their case to a British court.

The Human Rights Act forces authorities to think carefully about their actions and to make sure they are able to justify their decisions. For example, because there is a right to protest peacefully, the police or local authorities would have to have very good reasons to ban a demonstration, and would have to be able to show that there would be a serious risk to people's safety if the event went ahead.

Activity

Here are three examples of the use of the Human Rights Act. Decide whether or not you agree with the claimant that their human rights were being infringed.

1

Woman loses right-to-die ruling

DIANE PRETTY, who is terminally ill, today lost her legal battle for the right to commit suicide with the help of her husband.

Five Law Lords ruled the Human Rights Act had no effect on a refusal by the Director of Public Prosecutions to guarantee her husband Brian freedom from prosecution.

Assisted suicide, said Lord Bingham of Cornhill, was against the law and no-one had the power to suspend or abandon laws without parliamentary consent.

From the *Independent*, 29 November 2001

2

Christian schools ask for right to hit pupils

Christian independent schools yesterday asked the high court in London for the right to smack pupils on the biblical grounds that 'the rod of correction imparts wisdom'. The group of headteachers, teachers and parents believes that banning corporal punishment breaches parents' rights to practise their religion freely under the Human Rights Act.

Corporal punishment in independent schools was banned in 1999, twelve years after it was outlawed in state schools. But John Friel, acting for the claimants, told Mr Justice Patrick Elias that the group 'believed as part of their religious worship and part of their religious belief, that corporal punishment is part of their Christian doctrine'.

From the *Guardian*, 3 November 2001

3

Cox to sue Sunday People

Radio 1 DJ Sara Cox is to sue the *Sunday People* and the photographer Jason Fraser under the European Human Rights Act, after rejecting an apology by the paper last week . . . It is understood Ms Cox felt that the paper's apology, published last Sunday, did not go far enough to compensate her for the photographs, published the previous week. Ms Cox and her husband, DJ Jon Carter, were photographed at a private villa in the Seychelles by a photographer acting for Mr Fraser without their knowledge.

From the *Guardian*, 29 October 2001

1.8 Who are the British?

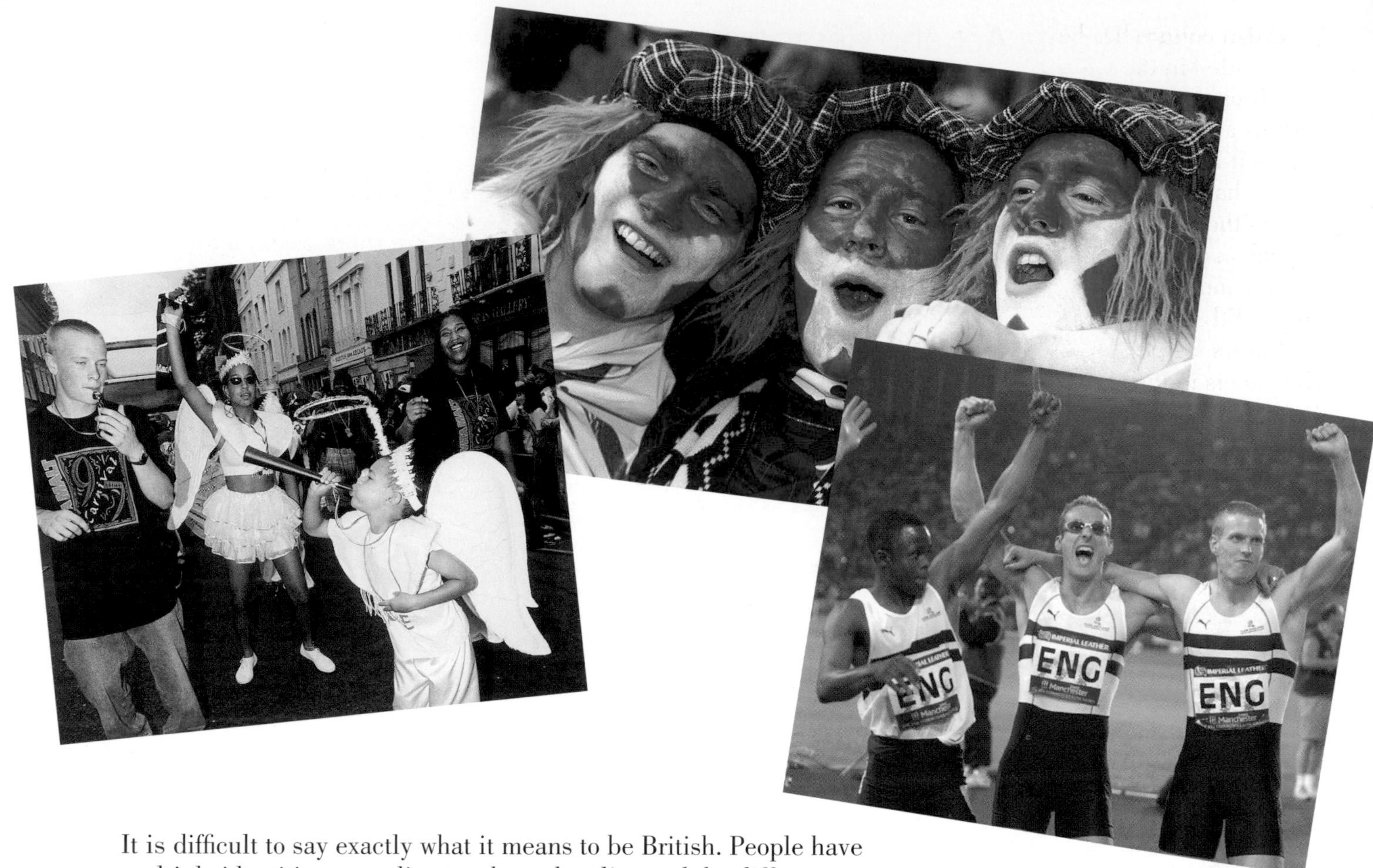

It is difficult to say exactly what it means to be British. People have multiple identities according to where they live and the different groups to which they belong. People who live in Scotland and Wales might identify themselves as British but also as Scottish or Welsh. Regional divisions in England might mean that people see themselves as a northerner or southerner and more particularly as a 'Geordie' or a 'Londoner'. Each person has a distinctive combination of identities that make them who they are. There has been a lot of discussion in the newspapers about what this means, and some well-known people were asked to sum up what they thought it meant to be 'British'.

John Major, former Prime Minister
'Britain is a nation of long shadows on county cricket grounds, warm beer, invincible green suburbs, dog lovers and – as George Orwell said – "old maids bicycling to Holy Communion through the morning mist".'

Claire Rayner, writer and broadcaster
'People define themselves as coming from Yorkshire or Lancashire, or as being cockney, like I am, rather than coming from Britain as a whole. There is a certain snottiness in trying to define "Britishness". If anybody asked, I would say I am a Londoner and a European.'

Sunder Katwala, columnist
'The central point . . . is that the old symbols of church, Queen and country don't work for many Britons of all ethnic backgrounds, white and non-white.'

Discuss

1. What do you think it means to be 'British'?
2. Do you identify more with your region than your country? Why?

British culture has been enriched by the different ethnic groups that have settled in the UK over many centuries. They and the cultures they have brought with them have become an integral part of British life. Curries and Chinese takeaways are as popular as fish and chips. But of course it is much more than this – literature, music, food, dance and theatre have all been altered and enhanced by influences from all around the world. The world of music, for instance, which has such an impact on young people, has for over a century been influenced by jazz, rhythm and blues, reggae and rap, which originate in Black American music. Ethnic groups have brought enterprise, skills and talents to British society, creating jobs and businesses. Examples are the Huguenots in the sixteenth century, West Indians and Asians after 1945, as well as refugees from more recent conflicts in Bosnia, Kosovo and Afghanistan.

Contribution of ethnic minorities

- Over two–thirds of independently owned local shops belong to people from ethnic minorities.
- Britain's National Health Service is heavily dependent on ethnic minority doctors, nurses and auxiliary staff.
- Additionally about 23% of doctors were born overseas.
- 24% of restaurant employees were born overseas.
- Sol Campbell, Ashia Hansen, Denise Lewis, Nassar Hussein and Audley Harrison rank among Britain's top sports stars.

Commission for Racial Equality

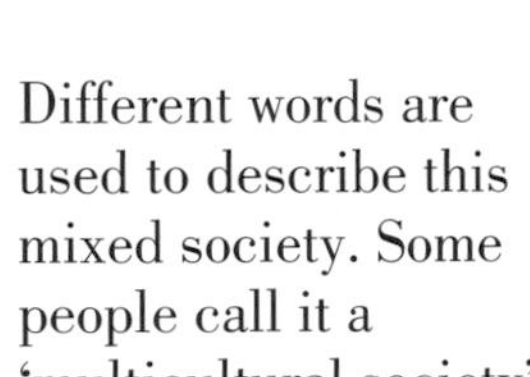

Different words are used to describe this mixed society. Some people call it a 'multicultural society'. Others talk about Britain being a 'diverse' society. Diverse means 'varied'. Diversity brings excitement, change and vibrancy to society. Ethnic diversity can also bring conflict between ethnic groups, as different cultures, understandings and religions collide. For example, conflicting loyalties can develop as young people from one ethnic group, who are brought up in Britain and are surrounded by other groups, reject the traditional culture of their parents. However, diversity also means that people learn about other people's way of life when they meet and talk to each other in schools, communities and work places.

Population of Great Britain by ethnic groups 2000–01

	Millions
White	53.0
Black Caribbean	0.5
Black African	0.4
Indian	1.0
Pakistani	0.7
Bangladeshi	0.3
Chinese	0.1
Other groups	1.1

Social Trends 2002, ONS

How did Britain become such a diverse society?

For centuries people have come to Britain from many parts of the world for all sorts of reasons:

- The Romans, Anglo-Saxons and Normans came as invaders.
- Others came to trade or work here, such as the Flemish weavers in the fourteenth century.
- Many came to escape war, famine or religious hatred in their own countries, for example the Huguenots escaping from France in the sixteenth century, Irish people fleeing the famine of the mid-nineteenth century, and Jewish people fleeing from persecution in Russia and Eastern Europe at the end of the nineteenth century.
- People from countries such as India, Bangladesh, Pakistan and the West Indies were invited here after the Second World War because there were not enough people to do all the jobs. The British government encouraged immigration to help to solve the acute labour shortages created by post-war reconstruction and a dynamic, booming economy.
- In recent years people have come from many other parts of the world to escape civil war and oppression and to seek a more prosperous lifestyle.

During the eighteenth and nineteenth centuries, Britain built up a huge empire and ruled large parts of the world as colonies, for example in India, Africa, China and the West Indies. Lots of Britons – English, Scots, Welsh and Irish – went to live in the colonies to govern or to make their fortunes in farming, mining or trade. So Britain has a special relationship with the people who come from the former colonies. Many thousands fought for Britain in the two world wars of the twentieth century. For instance, over one million Indians died fighting for the British in the First World War.

After the Second World War, when British colonies became independent, many of them decided that they did not want to lose all their links with Britain. They joined the Commonwealth, which had grown out of the old British Empire. The Commonwealth is a voluntary organisation in which the 54 independent states involved have a special relationship. They co-operate to promote the common interests of their peoples.

Because of its connections with other parts of the world, Britain has always been a place where people whose roots lie elsewhere have lived and these have always been diverse communities. For instance, in 1764 there were about 20 000 black people living in London. Today, well over 3 million people in Britain call themselves 'black', 'Asian', 'Chinese' or say they belong to another ethnic group. Nearly half were born and brought up in Britain, which is now their country of origin.

Activity

1. Why do you think that 'national identity' can be a problem in a diverse society like Britain?
2. Using some of the following headings, and working in small groups, produce a pack of photographs, articles and quotes, perhaps from your friends and relatives, about being British. Make sure your pack recognises the cultural diversity of this country.

people	**food**
language	**culture**
leisure	**politics**
interests	**work**

section 2

How does the justice system work in England and Wales?

Key words
- appeals
- civil law
- criminal law
- prisons
- sentencing

All societies need laws to control people's behaviour and to protect them from each other. Laws are rules that are enforced by the government through the police and the courts. How they are enforced varies from country to country. In this section, you will find out about the justice system in England and Wales.

You will learn about:

- civil and criminal law
- the role of the police
- the rights and responsibilities of the citizen in relation to the police
- the criminal justice system.

You will use the following skills:

- researching current legal issues
- justifying and expressing an opinion, orally and in writing
- contributing to class discussion
- understanding and explaining other people's points of view.

2.1 How does the law affect you?

Whether you are young or old, the law affects you every day of your life. It prevents you from doing exactly what you might like to do, but it also protects you from the actions of others.

Activity

Look at each of points A–F on pages 22–23 and, in small groups, discuss the questions for each one.

A Minimum age

- Why is there a law to control at what age young people can be served alcohol?
- List other laws that control the age at which you can do something.
- Do you think such laws are a good or a bad idea? Give your reasons.

NO ALCOHOL TO UNDER 18s
IT'S THE LAW!

B Driving

- Why are there laws to restrict the speed of vehicles?
- List other laws that control the driving of vehicles, such as having a licence and insurance.
- Do you think the current laws are reasonable? Give your reasons.

C Litter

- Why are there laws to prevent the dumping of waste?
- List other laws designed to protect the environment.
- Would you introduce more laws to protect the urban and rural environments? If so, what would they be? If not, why not?

LITTER.
DON'T GO HOME WITHOUT IT.
MAX. FINE £1000
WEALDEN DISTRICT COUNCIL

D Theft

Phone thief gets four years

A 23-year-old man has been sentenced to four years in jail for a mobile phone robbery just one day after the UK's most senior judge called for tougher sentences on handset thieves. The Lord Chief Justice, Lord Woolf, said offenders should expect a jail sentence of up to five years as part of a crackdown on the growing problem.

- What do you think about the jail sentence for this offence?
- Why do the courts decide to hand out tougher sentences for some offences?
- For which offences would you make punishments really tough?

E Family life

- When parents divorce, the courts can force one parent to pay maintenance or control parents' access to children. Do you think this is right?
- Can you think of other ways in which the law intervenes in family relations?

F Neighbours

Noisy neighbours face crackdown

Noisy neighbours who make fellow residents' lives a misery are to be targeted by new laws being considered by ministers. Plans are being unveiled to make it easier for local councils to take action against people making a din late at night.

- Do you think there should be laws to deal with noisy neighbours?
- Neighbours can fall out about a lot of things, for example noise, fences, shared facilities like guttering and drainage. What do you think are the best ways of solving these disputes?
- Do laws help to solve such problems, or do they make things worse?

In England and Wales, at what age can you:

1 Vote
2 Drive a car
3 Get married
4 Own a house
5 Buy tobacco
6 Give consent to heterosexual sexual activity
7 Play the National Lottery
8 Get the full rate of the National Minimum Wage?

Answers: 1 18; 2 17; 3 16, with parental consent; 4 18; 5 16; 6 16; 7 16; 8 22.

2.2 What is the law?

The law is divided into criminal and civil.

Criminal law covers actions that are regarded as crimes against society as a whole such as theft, murder, speeding and damage to property. If someone is accused of committing a crime, the police will arrest them, charge them (if there is sufficient evidence), and they will be put on trial in a **criminal court**. The prosecution is carried out in England and Wales by the Crown Prosecution Service, on behalf of the state.

Civil law covers disputes between people and is usually about rights. So consumer rights, issues about marriage and divorce, accidents at work, contracts between companies and disputes between neighbours come under civil law. Usually civil cases involve situations where someone feels that damage has been done to them. This person, called the **plaintiff**, brings a case against the other person, called the **defendant**. The case is heard in a **civil court**. The plaintiff can bring a case to court him or herself and must try to prove that the defendant is responsible (liable) for the damage caused and so should pay compensation. Examples of these claims might be over a motor accident or damaging someone's reputation by writing something negative about them.

Solicitors and barristers

If you are involved in a dispute with someone, you can go to a **solicitor** for advice about the law. He or she will represent you but you will usually need to pay a fee. Sometimes, the solicitors for the two sides can work out a settlement without having to go to court. If the matter does go to court, the solicitor may arrange for a **barrister** to represent you. Barristers argue out the case before a **judge**.

Activity

Look at the following cases and decide which might be heard in a criminal court and which might be heard in a civil court.

1 A young woman is accused of stealing clothes from a shop in her local high street.

2 A person moves a fence and takes some of the land from the garden of the neighbour next door.

3 Two young men have a fight and one is badly hurt.

4 A newspaper publishes something unpleasant about a celebrity in a newspaper. The celebrity says it is not true and accuses the newspaper's editor of publishing lies.

5 Someone giving evidence in a civil case is accused of telling lies in court.

6 A drunk driver has an accident and the passenger in the car is seriously injured.

7 A couple who are getting divorced disagree about how to divide their property. One demands a bigger share.

8 A crowd of football fans damages the property of a public house near a football ground.

9 A worker is sacked for what she believes to be racist reasons.

10 A burglar breaks into a house and steals a lot of jewellery.

Libel

One example of a civil offence is libel. If someone writes or broadcasts something about a person that is not true, that person can sue for libel. The person must be able to prove that the statement is unfair or inaccurate. Famous people or firms often claim they have been libelled and sue for damages in court. They are not always successful.

In one famous example dubbed the 'McLibel Case', McDonald's sued two protesters, Dave Morris and Helen Steel, because they gave out leaflets criticising the company. The case was the longest libel case in legal history. McDonald's won the case but it still created a lot of bad publicity for the company.

The BBC website reported the case as follows:

news download>>>

The pair fought a ten-year battle against McDonald's which ended in a 314-day libel trial, the longest in English legal history. McDonald's brought the case saying the pair had handed out a libellous London Greenpeace campaign leaflet entitled 'What's Wrong with McDonald's?'.

It accused McDonald's of exploiting its workers, damaging the environment and giving its customers food that led to heart disease.

The court ruled the burger chain had been libelled by most of the allegations and Ms Steel and Mr Morris were ordered to pay McDonald's £60000 damages. That sum was reduced to £40000 following a ruling by the Court of Appeal.

The court case is believed to have cost the burger chain £10m which it has no chance of recouping [getting back] as Mr Morris and Ms Steel are described as unwaged.

From BBC News Online, 31 March 1999

The law of libel can be used by anyone. If you think you have been libelled, you can sue, although, if you lose, you may end up with large legal costs.

Here is a letter written to a legal advice columnist for a national newspaper, by someone who thought he had been libelled by a television programme, together with part of the answer.

Q

Dear Gary,

A couple of years ago I spent seven days in a young offenders' institution for non-payment of a fine. A television programme was being made while I was there and, without my knowledge, I was filmed messing about with the lads going back to my cell.

This scene was used on TV with a caption saying 'Natural Born Killers'. This has made my life hell and I have been assaulted numerous times by people who think I am a killer.

What can I do about this?

A

Gary says...

You have a good chance of winning a case for defamation against the TV company involved, but must bring proceedings as soon as possible. You could even prevent further airings of the show with you in it. If reasonable viewers think you are portrayed as a killer you would get substantial damages in the thousands.

Activity

Suppose you were Gary replying to letters A and B, what would you advise the people in each case to do?

Possible remedies:

- Sue for compensation.
- Public apology on air or in newspaper.
- Receive an apology and out-of-court settlement (money).

Points to remember:

- The plaintiff has to be able to prove that the statement about them was unfair, inaccurate and damaging.
- The other side has to prove that what they said about the plaintiff was true.
- Whichever side wins, they can still end up paying huge legal costs.
- An apology might be enough to settle the matter.

Letter A

Dear Gary,

I'm an actress in a well-known soap on TV. Last week a newspaper claimed it had spoken to people who had been at wild parties at my house during which large quantities of drugs were taken. I admit that I've had some lively parties, but as far as I know, no drugs were taken. This is really serious as I could lose my job because the TV company that produces the show says any actors found to be using drugs will be kicked off the show. What can I do?

Letter B

Dear Gary,

I run a butcher's shop in the high street of a large city. A customer who doesn't like me went to the local newspaper and complained that I was selling illegal meat that could damage people's health. The newspaper wrote an article about it and now people have said they are not going to buy meat from my shop any more. I've lost a lot of money already. I have never bought illegal meat in my life. Can I sue the newspaper?

Discuss

1. How did McDonald's suffer from the libel case brought against them?
2. In the light of your answer to question 1, do you think McDonald's were right to take Mr Morris and Ms Steel to court?
3. What advice or warnings would you give someone who is considering taking libel action?

2.3 Would you make a good police officer?

It is the job of the police to enforce the law. When a crime has been committed, it is investigated by the police. If enough evidence is available against a suspect, the case is brought to trial in England and Wales by the Crown Prosecution Service. However, the police have many other jobs. A recent survey found that, on average, police officers spend 43% of their time in the office, often doing paperwork. They are also involved in searches for missing persons and animals, investigating burglar alarms, working with schools and other community groups, and giving evidence in court.

Read about a day in the life of a typical police officer.

Activity

1 What aspects of police work are described and shown in 'Late shift'?
2 If you had the responsibility of improving the job of a police officer, what changes might you make to remove the frustrations? Make a list of recommendations to send to the Home Secretary (who is the government minister responsible for the police in England and Wales).

Late shift

After an initial briefing for half an hour, I am called straight to a reported robbery in the town centre. The victim is a confused elderly lady whose bag has been snatched. I try to calm her down and take a statement but she is in too disturbed a state. A shopkeeper gives a statement describing the suspect. I drive the victim to her sheltered housing and contact the support staff there to tell them to check on her during the day. I would like to spend more time with the victim but know I have to get the paperwork done before the end of my shift. I return to the scene of the incident to take a full statement from the shopkeeper. The incident has taken an hour to deal with.

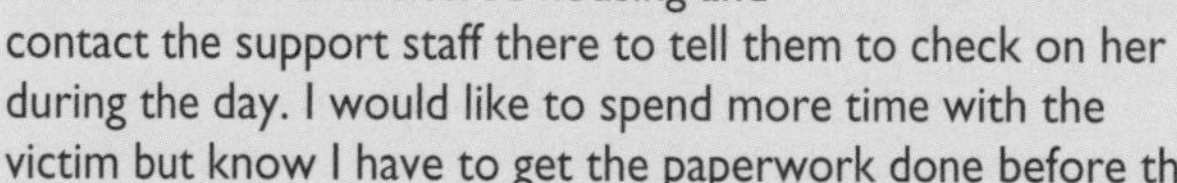

Back at the station I file a crime report, fill out the monitoring form for street robberies and try and grab some lunch. As usual I am left hanging on the phone for twenty minutes before anyone answers at the crime bureau to give me a crime number. The Robbery Squad won't take over the case until I have made all the initial enquiries and even then they might claim not to have the time. Consequently, it is difficult to get on with the paperwork while I'm hanging on the phone.

The crime reporting system is electronic but I have to wait my turn until a terminal is free. It takes twenty minutes for me to log through all the screens. I'm not the fastest typist so it usually takes me longer. In all, the reporting for the robbery takes me about an hour and a half, partly because I have to enter the same information several times.

I go on mobile patrol after responding to an alarm which, as usual, proves to be false. This wastes fifteen minutes.

I stop a driver on suspicion of drinking but the Breathalyser kit in my car doesn't work, so I have to wait ten minutes for a colleague to attend with a new kit. The driver proves to be just below the limit.

It's getting towards closing time and so the town centre is starting to get busy. I patrol the High Street where the pubs are concentrated. After half an hour I am called back to the station. As a WPC I am asked to attend the searching of a female prisoner. WPCs are often called to the custody suite to attend searches. If a juvenile girl is taken into custody a WPC is also required to be present. I am concerned to get back out on the street, as the pubs are pouring out and a couple of my colleagues are in strife. Unfortunately, though, I'm stuck in the custody suite for 45 minutes.

When I am able to get away, I am immediately called to assist in locating a missing twelve-year-old. Because he is a twelve-year-old he is a priority case. He is well known to the police, as this is the third time this month he has run away from his foster home. I spend the next 45 minutes filling in the missing person form. Despite the frequency of the event, it is not possible to transfer over information from the existing documentation. Nevertheless, for the next hour I look around several areas of the town known to me where he hangs out with groups of friends but can't find him. It is frustrating to know that even if I were to find him, with the local authority seeming to do little to resolve the situation, he will abscond again.

I return to the station at the end of the shift in time for the hand-over briefing which takes about half an hour.

'A day in the life of the 'typical' police officer', from Police Research Series, 2001

35 000 people each year apply to become police officers, but only 5000 are accepted.

Could you be a police officer?

Becoming a police officer is a lot harder and more challenging than most people ever imagine. It is tougher on your body, more taxing on your brain, more draining on your emotions and more demanding on your whole life. Do you think you could do it?...

How fit are you?

Could you chase a shoplifter up the stairs of a tower block? Try running up and down a flight of stairs a few times to see how fit you are. Lack of physical fitness is probably the main reason why we turn people down and they are often amazed when we do. We will put you through a medical that really tells us what shape you are in.

How observant are you?

Could you tell the height of a suspect in ten seconds? Or their weight? What they were wearing? Was that just a piece of wood or a sawn-off shotgun? A conviction and possibly someone's life depend on a police officer getting it right.

So one of the things we'll look for in your Initial Recruitment Test is how carefully you can observe scenes and how accurately you can record details. While you don't actually need any formal academic qualifications, we will test your command of English, your ability to handle numbers and how logical you are.

How sensitive are you?

We're here to serve the community. This means behaving sensitively and with compassion to every man, woman and child we meet. You need a lot of physical and mental stamina to be a police officer. When the pressure's on, you can count on 100% support from your colleagues. But sometimes you will face tricky and dangerous situations, possibly on your own.

- Could you tell a mother that her six-year-old daughter has been killed by a drunken driver?
- Could you help your colleagues break down a door on a drugs raid?
- How cool could you be if people start shouting racial abuse at you?
- Could you arrest an old woman caught stealing in a supermarket because she could not afford to buy food?

Rules are rules and the law is the law, but every police officer has to use his or her own judgement. Could you?

An advertisement in a recent campaign carried out by the Home Office aimed at recruiting more police officers.

The role of the police is to:

- prevent crime
- investigate incidents
- arrest suspects and bring them to court
- protect the public and their property
- keep public order.

Activity

Use the information on page 28 and the advertisement here to write a job specification for a police officer using the headings below. When you get to the part on personal qualities:

- look carefully at the qualities suggested in the advertisement
- use your own ideas about the qualities you think are important for a good police officer – think about the work of the police officer described on page 28.

Job specification for a police officer

Job title: Police Officer

Duties:

Working hours and conditions:

Personal qualities required:

Race and the police

One very sensitive issue in policing is racism. This was brought to the forefront of public discussion by the Stephen Lawrence case. Stephen, who was eighteen, lived in South London. He was black. In April 1993, Stephen was waiting with a friend for a bus when a gang of five young white men surrounded him and stabbed him. He collapsed and died shortly afterwards. The police were accused of not taking the crime seriously enough in the early stages of the investigation.

An inquiry led by Sir William Macpherson was later held into the murder and into the ensuing accusations of racism in the police force. The Macpherson Report found that the police had failed to recognise the murder as a 'racially motivated crime' and had treated the crime with a lack of urgency and commitment. It claimed that institutional racism (see definition below) in the Metropolitan Police force was partly responsible for this.

The report went on to suggest ways of tackling this and dealing with racist incidents, particularly the reporting and recording of such incidents. It also suggested that the procedures for 'stop and search' should be changed as many black people feel that they are unreasonably singled out by the police for random searches. It recommended changes in police training and in the recruitment and promotion of the police so that applicants would not be discriminated against on the grounds of colour, or of ethnic or national origin.

Institutional racism as defined by the Macpherson Report: 'The collective failure of an organisation to provide an appropriate and professional service to people because of their colour, culture or ethnic origin. It can be seen or detected in processes, attitudes and behaviour which amount to discrimination through unwitting [not deliberate] prejudice, ignorance, thoughtlessness and racist stereotyping which disadvantage minority ethnic people.'

What do you think this means?

Recruitment

There are very few police officers from minority ethnic groups in the police force. London has the largest percentage of people from ethnic minority groups in the UK – 30% in inner London and 22% in outer London. However, only 4.9% of police officers in the Metropolitan Police force are from these groups. Some people say this is because the police force is not welcoming to minority ethnic groups and this discourages black or Asian people from applying.

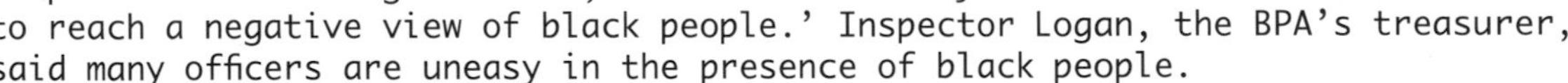

Black officers tell of racism

Black Metropolitan Police officers say the police should 'name and shame' senior officers who are not prepared to act against racism. Senior members of the Black Police Association (BPA) were giving evidence to the Stephen Lawrence inquiry. They said the service needs to stamp out what is called a 'canteen culture' of racial stereotypes and banter . . .

BPA chair, Inspector Paul Wilson, said most officers were not from multicultural backgrounds and the nature of their work reinforced any prejudice. 'Many police officers only meet black people in confrontational situations or dealing with crimes such as stop and searches. So it is right to assume that their view of black people is shaped through these meetings, and given that there are very few black people within the organisation, it is all too easy for them to reach a negative view of black people.' Inspector Logan, the BPA's treasurer, said many officers are uneasy in the presence of black people.

From BBC News Online, 25 September 1998

Activity

1 Why do you think the inquiry into the murder of Stephen Lawrence has been such a milestone in the way police deal with racist incidents?

2 What reasons are given in the BBC website report to explain why some police officers hold racist stereotypes?

3 What do you think might be the advantages of having a higher proportion of police officers from different ethnic minorities?

4 Here are four measures that could encourage more black and Asian people to apply to the police force:
   - **a)** run a big advertising campaign to attract them
   - **b)** set targets for the number of black and Asian police officers in any one force. For example, make sure that 8% of police officers are from ethnic minorities
   - **c)** provide extra training and guidance to ensure that black and Asian people reach the entry standards
   - **d)** use 'affirmative action' to make sure that black and Asian officers get promoted quickly to important posts in the force.

   Draw up a table to show the advantages and disadvantages of each option.

5 Can you think of any other measures that would help? Add them to your table.

6 Do you think any of the ideas suggested should definitely **not** be used? Explain why.

Do the police need some help?

The police have a big job to do. Traffic wardens have already been given some of the workload that used to be handled by the police, such as traffic duty. Special constables, who have full police powers, are part-time, voluntary police officers, and can be called in when the force is stretched.

Now Police Community Support Officers have been appointed in some areas of England and Wales to take over certain police duties and leave the police free for more skilled work. They wear a uniform, which is similar to, but not the same as, a police officer's.

The intention is to make people feel safer by having visible, uniformed officers on the streets. Police Community Support Officers are employed by their local police authority and help regular police officers with routine patrolling. They are empowered to obtain the name and address of any person acting in an anti-social manner, confiscate and dispose of alcohol and tobacco from young persons, and issue fixed penalty notices for dog fouling or dropping litter. In some, but not all areas, they have the power to detain suspects. Their duties can also include:

- house-to-house and missing persons inquiries
- victim support
- analysing CCTV footage
- dealing with street-corner youths
- checking on truants and people with curfew orders
- dealing with abandoned vehicles
- crowd stewarding
- reporting graffiti, vandalism and damage
- cordoning off crime scenes.

news download>>>

An officer of a different kind started patrolling the streets of Lincolnshire at the end of January 2003 – the new Police Community Support Officer (PCSO).

The completely new Community Support Officers will soon become a familiar face walking around the towns and villages of the county. These are not regular police officers but people employed and trained by Lincolnshire Police to help patrol the streets, deal with minor incidents of public disorder and tackle the quality of life issues such as anti-social behaviour.

The Police Community Support Officers will support the work already done by regular officers. They will be a highly visible uniformed presence, dressed in a uniform similar to but distinct from that of regular police officers. For example, they will have a reflective blue cap band, yellow and blue jacket and reflective labels identifying them as Police Community Support Officers.

From Lincolnshire Police website, 1 February 2003

Some members of the police force are very unhappy about the idea of these Police Community Support Officers, but others are in favour of them.

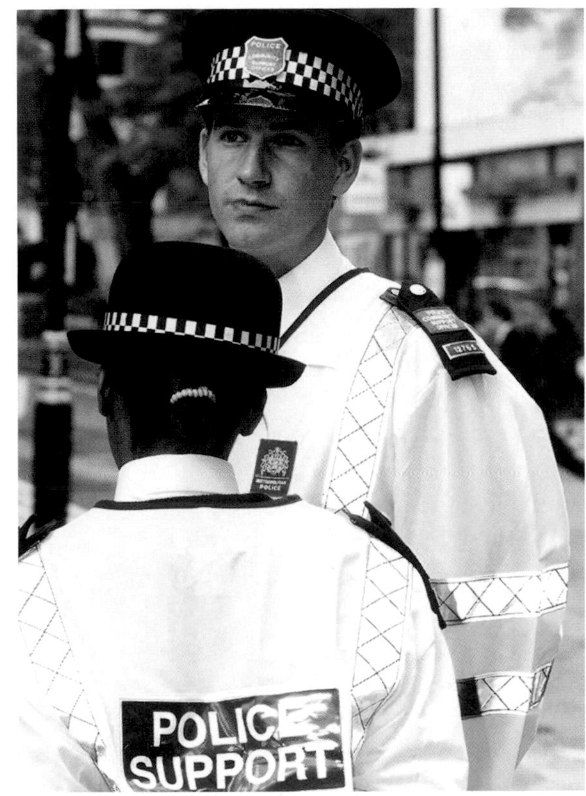

Activity

1. Read the following arguments for and against Police Community Support Officers. Decide which arguments you agree with, and which you disagree with.
2. Hold a debate in your class on this motion: 'This house supports the introduction of Police Community Support Officers to help the police force.'
3. At the end of the discussion decide:
   - a) what duties might be usefully carried out by Police Community Support Officers
   - b) what powers they should **not** have.

1 In order to beat crime we need people to get together to fight the criminals. The PCSOs can help motivate people to do this. For example, to help fight the presence of drugs on estates.

2 You can't allow people who are not properly trained to act like police officers. Even suspected offenders deserve protection by law.

3 PCSOs do not have the benefit of police training in the law and people's rights, so they end up breaking the law themselves.

4 The police are too busy to patrol some areas. PCSOs could patrol and save the police a lot of time as well as make local people feel safer.

5 When people feel that the police cannot or will not protect them, they will do the job themselves. Then we will have vigilantes on the streets, so it's better to have PCSOs with some training.

6 Crime is low in areas where people have organised themselves into watch schemes. Criminals are worried by schemes like these and less likely to go to areas where PCSOs are operating.

7 A lot of problems are caused by the anti-social behaviour of young people. PCSOs will be local people who can talk to the young people and diffuse the situation before it becomes a problem.

8 The police need to be freed up to deal with the serious criminals and incidents for which their training is vital.

9 PCSOs might act like vigilantes, bullying others in order to feel powerful themselves.

10 There are never going to be enough police to bring some areas under control.

2.4 Rights on arrest

Most of us are likely to be involved with the police at some time in our lives. It may be as a victim after we have been burgled or after a violent incident. But we may also be on the other end of police attention and end up as a suspect in a crime or guilty of some public order offence like causing noise late at night. Whether we are innocent of any crime or a suspect, it is important that we are treated properly – it is part of the basic rights and freedoms of a democratic society.

In the UK, there are clear rules about how we should be treated if arrested.

In the street

- You can be stopped by the police and searched if they have reasonable suspicion that you are carrying controlled drugs; offensive weapons (firearms, sharp objects); stolen goods.
- If you are attending a sporting event, a rave or a demonstration police do not require reasonable suspicion to be allowed to search you.
- You can be arrested and have charges brought against you if you resist being searched.
- You can only be forced to go to a police station if you are arrested.
- You can ask for police identification or a warrant card.

- You can ask why you are being stopped and searched.
- You can ask for a copy of the record of search.

When arrested

- You should be told why you have been arrested.
- You should be treated humanely and with respect.
- Someone should be notified of your arrest. (You do not necessarily have a right to a phone call.)
- You should be able to see a solicitor.
- The police can keep you for 24 hours without charge, although for serious offences this can be 36 hours.
- If you refuse to have your fingerprints taken, the police can apply to a magistrate in England and Wales to compel you to agree.
- The police can apply to a magistrate for a longer period of detention – usually up to 72 hours.

Police caution on arrest
You do not have to say anything. But it may harm your defence if you do not mention when questioned something which you later rely on in court. Anything you do say may be given in evidence.

When interviewed and charged

- The interview will be tape-recorded. You have the right to have a solicitor present during the interview.
- After the interview, the police may:
  - release you without charge
  - release you on police bail
  - charge you
  - release you after a formal caution
  - remand you in custody.
- If you are charged, the custody officer will read out the charges against you and ask if you have anything to say. You will receive a copy of the charges and a date of the court appearance.
- You may be fingerprinted and photographed.

In your home or other premises

- Premises can be searched if the police believe that evidence can be found there to help enquiries.
- Premises can be searched with the consent of the occupier.
- A warrant can be obtained from a magistrate, but no warrant is required if police are: seeking an escaped prisoner, protecting a life, stopping serious damage to property, arresting someone, seeking evidence after an arrest, seeking a terrorist.
- You can be present during the search unless you are hindering the investigation.
- The police should give details of their powers to search premises.
- The police should not use unreasonable force.
- A record of the search should be kept.

Activity

1 Work in pairs. One of you should write down the powers that the police have, the other the rights of the suspects. You could use a chart like the one below or write separate lists.

Police powers	Rights of the suspect

2 Choose two points from the list you are working on and explain to your partner why they are important.

3 Do you think there is a fair balance between police powers and suspects' rights? Discuss your ideas with the rest of the class.

How well did they do?

Activity

PC Smith and WPC Jones are young police officers. Usually when they go out on patrol nothing much happens. But on one particular day, during the afternoon and evening shift, they encounter a number of incidents. They have very little time to make judgements.

Your task, working in pairs, is to decide how well they did and to spot any mistakes they made. Use the information on the previous two pages to help you.

PC Smith and WPC Jones left the police station at around 2p.m. Their first area of patrol was the High Street. They were soon approached by a shopkeeper who said that clothes had been shoplifted from his boutique and pointed out a woman who had, he said, been in his shop shortly before. She was carrying a bulging bag.

Incident 1

The police officers went up to the woman and said that they wanted to search her bag. She refused, saying they had no reason to. However, they made her open her bag. There were no stolen clothes in it.

Did they have the legal right to search her bag?

The next part of their patrol took them past a school. The pupils were on their way home. Outside there was a fight going on and someone shouted: 'He's got a knife!' The police officers rushed forward.

Incident 2a

The fight stopped when they arrived. They spotted a very aggressive looking boy of seventeen. There was a knife at his feet. He said it was not his although other students said it was. Smith and Jones decided to take him and the knife to the police station to question him. He refused to go but they took him anyway.

Did they have the legal right to do this?

Incident 2b

At the station they questioned the boy but could not get him to admit anything. They said they wanted to take his fingerprints and compare them with those on the knife. The boy refused. At this point they decided that there would not be enough evidence for an arrest and they let the boy go.

Could they have forced the boy to have his fingerprints taken?

Were they within their rights to question the boy?

Late in the afternoon they saw a gathering of people being addressed by a known member of a racist group who was complaining about refugees coming to the UK. A group of local residents shouted back and a serious argument started.

Incident 3

It looked as though it might turn violent until Smith and Jones stepped in. They arrested the speaker on the grounds that he was inciting racial hatred.

Were they within their rights to arrest the man?

At the end of their patrol, when it was quite dark, Smith and Jones were walking past some houses when a man emerged from an alley carrying a video recorder. He could not give a convincing account of how he got the video or why he was carrying it about.

Incident 4

They called in some other officers and went to the man's house. His mother opened the door. They said they wanted to search the house for stolen goods. She agreed and they found a number of items in his room that they thought might have been stolen.

Were they within their rights to search the man's house?

Activity

Work in threes. One of you should take on the role of the suspect of a crime, one an arresting officer, and one an observer. Role play a street arrest for a suspected robbery. Both the police officer and the suspect should act responsibly. If either is unreasonable, it could harm their future position in court. The observer should note down any mistakes made by the suspect and by the police officer and should report what has been noted at the end of the role play.

Observers could describe what happened in their role plays and the issues discussed. The role play will help you prepare for the following discussion questions.

Discuss

A police officer's job is not easy. They have to make complicated decisions very quickly. Police officers don't always get it right but they need enough powers to be able to do their job well and so help create a safe and secure society.

1 Do you think any of their powers should be extended? Which ones and in what circumstances? What would be the advantages? The box below gives you some ideas that have been suggested for extending police powers. Which ones do you agree with?

Should the police be allowed to:

a) hold suspects much longer, say up to 72 hours, before charging them
b) hold suspects indefinitely for serious offences such as child murder or terrorism (if they get a magistrate's agreement)
c) make suspects give DNA samples if there has been a rape
d) arrest people who refuse to give them their name or who they suspect have given a false name?

2 Do you think any of their powers should be reduced? What would be the advantages?

3 Are there any powers that you would give the police that they don't have now?

2.5 How does the youth justice system work?

Youth justice in this country is based on three main ideas:

1 Young offenders should **take responsibility** for their behaviour and offences, and should learn to behave more responsibly in the future.
2 Young offenders should **make amends** to the victims of the crime or to the community.
3 Guidance and support should be offered to the offender to get them back into society and **help them develop** as law-abiding citizens.

This is called **restorative** justice because it aims to 'restore' young offenders to society and make them pay some sort of restoration to the people and community against whom they have offended.

The diagram here shows the main features of the youth justice system in England and Wales.

The process of youth justice

Informal warning

If a young person between ten and seventeen years old is believed to have committed a criminal offence, the police can give the offender a 'telling off' or informal warning. This is usually for a first or minor offence.

Reprimand

If the offence is more serious they will get a reprimand. This is given at a police station in the presence of an appropriate adult. You cannot get more than one reprimand.

Final warning

If they offend again or have committed a more serious offence (and have admitted they did it), they will be given a 'final warning' which means they will be referred to a Youth Offending Team.

The decision by the police to give a reprimand or a final warning depends on:

- the seriousness of the offence
- whether the young person has been in trouble before.

Youth Offending Team (YOT)

The team is made up of members of the police, social services, education, probation and health agencies in a local area. Some teams are very large with over 50 members; others will have around ten members of staff. Five or six people may work with the young offender, although one or two will take particular responsibility for him or her. The team will arrange a programme to 'rehabilitate' the offender – to try to change the young person's attitudes and behaviour. The programme will cover things like:

- reasons why the young person got into trouble
- counselling
- help for parents to become better at controlling the young person
- community activities
- an apology to the victim or mending any damage done
- improving school work and attendance.

A Youth Court

Activity

1 Match each person, numbered above, with one of the following roles:

- witness
- magistrate
- justice's clerk
- prosecutor
- usher
- YOT member
- young person (defendant)
- parents
- solicitor
- victim

2 Write a sentence to explain the role of each of the people involved in the Youth Court.

If the offence is serious, or it is a second or third offence, the young person will be charged and sent to the Youth Court.

Youth Court

The Youth Court is a type of magistrates' court designed for young people under the age of eighteen. It is less formal than adult courts. The magistrates are specially trained and they can pass a different range of sentences. The cases are held in private; members of the public are not allowed in. Parents are generally expected to attend. If the young person is found guilty the magistrates can impose a range of sentences from fines to custodial orders where the offender is imprisoned in a secure unit.

Activity

1 What do you think should happen to each of the following offenders? Think about how old each offender is, what they have done, whether they have offended before and how serious the offence is. Should they:

- get a Reprimand
- get a Final Warning and go to the Youth Offending Team
- be sent to the Youth Court?

2 What programme or sentence from a Youth Court would you give these offenders?

Case study 1: *John*

John is fourteen years old. He has been picked up by the police for joyriding. He was part of a group that took a car and drove several kilometres along country lanes before abandoning it in a town centre. John says he just went along with two older boys who took and drove the car. It is his first offence. However, he has also been taken home by the police late at night for causing disturbances on the estate where he lives.

Case study 2: *Sarah*

Sarah is fifteen. She has been truanting from school and with several mates has been causing a disturbance in the local shopping mall. Shopkeepers and the public have complained. Recently the group did some damage to the plants and flowers in the centre of the mall.

Case study 3: *Michael*

Michael has been caught mugging other young people for their mobile phones. He has admitted at least three cases. He has made people hand over their phones by threatening them and handling them roughly. But he has never hit anybody or used any weapons.

3 Work in pairs.
  a) Make up three crimes that might bring three offenders before the Youth Court.
  b) Swap them with those of another pair and decide which of the magistrates' sentences you would give to the other pair's offenders.

4 What do you think of the different kinds of orders and sentences that are now given to young offenders? Do you think that they are too soft or that they are a good way of rehabilitating young offenders?

Magistrates can impose the following sentences in a Youth Court:

- Fine or compensation to be paid to the victim.
- Parents 'bound over' to exercise proper control over the offender and make sure he or she follows any community orders. They forfeit £1000 if the young person offends again.
- Reparation Order – could involve repairing damage, writing an apology, meeting the victim face-to-face to talk about the crime.
- Action Plan Order – the Youth Offending Team draws up a three-month programme, which might involve:
  - taking part in activities such as anger management classes or drug/alcohol misuse programmes
  - presenting themselves at specified times and places
  - staying away from specified places, e.g. shopping centres
- Attendance centre – attending a centre, usually run by police, for two hours twice a month for a total of between 12 and 36 hours.
- Curfew order – remaining in places at certain specified times, for example at home after 9p.m.
- Supervision order – supervised by a social worker, probation officer or YOT member (for three months to three years).
- Custodial Detention – the court may sentence a young person over the age of twelve to a period of time in custody, half in a secure unit, half under supervision in the community. If the offender is over fifteen, he or she could be sent to a young offenders' institution.

At what age are children criminally responsible?

In England, Wales and Northern Ireland the law says that children under the age of ten are not 'criminally responsible'. (In Scotland, the age is eight.) That means that the law treats children under this age as though they probably do not understand that what they have done is wrong. If a child under the age of criminal responsibility does commit a serious crime, social services will deal with the case. However, everyone over this age can be arrested, tried and, if found guilty, punished.

In 1993, James Bulger, a two-year-old boy who was out with his mother in a busy shopping centre, was abducted and murdered by two older boys. The two boys, Robert Thompson and Jon Venables, were both aged eleven when they were convicted of his murder. They were considered to be 'criminally responsible'.

The case provoked, and continues to provoke, very strong emotions. Some people say that the two boys must be evil and that they certainly knew that what they were doing was wrong. Others say that both of the boys had had very unhappy childhoods, and that they were too young to be tried in an adult court.

The case tells us a lot about the way we view child criminals. Here are two opposing views on what the age of criminal responsibility should be. Both views relate to the Bulger case.

Children of ten know the difference between right and wrong. They know you don't hurt small children. The killing of James Bulger was a planned and covered up crime. Any parent will tell you there are cases where children play rough and get hurt, but they know it's wrong to kill a child and Thompson and Venables knew that, otherwise they wouldn't have covered it up and lied about it. We have children as young as eight, or even six, terrorising people on estates such as the one I live on. I also think parents should be held responsible for their children's behaviour.
I think the age of criminal responsibility should be ***lowered to eight.***

Lyn Costello *Mothers Against Murder and Aggression*

My five-year-old daughter, Silje, was killed by two boys near our home in Trondheim, Norway. The boys stripped, stoned and beat Silje and left her for dead. I do not understand why and I will never recover, but I don't hate the boys. I think they understood what they had done, but not the consequences. It was a year after the killing of James Bulger, and the two incidents were compared in the press. In Norway, where the age of criminality is fifteen, the boys were treated differently. The boys went back to school, were helped by psychologists and have had to learn how to treat others to fit back into society. I think the age of criminal responsibility should be ***raised to fifteen.***

Beate Raedergard Mother whose child was killed by young boys

Activity

1. Do you agree with either of the viewpoints expressed below? If so, say why.
2. If you don't agree with either, what is your view?
3. Murder is clearly very serious but it is an extreme case. What about less serious crimes? Should there be a different age of responsibility for crimes such as:
   - stealing sweets from shops
   - causing trouble on an estate
   - drawing graffiti
   - damaging property?
4. Prepare a case to make to the whole class, explaining whether you think the age of criminal responsibility should be raised, lowered or kept the same, and why.

2.6 How do the courts work?

A number of factors affect which court a case is heard in:

- whether the case is a criminal or a civil one
- whether the case is a first hearing or an appeal against a previous decision
- how serious or complex the case is.

Court of Appeal

If a defendant does not think he or she has had a fair trial, or that their punishment is too harsh, they can take their case to an appeal court. Everyone has the right to appeal but there has to be a good reason for it, for example new evidence or the mishandling of the first trial by the judge. Appeals are heard by judges; there is no jury.

CRIMINAL

Criminal courts

Most criminal cases start off in the magistrates' court (see panel below). If the offence is serious, it usually then passes on to the Crown Court.

Magistrates' Court

More than 90% of all criminal cases are dealt with in magistrates' courts. These are the less serious offences such as: illegal parking, speeding, the theft of small amounts, fighting in public, being drunk and disorderly. They are called 'summary' offences. Magistrates also deal with a small number of civil cases, especially the granting of licences to clubs, pubs and betting shops.

Usually three magistrates sit on the 'bench' to hear the case and, for summary offences, they decide guilt and sentence. Most magistrates are 'lay' magistrates, called 'Justices of the Peace'. They are ordinary members of the public, not professional lawyers, who take on the job of magistrate on a rota, about twenty times a year. They are not paid for the work, although they can claim expenses. A professional lawyer can advise them on points of law. This is the 'clerk of the court'.

Crown Court

These courts are held in cities and towns around England and Wales. A judge is in charge of proceedings and a jury decides whether the defendant is guilty or not. Cases such as theft and assault are tried by circuit judges or recorders (part-time judges). Very serious offences, such as murder, armed robbery or rape, are tried by High Court judges in larger courts like the Old Bailey.

If the offence is serious, it usually passes on to the Crown Court

House of Lords

The highest court in the land is the House of Lords. Judges called Law Lords will hear appeals on important points of law that may be of great interest to the general public. For instance, it might be to do with whether a person has the right to an assisted death.

Activity

To which of the courts would the following cases go:

a) A driver who has been caught speeding four times.

b) A man charged with burglary and manslaughter – he broke into an old man's house and stole goods worth £800. The old man had a heart attack as a result of the break-in, and died shortly afterwards.

c) An actress is suing a magazine for £500 000 because it published photographs of her wedding without her permission.

d) A man wants the right to an assisted suicide because he is paralysed by a disease which is slowly killing him. He has been refused permission by the High Court and the Court of Appeal.

e) A woman convicted of causing the death of her baby claims she has new medical evidence to prove her innocence.

Court of Appeal

If the people concerned do not agree with the verdict, then civil cases can be taken to appeal.

CIVIL

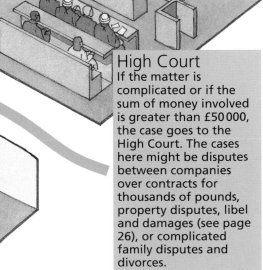

High Court

If the matter is complicated or if the sum of money involved is greater than £50 000, the case goes to the High Court. The cases here might be disputes between companies over contracts for thousands of pounds, property disputes, libel and damages (see page 26), or complicated family disputes and divorces.

County Court

Most civil cases are dealt with in the County Court. A judge, usually sitting without a jury, decides these cases. They may be matters such as disputes between neighbours, undefended divorces, or contracts where not too much money is involved. If claims are under £5000, then they are settled in the **small claims court**.

Trial by jury

Jury
A jury in England and Wales is made up of twelve people from all walks of life. Anybody between 18 and 65 who votes in elections can be called to do jury service. They are paid a small amount of money by the court for attending. It is compulsory, although people in certain professions can be excused, such as doctors, vets or soldiers, as well as people in special circumstances, for example if they care for someone all day or have difficulty reading.

Magistrates' courts deal with minor offences. When more serious offences – called **indictable offences** – are involved, they are passed on by the magistrate to the Crown Court. But there are also some offences which are called **either-way offences**. An example is theft, which might be shoplifting goods worth a few pounds or stealing the life savings of an elderly person. In some of these cases, the defendant can choose to be tried by the magistrate or to have a trial by jury in a higher court.

Trial by jury is a much slower and more expensive business than just having a judge or judges who make decisions. Some cases cost hundreds of thousands of pounds. Some people say that many defendants who ask for a jury trial are trying to spin out their case, hoping witnesses will disappear or the prosecution will drop its charges. Then, when the actual day of the trial comes, they plead 'guilty'.

There is an argument that some offenders should not always be given the choice of whether to have a jury trial, especially if they are repeat offenders. However, the civil liberties organisation, Liberty, believes that the right to jury trial is a cornerstone of our democratic society because it makes sure that people are judged by their fellow citizens. Having twelve people on a jury drawn from a variety of backgrounds lessens the likelihood of an error and ensures that the decision reflects the views of the community at large.

Activity

Work in pairs. Decide which of the arguments below are **for** trial by jury and which **against**. Add any other arguments, either for or against, that you can think of. Then, as a whole class, discuss the following questions:

1. What are the main problems with trial by jury?
2. Why would some people argue it is the only way of making sure everybody gets a fair trial?
3. Why would it be easier to have an experienced judge or judges dealing with certain cases? This is what many countries do.
4. Are you, on balance, in favour of or against letting everybody who wants to, have a jury trial?

1 Having a jury of ordinary people is the best way of ensuring that everybody agrees that trials are fair and not controlled by rich and powerful people who all know each other.

2 Trial by jury is very expensive.

3 Jurors can be bribed, threatened or intimidated by friends of the accused person.

4 A jury is likely to be made up of a mix of people from different backgrounds – social, ethnic and religious.

5 Jurors may read stories in the newspapers about their trials or similar cases which could influence them.

6 It is important that people see that the criminal justice system is fair. If people stopped believing in the fairness of courts, respect for the law might break down.

7 Jurors may have very fixed opinions about people accused of being criminals and not really listen to the evidence to decide if the person is guilty or not.

8 Since juries are made up of ordinary people, they are more able to understand the situation faced by the defendant because they or their families may have faced similar circumstances.

9 Justice should be swift. A magistrate can hear a case quickly and decide guilt or innocence. Trial by jury can take months and months before it even starts.

10 Judges can be out of touch because they live mostly in a world of other judges and lawyers where they do not meet ordinary people. So the decision of the jury reflects more what people outside the courts think.

A better way of sentencing?

If an offender is found guilty in a court of law, it is the job of the magistrate or judge to decide on the sentence, or punishment.

The sentence depends on the offence and the circumstances under which it was committed. Magistrates and judges can award sentences from absolute discharge, community service and probation, right up to life imprisonment. They receive training and guidance on sentencing, but only recently has there been any discussion about involving the victim in the offender's sentence.

This article describes an experiment in Canada, where the judge decides on a sentence by consulting everyone involved, including the victim.

Justice in the Round

There is no judge's bench. No robes or wigs. No formal submissions from prosecution and defence to influence the judge's sentence.

A circle of between 20 and 30 people is discussing the appropriate sentence for 'Mr Green', a physiotherapy student. He has pleaded guilty to robbing a petrol station and threatening a young woman with a knife – a crime for which he could normally be jailed for three years.

The circle includes his wife and other family members, a fellow student, his football coach and his legal representatives. Also present are the victim, her parents, boyfriend and other supporters and her counsel. The policewoman involved in the case has a say; so do a representative of the local victim support group and an alcoholism and drugs counsellor.

Facilitating the circle is a red-haired, elf-like figure – Bria Huculak, a judge from Saskatchewan. She was appointed a judge in 1992 at the age of 40 and shocked the Canadian legal system by beginning to consult the community about appropriate sentences for certain defendants pleading guilty.

She and her colleagues began using sentencing circles. What they now have is a process that is a mixture of victim/offender mediation, ancient traditional peace-making circles and democratic discussion. The aim is to identify the harm done and to work out appropriate ways of responding to it, and, if possible, repairing it.

The process may take six or seven hours. Sometimes, sentencing circles recommend to a judge novel forms of sentence. Prison sentencing is much reduced. One offender, whose drunk and dangerous driving had caused the death of his father, had to spend the next year or so explaining his crime and waywardness to public meetings of young people as part of his punishment.

From the *Guardian*, 9 May 2001

Discuss

1 What are the advantages of this approach to sentencing?
2 What might be the disadvantages?

Activity

Sentencing circle role play
If there are not enough roles for everyone in this role play, some can be observers making notes on how everyone behaves in their role.

The situation
Jake Lewis is accused of stealing a car and driving it dangerously. He crashed it while being chased by the police, and his girlfriend, Courtney, was injured. She has also been accused of being an accessory to the crime. Jake has admitted to the crime. You are members of the sentencing circle. You must now reach a decision about his sentence.

Susanna Pike – the judge in this case, who knows that Jake could qualify for a custodial sentence, especially since this is not his first offence, and his girlfriend, a minor, was injured. Susanna leads the discussion.

Jake Lewis – 22 years old, unemployed, from a large housing estate in an inner city. He has admitted to stealing a car, driving it without insurance and crashing it into a tree. He has stolen cars before, but never crashed them.

Courtney Johnson – 17 years old, Jake's girlfriend, employed in a clothes shop. She has admitted to helping him steal the car and being a willing accessory. She was in the passenger seat, and received cuts to her face and a broken jaw.

Jake's mother – who Jake lives with, is very worried about him and wants him to stop stealing cars. She thinks that Courtney is a bad influence on him.

Courtney's parents – blame Jake for the injuries their daughter has received and want him to receive a harsh punishment to get him away from Courtney.

Tariq Coles – the owner of the car, which he bought very recently. It was his pride and joy. He only had third party insurance, so he may not be able to afford to replace it.

Constables O'Malley and Ferguson – the police officers who pursued Jake after the report of the theft by Tariq, the owner of the car. They had to assist at the scene of the crash and call the ambulance for Courtney.

Jake's solicitor – who will argue for a non-custodial sentence.

Solicitor for the prosecution – who will stress Jake's previous record and the need to deter him from more car crime.

Several witnesses – some who saw the car being driven erratically and one who witnessed the crash.

Neighbours of Jake and his mother – who are fed up with car crime on the estate and know that Jake is a ring-leader. They are convinced he was involved in a similar offence earlier this year where a nine-year-old girl was seriously injured when a stolen car ran out of control and hit her on the pavement.

Courtney's employer – who has come to say that she is a good worker, liked and trusted by her work colleagues, and that she gets on well with customers.

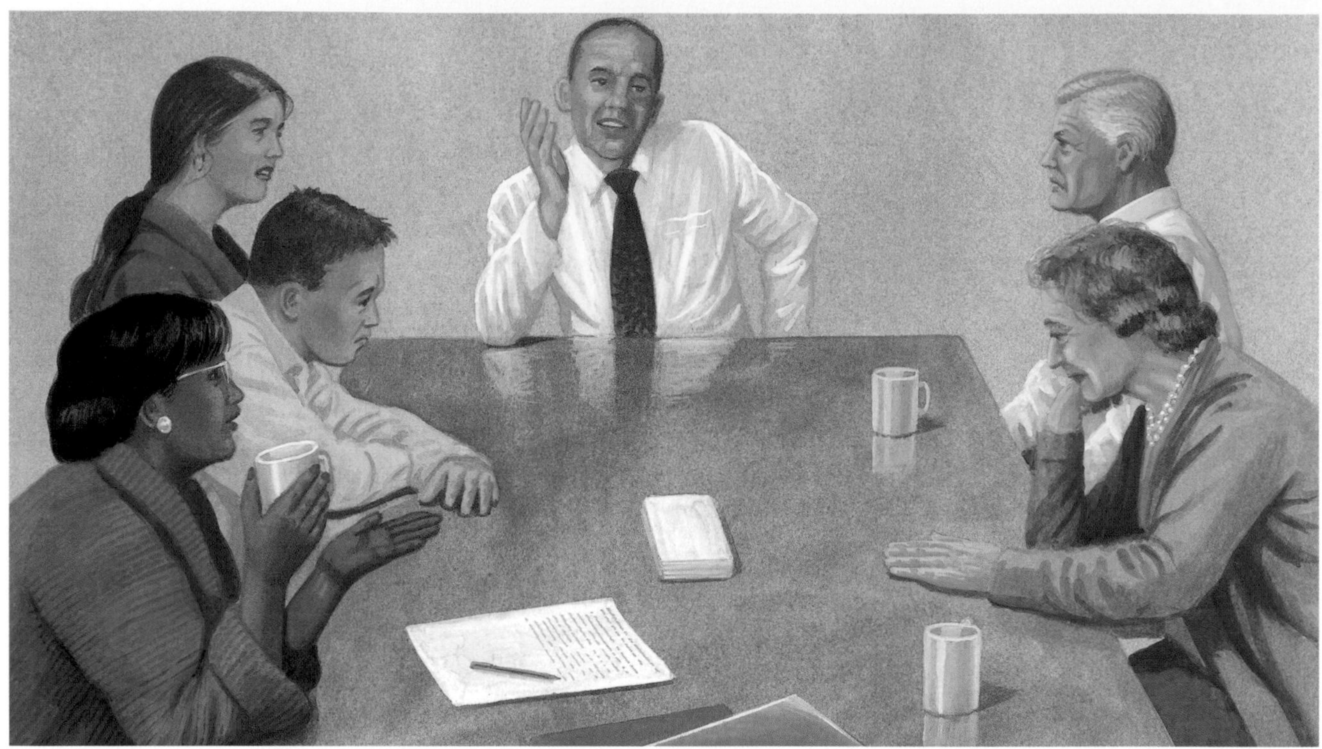

Mediation

In Britain we do not have sentencing circles but there is a trend towards mediation – offenders meeting their victims to face up to the pain, damage or loss they caused another human being. Many offenders do not realise how much they make other people suffer. This mediation is in addition to, not an alternative to, punishment.

Discuss

What do you think about the idea of offender/victim mediation?

a) How could it help the offender?
b) How could it help the victim?
c) For which of the following offences do you think it would be most suitable? Give reasons for your choices.

When a boy has been bullied and assaulted by an older boy who has stolen his mobile phone.

When goods have been stolen from a corner shop.

When a drunk car driver has injured somebody who is now unable to walk.

When a man has attacked a young woman at knife point.

d) Do you think mediation is a good idea for young offenders between the ages of ten and seventeen? Explain your answer.

2.7 Going to prison

Most people agree that a **custodial sentence** (being sent to prison) is the most serious. People can be imprisoned for many different kinds of offences. The vast majority of prisoners spend a short time in prison (less than one year). However, some prisoners have to adjust to living in prison for many years. The number of people in prison continues to rise. There are now more than 70 000 people in jails in the UK.

People disagree about the purpose of a prison sentence.

Restitution

A It is important that the victims of crime and society as a whole feel that the offender has made amends for their crime. This means they have 'served their time', admitted their guilt and are sorry for what they have done. It puts things right.

Deterrence

B We must put people in prison for certain crimes so that other offenders will be deterred from committing those crimes – they know what will happen if they are caught.

Retribution

C Prison teaches criminals a lesson. If they have done wrong, they should pay the price.

Reform

D Prison can provide offenders with education and training to help them get back on their feet when they leave prison so that they can 'go straight'.

Prevention

E At least while people are in prison they are not committing any more crimes. The rest of us are safe from them for a while.

Activity

Statements A–E express different reasons for sending an offender to prison.

1 Give each statement a mark from 1 to 5 (1 = disagree strongly, 5 = agree strongly) to show how much you agree with each view.

1	2	3	4	5
disagree strongly	disagree	not sure	agree	agree strongly

2 Carry out some research among your friends and family to find out which of these statements is most commonly agreed with. Use the same scale.

3 Compare results across the class and make a chart, perhaps using IT, to show which of the statements are most strongly agreed with.

4 How do your views compare with the overall sample?

5 What other arguments for and against prison can you think of, for example:

- the high cost
- doesn't prevent people re-offending
- turns people into hardened criminals
- community service works better with many offences.

What is it like inside a prison?

Prisons vary. Prison Inspectors regularly visit prisons to review conditions – particularly things like bullying, racism, quality of food, cell space, education and training, provision for exercise, health care, etc.

One woman's experience

Below is one account of a short stay inside a women's prison.

Rebecca (not her real name), in her late teens, spent six months on remand at Holloway women's prison in London on drugs charges.

'I was shocked when they sent me to prison. I couldn't believe it. It was the first time I was separated from my family and it was difficult to cope. Holloway is not a good place to be. There were no televisions in cells and no electricity points to plug in a radio. We were banged up for long periods each day, especially at weekends when there were staff shortages.

'Sometimes it was three or four days before you could have a bath. You had to make do with washing from a bucket. At first I was in a cell by myself, but I wanted to move to be with other people. We played cards and talked to pass the time. I also read a lot.

'They normally woke us around 7 a.m. We had breakfast at 8 a.m. If there were enough staff you got half an hour's exercise in the fresh air.

'Sometimes we were forced to take our lunch back to our cells. And if there weren't enough officers we had to be back in our cells early, sometimes by 4 p.m., especially at weekends. The food wasn't very good. It was difficult not being able to have something to eat or a cup of tea when you felt like it.

The first month was very hard, but you do get used to it. If you're quiet and don't bother other people, you will be fine. I got in one fight but the officers stopped it.'

From the *Guardian*, 27 November 2001

One man's experience

In 1994 professional golfer John Hoskisson killed a cyclist in a drink-drive accident. He was sentenced to three years in prison. In his book *Inside* he describes his experiences in two prisons.

Wandsworth

The cell door flew open and three of Wandsworth's most feared warders charged in. 'Against the wall,' they screamed, truncheons drawn. For a split second there was pandemonium but in that time I saw Jimmy Baker, one of my cellmates, whip a small parcel of heroin out of his pocket and swallow it.

Minutes later we were all back in the cell – the beds had been overturned, mattresses were split open, pictures ripped off the wall and the sheets left in a pile on the dirty stone floor.

Later Jimmy picked up his slop bucket and with practised ease retched up the contents of his stomach including the parcel of heroin he had swallowed. I told him I'd have to ask him to move out if he smoked heroin. 'Do that and I'll knife you,' he said.

I've never been so fearful of my safety. As the night progressed he became more volatile, screaming obscenities. Sleep was impossible and I could not disengage my mind from the terror of my incarceration with this loathsome, drug-crazed creature.

Cordingley

The bonus of a C-category prison is being allowed to wear one's own clothes; the downside was that because inmates were supposedly more trustworthy, officers left each prison landing unsupervised. Consequently the place was filthy. Stale mouldy food littered the floor, dustbins overflowed, and the windows were so dirty hardly any light filtered through.

The next day was my first induction – setting objectives for each prisoner. I asked for education opportunities and to keep fit in the gym. I was to be disappointed. The gym was minute and decrepit with gaping holes in the floorboards. As for education, because of savage budget cuts, only 20 out of 280 inmates were on courses. No trades were taught. GCSE English was the most advanced course you could take.

Everyone at Cordingley was expected to work. I was assigned to the metal shop. The whole thing was farcical. After a cursory explanation, the supervisor left me at my huge pressing machine with just the comment: 'Do the best you can.' It took me five minutes to learn the job. Ten minutes to invent a quicker way of doing it. Fifteen before I received a warning: 'Hey you – you're working too hard.' At the end of the first week we had produced 2000 pieces; 1800 pieces had to be scrapped because they'd been badly made.

Every week I saw prisoners released back into the outside world with nothing to show for their time inside except a £46 discharge grant. Regularly they were rearrested within days.

It's been a real eye-opener, prison. Perhaps it's now time I made some sort of comment. One thing's for certain – prison is essential. There are some dangerous people in here; the public has a right to be protected. But it's no good putting everyone in the same boat.

Extracts from John Hoskisson's *Inside*, 1998

Activity

1 Some people think that prison should be tough, to make people determined not to go back. They often say 'prison should not be like a holiday camp'. What do you think about the conditions Rebecca and John describe?

2 Which would be the worst parts of imprisonment for you: loss of freedom, the basic conditions, fear of possible fights and bullying, being told what to do by officers, or something else?

2.8 Reducing crime

One measure by which people judge the quality of their lives is the amount of crime they think happens. Fear of crime is greater than it used to be. This might be because we hear about crime more frequently on television and in the newspapers. Whatever the reasons, many people, particularly the elderly, think that things are much worse now than they were in the past.

So, are the instances of crime increasing? And if so, by how much? This is a difficult question to answer. The British Crime Survey (BCS), which produced diagrams A and B below, gets its information from interviewing a cross-section of people about their experiences of crime. The survey is often regarded as a more accurate picture of crime rates than figures from the police.

Activity

1. Look at diagram A. What have been the trends in crime from 1981 to 2000?
2. Look at diagram B.
   a) What are the three largest categories of crime?
   b) What is the percentage of violent crime against the person (mugging, wounding and assault) rather than against property?
   c) Do any of these figures surprise you?
3. Do you think people are right to be more worried about crime?

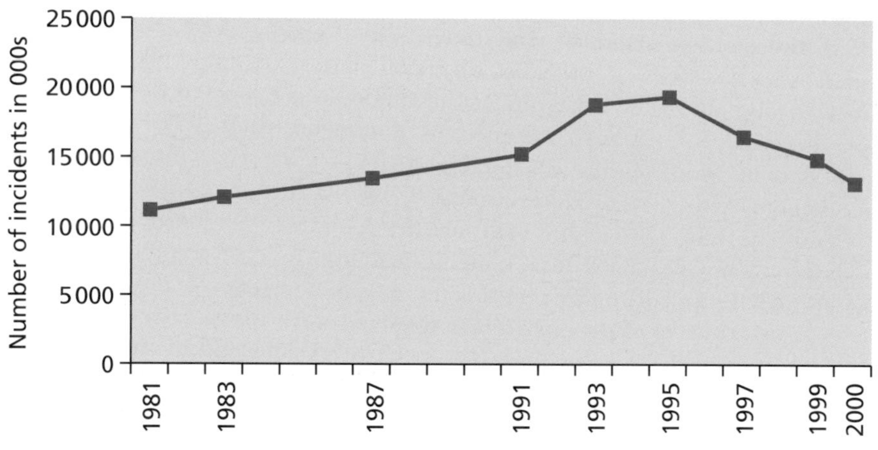

A BCS, trends in crime, 1981–2000

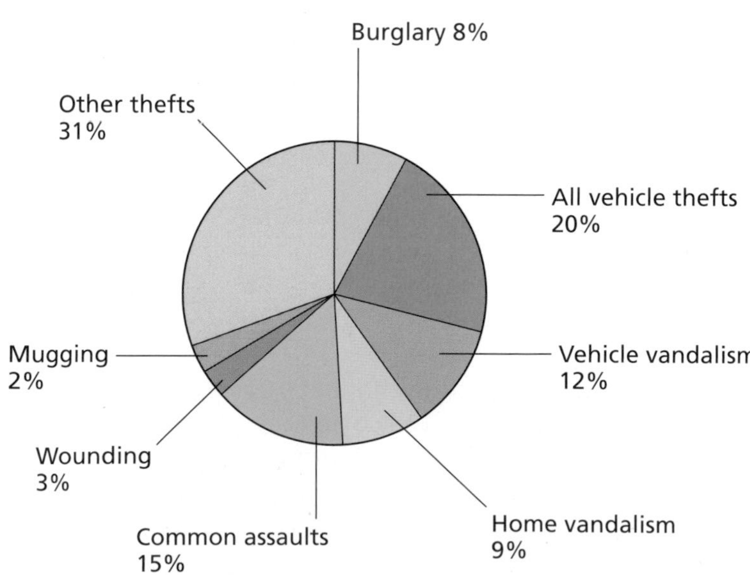

B BCS, breakdown of crime by offence category, 2000

The British Crime Survey estimates the number of crimes committed from its interviews with a sample of people. Surely, you would think, official figures from the police are more accurate? The problem is that:

a) people often do not report crime to the police
b) the police sometimes change the way they record crime.

The following table compares the numbers of crimes recorded by the police and those estimated by the British Crime Survey for the year 2000. (Note that the table is in thousands, so in the first row 481 000 cases of vandalism were recorded by the police and 2 608 000 by the British Crime Survey – this means that the police figure is only 18% of the BCS figure.)

Crime figures for 2000

	Crimes recorded by the police (000s)	**British Crime Survey (BCS) estimates (000s)**	**% of BCS recorded by police**
Property crime Vandalism	481	2608	18
Burglary	409	1063	38
Attempts with no loss	106	660	16
Burglary with loss	303	403	75
Vehicle thefts	938	2619	36
Thefts from vehicles	478	1626	29
Thefts of vehicles	235	337	70
Attempted vehicle theft	224	656	34
Bicycle theft	119	377	31
Theft from the person	88	629	14
Violent crime Wounding	195	417	47
Robbery	78	276	28
Common assault	193	1890	10
All property and violent crimes	2501	9879	25

Source: The 2001 British Crime Survey (*Home Office Statistical Bulletin*)

Discuss

1 Taking into account all the information above and your answers to the Activity, why do you think it is so difficult to tell whether crime is going up or down?
2 Do you think that crime is on the increase in the area where you live? What reasons do you have for saying this? Would your views be influenced by knowing what the crime figures were for your area? Try to find them out by looking at your local police force website.

Activity

1 The table on the left suggests that, on average, only 25% of all crime is reported to and recorded by the police. What reasons can you give for this?
2 Look at the recorded percentages for common assault (10%) and vandalism (18%). Why do you think such a low percentage of these is recorded by the police?
3 Look at the theft of vehicles where the percentage is very high (70%). What reasons can you suggest for this?
4 What would happen to official police figures on different types and amounts of crime if the following things happened?
   - People started to think differently about an offence and reported it more often, for example assault, such as somebody being hit outside a pub.
   - The police decided to crack down on a particular offence and were more likely to look out for it and follow it up, for example drink-driving.
   - The police and public began to think of an offence as less serious and to be more tolerant of it, for example use of soft drugs.
   - The police installed a large number of speed cameras on many roads.

Zero tolerance

A lot of people think that the answer to crime is to get tough – the tougher you get, the less crime there will be. The idea behind zero tolerance policing is that if you crack down on minor crimes like graffiti and vandalism, you prevent more serious crime from taking hold in an area. Police officers go after so-called 'quality of life' offences: misdemeanours such as drinking in the street, graffiti, playing music too loudly or even jay-walking. This sends out the message that any unlawful act will be punished. Rudy Giuliani, when he was mayor of New York, claimed to have cleaned up crime-ridden parts of the city through tough policing and zero tolerance.

Rudy Giuliani, Mayor of New York, 1998–2001

Discuss

What do you think are the best ways of reducing crime?

Activity

1 Sort arguments A–H into those **for** zero tolerance, and those **against**.
2 Which side are you on? Do you think it would work in this country? Give your reasons.
3 Write a newspaper article on zero tolerance, explaining what it is and your view on why it would be a good or a bad thing to introduce in Britain.

A Criminals need to know that law-breaking of any kind will not be tolerated. If they learn that lesson early on they won't be tempted into a life of crime.

B Many of the offenders picked up under zero tolerance are victims as much as they are offenders – drug addicts, unemployed, homeless and damaged people. They need help, not punishment.

C Zero tolerance really gives the police almost limitless power to stop, search and harass anyone in a poor community. Minority ethnic groups often feel 'picked on'.

D Zero tolerance policing is very expensive and requires huge numbers of police officers, who are all focusing on catching minor criminals instead of following up corporate crime, large-scale drug dealing and organised crime.

E If young offenders are removed from a criminal environment before they sink into a life of crime, they are more likely to have happier and more successful lives. A custodial sentence can offer them the chance of an education.

F Making sure relations with the police are good and that people are respected and consulted about what should happen in the area – that reduces crime, not the constant fear of arrest.

G Crime costs the country huge amounts of money, especially minor crimes like graffiti and petty theft. Everyone benefits if these activities are stopped.

H Residents often want the police to crack down on crime, especially street prostitution and drug-dealing. Residents are frightened of the criminals, not the police.

section 3

Local government and community

Key words
- community
- neighbourhood
- regeneration
- voluntary organisation
- volunteering

What part can you play in your community?

Being part of a community makes you feel that you belong. It gives you an identity. This section looks at how citizens fit into communities and how you can help make your local community a better place to live.

You will learn about:

- the idea of community
- who provides what a community needs
- voluntary organisations
- ways that local people can get involved themselves
- local taxation and local decision-making
- regenerating communities
- Local Agenda 21.

You will use the following skills:

- analysing information
- discussing your ideas
- presenting and explaining your ideas
- making decisions
- using your imagination to consider how other people might feel in different situations
- taking part in activities and reflecting on this.

3.1 'Community is good for you!'

A community is a group of people with a shared identity or interest. Most of us belong to lots of different communities. Here are Janice and Aktar. They belong to many different communities.

internet chat room

chat room

friends

school

neighbours

Aktar

Janice

work

football fan

religion

Girl Guides

Activity

1 What different communities do Janice and Aktar belong to?

2 Copy and complete a diagram like this to show all the communities that you feel you belong to.

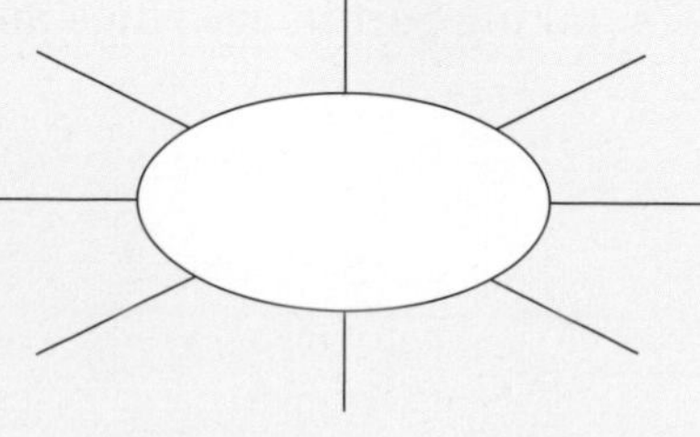

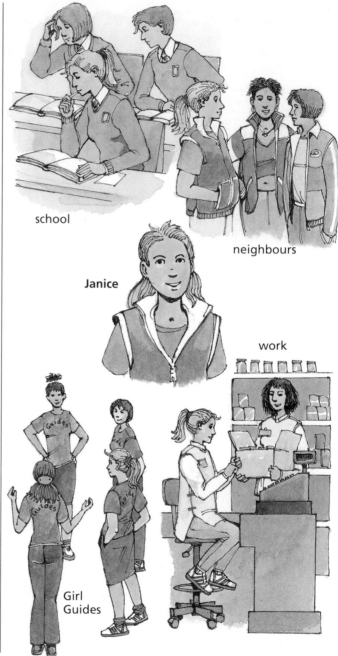

The communities you belong to help you to develop your sense of identity (who you are and how you see yourself). A sense of belonging comes from shared interests and shared values (things you think are important). These are developed in areas such as:

- school and the area you live in, the friends you make and the interests, such as music, that you have in common
- work where you spend a lot of time and form friendships
- religion in which you share a set of beliefs with others
- a minority ethnic community in which you share the same beliefs and culture as others
- local issues groups, where people share interests and goals, e.g. when people get together to demand safety on roads.

When we talk about our local community we are usually referring to the area we live in, our neighbours, the shops we go to, and so on.

Community is good for you
Researchers have found that being part of a community makes people more content. People like to have other people to talk to, say hello to; to feel that others share their interests. More than this, it seems that the more communities we are involved in, the more satisfied we are with our lives.

Activity

1 Think about the communities you have seen in soap operas on TV like *Hollyoaks* or *EastEnders*. What are the things that link these people and make them into a community?
2 What different types of community are represented in each of these photographs?

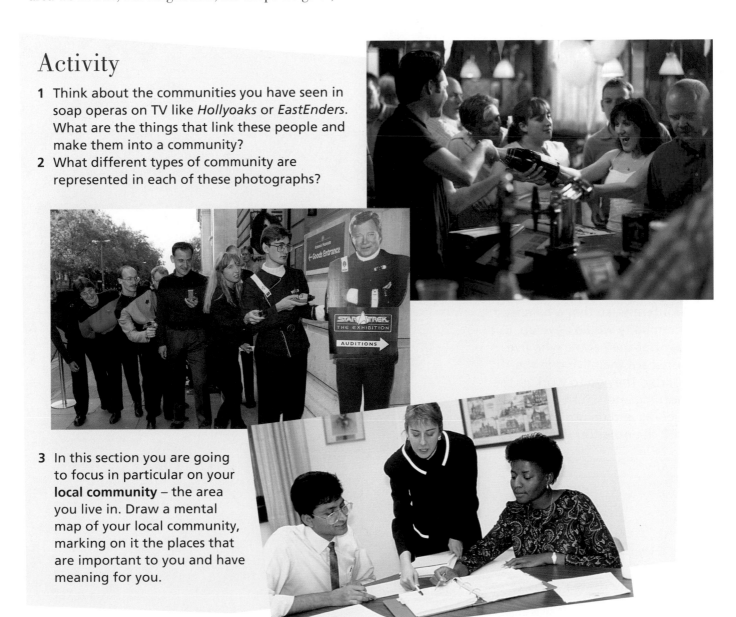

3 In this section you are going to focus in particular on your **local community** – the area you live in. Draw a mental map of your local community, marking on it the places that are important to you and have meaning for you.

How would you develop a sense of community?

Activity

A new area of housing has been built in the countryside over the last few years. It is on the outskirts of a large city – about thirty kilometres from the centre – but far enough away to seem like a place on its own. There are all sorts of houses:

- expensive ones with drives and gardens
- starter homes for young couples
- affordable housing for families supported by the council and a housing association
- rented council housing in several low-rise blocks
- flats for single people
- a retirement complex.

The people who planned the area wanted to make sure that there was a wide range of people of all ages with all sorts of interests, so that a balanced community would develop. But many of the people who live here earn their living in the city nearby. They go to work in the morning and return in the evening and do not really mix with the other residents.

How can you help this area to develop a sense of community? Look at the community buildings on the right. Choose four of these to add to the area to help the local people to mix and develop their sense of belonging to the area. Think about:

- which ones would bring people together
- how you could cater for different age groups
- what would give the community a sense of purpose
- what would make the inhabitants feel they shared a common interest.

1 Which four buildings would you choose? Why?
2 Which buildings do you think are not important?
3 Choose one other community building or space, not shown here, that you think the area should have.
4 If you were to choose the school as the main focus for community development, what programme of events/meetings could you plan to develop community feeling?
5 What community places do you have in your area that bring people together?

Community buildings

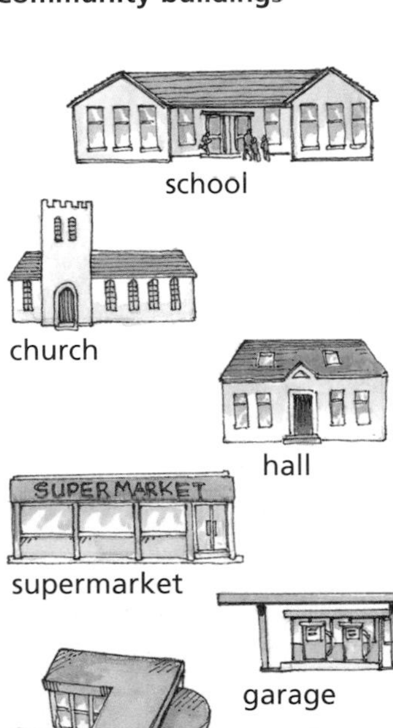

school

church

hall

supermarket

garage

youth centre

post office

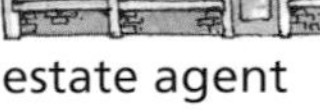

estate agent

internet café

antique shop

bank

garden centre

pub

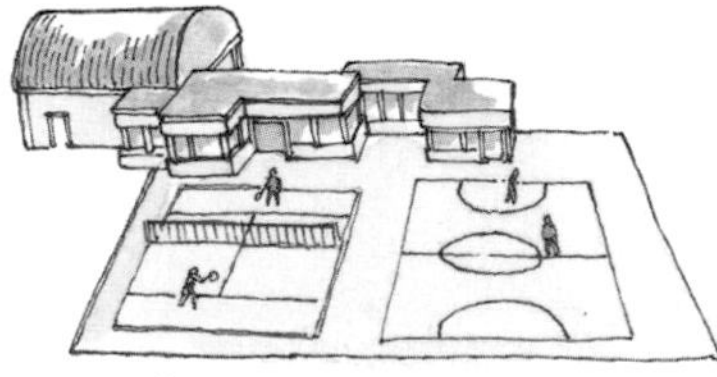

recreation centre

Parallel communities

In May 2001, the town of Bradford saw some of the worst riots that have taken place in England for the last fifteen years. Gangs of Asian and white youths fought running battles in the streets. Shops were set alight and property was vandalised. An enormous amount of damage was done. Similar riots took place in Burnley in June 2002.

Sometimes people living in an area do not mix with other people who live near them. They live in 'parallel communities'. They go to different shops and schools and live separate lives. They never get to know each other. This separation can breed misunderstanding, fear and hatred. It can lead to conflict between the communities. In Northern Ireland, the Catholics and the Protestants have long lived in parallel communities, separated from each other, and that has helped lead to severe conflict between the two communities. In parts of England there has been rioting and conflict between Asian and white groups who live in parallel communities.

A

IGNORANCE, MISUNDERSTANDING AND FEAR

Oldham council was charged yesterday with doing little to challenge the racial segregation in housing and education that has gone on in the town for 30 years...

In a bleak analysis of segregation, [a report] says that Pakistanis and Bangladeshis who came to work in the town's mills chose 'to live with their own kind' in neighbourhoods such as Glodwick, scene of the worst riots on mainland Britain for 15 years. Segregated housing in turn led to segregated schools...

'Whether in school or out of school, there are few opportunities for young people across the communal boundaries to mix... Relationships between communities at adult level are largely confined to business transactions (shops, restaurants, taxis).

'Pakistanis, Bangladeshis and whites simply do not meet each other to any significant degree and this has led to ignorance, misunderstanding and fear. The divisions are such that we now have to ask the question whether people in different communities actually want to have much to do with one another.'...The report rejects suggestions of no-go areas for either whites or Asian people. 'There are areas where people, especially young people, of different communities feel uncomfortable...These might be considered "won't go" areas; there are no "no-go" areas in Oldham.'

From the *Guardian*, 12 December 2001

B

Divided communities

In Oldham. . .there are a small number of deprived estates where white children have never made an Asian friend or vice versa. Most primary schools are single race, and many secondaries are 99% white or 99% Asian.

For many people, the first prolonged contact with different cultures comes at sixth-form college. By then, isolation, poverty and unemployment have already cemented attitudes on race.

Asians – including Pakistanis, Bangladeshis and Indians – make up 11% of Oldham's population. But they make up only around 2% of the workforce of the local council, the town's biggest employer. The rate of mixed marriages in the town is less than 1%. Many Asians who have lived there for 20 years have never seen a police officer in their area. . .

Asif, 23, a trainee lawyer, will not walk five minutes north of his front door because he would cross into a white estate and that would be asking for a beating. He said: 'Some kids – even educated kids – never get to know white people except teachers. When the only whites you see are rushing through the streets having smashed your windscreen, or a skinhead chasing you down the road, people start to demonise whites in their minds. Race relations here are going back in time. You feel whites don't actually want to know you.'

From the *Guardian*, 12 December 2001

Activity

Read the newspaper extracts A and B.

1 What sorts of problems do the writers identify because of Oldham's 'parallel communities'? Think about the following:
- schools
- jobs
- housing
- religion
- relations between communities.

2 Many of the areas that have been affected by riots and disturbances are deprived areas where the housing is poor, there are few jobs, and people are unemployed and poor. So what can be done to lessen the tension between communities? The suggestions opposite have been made in an official report about how the situation in Oldham could be improved.
   a) Give your opinion about how well they might work.
   b) Suggest some ideas of your own.
   c) Do you think similar ideas could be used in other parts of the UK?

Make sure that schools are racially mixed.

Make sure that all ethnic communities are represented among council staff.

Clear and replace poor-quality housing much more quickly and make sure that new housing schemes are racially mixed.

Create opportunities to enable different ethnic groups (including white people) to mix.

Create more job opportunities for all of the people who live in the area.

Ensure that any Christian faith schools, which do not accept Muslims make available 20% of their places to non-Christians.

Put a big effort into teaching the English language to Asian adults and pre-school children.

A new style of community?

Welcome to Celebration

Take the best ideas from the successful towns of yesterday and the technology of the new millennium, and synthesise them into a close-knit community that meets the needs of today's families.

In Florida, USA, close to Walt Disney World Resort, The Celebration Company, a subsidiary of the Walt Disney Company is building a whole new town called Celebration from scratch. It is part of a growing trend in the USA called 'new urbanism'. Americans are building small towns that form their own tight community. The houses in Celebration resemble those built around 1900, they are close together with garages behind the houses and alleyways to access them. The idea is that the neighbours will get to know each other and all become good friends.

Celebration is built on four ideas:

- community
- health – it has its own hospital and a huge fitness centre as well as kilometres of cycle and walking paths
- technology – all houses are connected to the internet and to the latest technological developments.
- a sense of place.

Celebration has its own park, lake and golf course. The prices of houses are much higher than for similar homes in neighbouring communities. Also, you have to stick to the rules, which are tight: you can't change the colour of your house without agreement and your paintwork must not be chipped, you must mow the lawn to keep the front tidy, you must not repair cars on driveways, and so on. Homeowners agree to these 'guidelines' before they buy their homes.

Activity

Think about the Celebration community.

a) What would be the advantages of living in a community like Celebration?

b) What do you think it would be like if you broke the rules, for example painted your house a bright colour or left a mess on your front driveway?

c) What sort of people do you think live in communities like Celebration?

d) What do you like/dislike about Celebration?

Celebration – a place where memories of a lifetime are made. It's more than a home; it's a community rich with old-fashioned appeal and an eye on the future.

This is all part of the desire of many Americans to escape from the cities, which are less pleasant and more dangerous. For some time they have been building areas of housing that are protected by walls and fences so that the people inside them can feel safe. In many of these places all the needs of the residents are met by the services provided – shopping, house repairs, leisure and entertainment. Of course, it is only the well-off who can afford to live in these walled environments.

Today more than 8 million Americans live in gated communities. A similar trend is appearing in Britain. Many new developments for well-off people in city areas – London, Birmingham, Leeds and Cardiff – are being built behind protective walls and gates. Security cameras and guards are employed to make sure the areas are kept safe. They protect the residents from robberies and car-jackings and the dangers of the city. At the same time residents are cut off from their neighbours outside. In the development of the London Docklands in the 1980s, there was a lot of hostility from local people as they saw housing developments for the wealthy, surrounded by high walls, going up in the area they had lived in for years.

In Britain [today] gated communities are no longer a novelty...One of the largest, in terms of area, is...20 miles from Newcastle upon Tyne. Wynyard Woods began in 1994...Today the development boasts gates within gates. There are two main gates, one of which is closed after 7p.m. 'In addition many residents like to have a gate of their own in front of a high wall,' says Doreen Pate, sales director of Bellway Homes in the north-east. 'It gives them a sense of their own identity and space.'...

The development already boasts a pub-restaurant, supermarket, golf course, and a cricket pitch. A hairdresser's and a nursery are in the pipeline. So a gated community of just over 900 residents is already better supplied with facilities than many a long-established rural village.

From the *Guardian*, 30 January 2002

Activity

Now think about gated communities in Britain.

a) Why do people want to live in these communities?

b) Do you think that the people who live there like it?

c) What do you think is the effect of these communities on the attitudes of people who live next to them?

d) Would you like to live in one?

e) Do you think the growing number of such places is a good thing or a bad thing for British society?

3.2 Who provides what you need in the local community?

We all live in a local community, made up of the houses, the streets and the shops in the neighbourhood where we live and the places and facilities we use nearby. We have certain needs and we expect certain services. In any community some of these are provided by the local council and some by voluntary organisations.

What services does the council provide?

Most councils are divided up into separate departments that use names like the ones shown here.

Police and fire services

- These are provided by larger councils such as county councils

Social services

- Families and children, adoption and fostering, care of elderly people
- Youth services – young people who break the law
- Mental health care in the community

Planning and technical services

- Gives permission for new building – houses, flats, offices or other business premises
- Deals with housing improvement when people want to add extensions to their houses
- Is responsible for highways and pavements, and engineering works (such as digging up roads for pipes, putting in road humps)
- Takes measures to prevent crime, for example CCTV cameras

Housing

- Maintains and repairs houses and flats owned by the council
- Provides services on housing estates, for example caretakers, noise patrols
- Tries to resolve problems, so rogue, troublesome families might be evicted

Education

- Runs and allocates funds to schools under the council's control
- Decides who should be admitted to schools
- Advises parents about local schools and makes arrangements for pupils with special educational needs

Leisure and amenities

- Provides and maintains parks and open spaces, recycling centres, recreation and sports centres, libraries, cemeteries, youth clubs and schemes for young people

Environmental services

- Cleans the streets and collects the rubbish
- Is responsible for environmental health matters such as food safety, pest control and air quality
- Deals with noise pollution and may have a noise patrol
- Ensures that shops are selling safe products and not cheating people (trading standards)

Activity

Brainstorm the different services that your family and friends use in any one week. Include older people that you know, such as grandparents.

Voluntary organisations

There are thousands of people who do voluntary work every day. They do not get paid although their expenses are usually covered. The work they do varies enormously: working in charity shops, providing advice, running clubs for young and old people, helping people with their shopping or their household chores.

Voluntary organisations fill the gaps when councils and central government do not meet the needs of the community. There are thousands of these organisations. Here are just a few examples.

Age Concern
Works with old people, providing support to help them manage their affairs and make sure they get treated well. For example, gives help on insurance and getting repairs done

Shopmobility
Provides wheelchairs for use in shopping centres or arranges for volunteers to do the shopping for people who have trouble moving around or getting out

Citizens' Advice Bureau
Provides advice on a whole range of topics or directs people to where they can get the advice they need. In particular, helps people who get into debt

Community Service Volunteers (CSV)
Helps to set up community projects

Groundwork
Works with young people, often those excluded or in danger of being excluded from school. Involves them in a range of creative community projects which teach them skills for life and employment

Timebank
Allows ordinary people to offer their time to a 'bank' from which organisations needing volunteers can request their services

Divert Trust
Mentors young people in difficulties

Prince's Trust
Works with 18–25 year-olds to help them set up businesses

Women's Royal Voluntary Service
Runs shops, cafés and trolley services in hospitals; provides meals on wheels for the elderly

Activity

To which council department(s) or voluntary organisation would you send the following people to get the help they need?

A **'I am 78 and have bad arthritis. I can't get out to the shops to buy food.'**

B **'We've just moved into the area and are having difficulty getting our children into the local school.'**

C **'I want to open a club for young people, which I am building in a disused warehouse. Who do I need to see to get permission to make changes to the building, and organise safety measures like fire exits?'**

D **'The refuse men keep missing our street. The rubbish is piling up and up. We're all fed up with it!'**

E **'Our daughter has got into terrible debt using credit cards. She owes thousands of pounds and is desperate. We don't know how to help her.'**

F **'I want to do some voluntary work, but I can only spare a certain amount of time each week.'**

G **'Our neighbours are giving us hell. They play loud music, have parties and shout and scream in the street into the early hours of the morning.'**

H **'The young child in the house next to ours is not being looked after properly. He is often dirty and has a lot of bruises.'**

Getting involved – your own community project

You can make a contribution to your community and also achieve some of the coursework objectives for your citizenship studies course by getting involved in your own community project.

Identifying a project

You could:

- help on an environmental project, such as clearing a canal
- run an event to support a local charity
- visit elderly people
- run some events for children's groups or help out in a school where the children are severely disabled
- do a project while you are on work experience, perhaps on equal opportunities or trade unions in the workplace
- get involved in a current community action, for example campaigning for safe roads or protecting the environment.

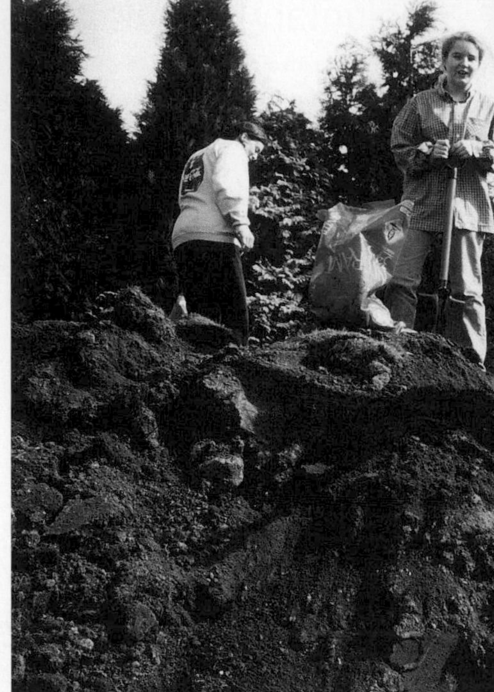

Changemakers volunteers working on a landscaping project

Think about

1 Do any local organisations need people to help? Invite representatives to talk about their aims and objectives and what you could do to help.
2 Is there a specific organisation you would like to work with? Contact them and find out if there is anything you can do.

A Changemakers project to paint a mural on a school wall

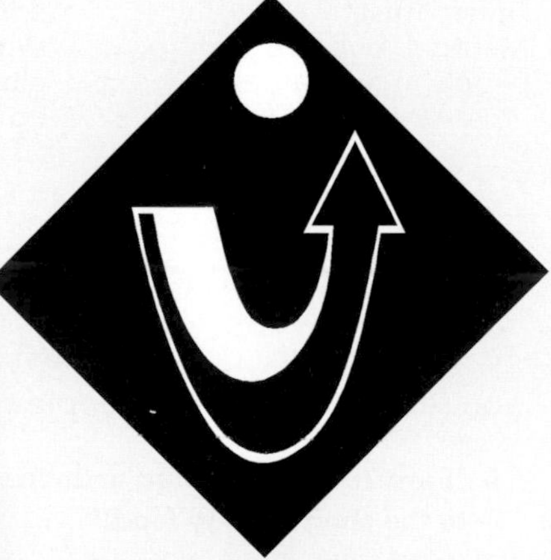

Changemakers is an organisation that works with young people in their communities. It helps them to address the issues that concern them in their own lives and to join with others in positive action to create change. Projects are designed and led by the young people themselves.

What can you gain from volunteering?
As well as learning important new skills, you gain confidence, make new friends and feel that you are making a worthwhile contribution to your community. But you can also learn a lot about the world in which we live. When you plan to start volunteering, think about the following questions:

- What do I already know about this topic?
- What are likely to be the needs of the people I will meet?
- How might I be able to help?
- Who already helps these people?

While you are engaged in your voluntary activities, think about some of these questions:

- Why is there a need for this work?
- Could better services be offered?
- How could I help to improve things? What would I need to do and who should I contact?
- What have I learned about this topic that I didn't know before?

You could carry out some research on the internet or by writing to charities and voluntary organisations to see what other people think.

Pupil project sparks public drugs inquiry

Pupils in a school in Satley, Birmingham, have been investigating drug crime, rats and educational achievement as part of a six-month investigation into the inner-city area's problems as part of their citizenship project. The pupils were asked to find out what problems affected their community and interviewed nearly 200 local residents as well as police officers and education officials.

Many residents expressed worries about the area's booming rat population, which has been feeding off piles of illegally dumped rubbish. The young people also found that people were concerned about the increased incidence of gun-related crime and drug dealing, as well as concerns among the local community about the city's education system.

The inquiry will reach its climax when the young people publish a report containing a series of hard-hitting recommendations. Birmingham's chief education officer has agreed to take the recommendations seriously, and will distribute copies to all the city's schools.

From the *Times Educational Supplement*, 7 March 2003

For your citizenship project, you will probably be working in a group or team.

1. Make a note of all the areas of volunteer work that you are interested in.
2. Discuss them in your group and choose two or three that you are really keen on doing. Put the one you like best at the top of your list.
3. Do some research on your choices, for example at the local library, on the internet.
4. When you know more about what is involved, discuss your options again and make your final choice.

Planning your project

Stage 1

- Look at what is involved in your project, what needs to be done and what problems might arise.
- Make sure that it is manageable. It is better to have a more limited and realistic set of objectives than try to be too adventurous. Ask for advice if you're not sure.
- Check if any money is involved and how this will be raised. You must be careful that you are not responsible for any bills.

Stage 2

- Roles – decide who in your team is going to do what.
- Decide if people are going to work on their own or in pairs.
- Try to match the skills of team members – what they are good at – to the tasks they have to do.
- Write down everybody's role and exactly what they are responsible for. This is very important in order for things to get done and ensures that there are no arguments later on.

Stage 3

- Draw up an Action Plan. This means that you:
  - fix the deadline by which the project has to be completed
  - make a time planner to show the months and weeks between the start of the project and the deadline
  - mark on the planner the dates by which things should be done
  - put in another column the name of the team member responsible
  - make sure each team member signs it and has a copy.

ACTION PLAN

Title of Project: Report to the council on facilities for toddlers

Names of team members: Jimmy, Jordan, Donna, Rehana

Month	Action	To be completed by	Who is responsible for task?	What will we need?	Comments
November	1 Write to two local playgroups to ask for permission to visit. 2 Find out what facilities parents of toddlers would like. 3 Request interview with local councillor.	8 November Visit playgroups 21 November 10 November	Jimmy and Rehana Jordan, Donna, Jimmy and Rehana Donna	Addresses of the playgroups A questionnaire An observation sheet Telephone number Access to telephone	May need to follow up letter with phone call. Practise telephone conversation first.
December	Interview councillor.	Fix date in December	Donna and Jimmy	Tape recorder	Prepare questions in advance.
January	Work in playgroups helping and observing toddlers.	Work experience week in January	Jimmy, Jordan, Donna and Rehana	Cameras Logbooks	
February	Analyse all information: questionnaires, observation sheets, logbook notes, tape recordings.	End of February	Jimmy, Jordan, Donna and Rehana	Help from teacher	Think about using software to display information and produce presentation.

Recording and evaluating your project

You need to record and evaluate your project as well, to judge how well you have done. This is particularly important if you are using this project as part of your GCSE coursework. Your teacher can give you examples of the forms you need to use.

What you did

Keep an **Activity log** of everything your team does during the project. It is important that you write things down as you do them. Don't do it all at the end.

- Keep a record of any meetings you have to plan your activities – with dates!
- Write down the activities with dates they were done and who in the team did them.
- Write down any review meeting you have with teachers and any presentations you make to the class.
- If you change the direction of the activity, write this down and say why you decided to do so.

Evidence

You have to collect **supporting evidence** to show what you've done. Make sure you do this from the beginning because the evidence might not be available later on. For instance, take lots of pictures when you do things – you won't be able to do it at the end, so carry a camera with you. The evidence can be collected in lots of different ways. Here are some:

- written work – any pieces of writing you undertake for the project
- photographs
- letters
- video or audio recording
- the minutes of meetings
- PowerPoint presentations
- any computer-produced material – scans, photos, information collected from the internet

Evaluation

In this part you assess how well you did, what you learned and how your project affected other people. Write up your evaluation under the following headings, using the questions for guidance.

1 Your contribution

- What part did you play in your team?
- Do you think you made an important contribution? (Explain what you did.)
- Were you a leader and/or did you make important decisions?
- Would you have done anything differently?
- How could you have improved your contribution?

2 The contribution of your team members

- What do you think about the contribution of other team members – did everybody play their part and meet their responsibilities? (Say what they did.)
- Were some members particularly important and/or made important decisions?
- Who do you think played the most important part in your team? (Explain why.)

3 What impact did your project have on others?

This really depends on what you did but here are some guide questions:

- Did the people involved enjoy what you did?
- Did other people benefit from what you did?

4 What have you learned?

- What are the most important points that you have learned about:
  a) yourself
  b) working in a team
  c) the issue?
- Would you have done anything differently?

5 How successful were you?

Write a short summary weighing up the things that went well, the things that went badly and the overall outcome of what you did. How successful do you think your team was?

3.3 Where does the money come from for council services?

Providing services like housing, schools and refuse collection costs a lot of money. Where does the money come from and is the way it is collected fair? Some money comes directly from the government, whilst some is collected from local businesses that pay a **business rate**. But a great deal of it comes from the people who live in the area.

Every household (with a few exceptions) has to pay **council tax**.

People who live in council houses and flats pay a proportion of their rent as council tax. People who live in rented houses and flats have to pay the council tax on the property they live in as if they owned it.

For people who own their houses, the amount is set every year according to the value of the house they live in. Each house is fitted into a band according to its market value (how much it will sell for). An adult living on his or her own can get a 25% discount.

Activity

1 Which is the more expensive area for council tax – Birmingham or Durham? Can you suggest any reasons for this difference?

2 Work out the council tax each family pays in the three examples on this page.

3 Do you think anybody is paying too much or too little tax?

4 Find out how your council spends the money it gets and how much it gives to different services.

Band (same across England and Wales) in £		Council tax in		
		Birmingham (£)	Durham (£)	Lewisham (South London) (£)
A	Up to 40 000	652	480	535
B	40 000–52 000	761	560	623
C	52 000–68 000	870	640	713
D	68 000–88 000	978	720	802
E	88 000–120 000	1196	881	980
F	120 000–160 000	1414	1041	1159
G	160 000–320 000	1631	1201	1337
H	More than 320 000	1957	1441	1604

Figures rounded to nearest pound

The Patels live in Birmingham in a large house with four bedrooms valued at £300 000. House prices have recently risen rapidly. The Patels are not very well off. Mr Patel works but his wife does not. He earns around £24 000 a year. They have three children who are all at state school.

Geraldine James lives on the outskirts of Durham, almost in the countryside, in a three-bedroom house valued at £87 000. She lives with her three grown-up children. All four of them are working in well paid jobs. Geraldine earns £22 000 a year and the others all earn over £20 000.

John and Mary Brighouse live in Lewisham so they can be near to their work in the City of London. They live in a four-bedroom house valued at £400 000 but they also have a large country cottage in Berkshire. They have two boys at private school. They both work, one in banking, the other in insurance, and they have a combined salary of just over £250 000.

Could local taxation be made fairer?

People complain about paying local taxes, yet they need and want the services that the taxes pay for. In fact, they also complain if the services are not good. However, most people accept that it is one of the duties of a citizen to pay taxes. But they want the taxes to be fair – they want to feel that everybody else is paying a fair share.

Activity

Look at the different arguments below. Decide which ones you agree with. Then have a class discussion on what you think is the fairest way of collecting money from people in a local area.

A Every single person uses the services, so every working person over eighteen should pay their share.

B Some people are much better off than others, so they should pay more.

C Better off people already pay a lot of money in income tax to the government, so why should they pay a local income tax? That means they will be hit twice.

D If everybody pays the same then poorer families get the worst deal.

E Poorer families use more of the local services, so it is right that they should pay more.

F It's better to use the house itself – the higher the value the more council tax the owner pays. Usually if the house is of much higher value then better off people live there. Also, you know who lives there and you know who you can collect the tax from.

G No system can be fair to everyone.

Activity

1 The chart on the right shows three ways in which local taxes could be collected. Study them carefully.
2 Look carefully at the four households on page 73 and make brief notes about:
   - the number of adults in the household
   - income
   - how much they use local services.
3 Then look at the table below to see how much they would pay under the three different systems.
   a) Which household suffers most under System A? Why?
   b) Which household suffers most under System B? Why?
   c) Which household suffers most under System C? Why?
4 Which households make most use of local services?
5 Which system do you think is the fairest?

The households

The people shown on page 73 all live in the same area, which is run by Durrington County Council. The County Council sets the local tax. The table below shows what it might set under different systems.

	Household 1	Household 2	Household 3	Household 4
System A House value tax	800	1 300	580	500
System B Tax per person (£250)	1 000	500	250	250
System C Local income tax	850	2 500	1 000	350

System A
House value tax
As in the case of current council tax, you pay tax based on the value of your house. Houses are put into bands of value and your council sets a tax for each band. People who live in the highest value houses pay the most.

System B
Tax per person over eighteen
Every person over the age of eighteen (not students in full-time education) living in a house would pay tax. So everybody pays the same amount.

System C
Local income tax
The amount you pay is worked out according to the income you earn. The more you earn the more you pay.

Household 1
John and Mabel Smith have two sons, an eighteen year-old, who is a trainee electrician and a twenty-one year-old, who is working. Mabel works part-time and the three men earn low wages. Their total income is £40 000. They live in a three-bedroom house in Apricot Avenue. They all make good use of the local services.

Household 2
Charles and Amy Thorpe live in a six-bedroom house in Prosperous Avenue. They have one child at a private primary school. Charles earns a very high salary – £150 000. Amy does not work. They use local services to a limited extent but not, for instance, education, which they pay for themselves.

Household 3
Rena Desai lives on her own in a two-bedroom flat which has gone up in value considerably in the last few years. She lives in Riverside Walk and she earns £50 000 per year. Rena does not use the local services very much.

Household 4
Matty Kane lives on her own with four children, all at secondary school. Matty works for the local council as an administrative assistant at County Hall, and earns £15 000 per year. She lives in a modern house in Ordinary Close on an estate on the edge of town.

Her husband died in an accident but the compensation she received allowed her to purchase her three-bedroom house. She and her family make full use of council services – schools, library, swimming pool, etc.

What do you know about your local council?

The council provides many of the services you use in your area. It is where decisions are made that affect the area you live in. But what do you know about it? Try the quiz below. When you have finished, check your answers with the information on pages 74–75.

Quiz

Answer True or False.

1 Councillors are paid officials who work for the council.
2 The council is elected every year.
3 A councillor is elected by the residents of a ward.
4 A ward is a geographical area within the boundaries of a local authority.
5 Every councillor has to belong to a political party, for example Labour or Conservative.
6 The political party which wins the election and has the majority of councillors is put in charge of running the council.
7 Local elections always take place on the first Thursday in May.
8 Council meetings take place four times a year.
9 The person in overall charge of the council workers in the town hall is called the Chief Executive.

3.4 Who makes the decisions in your local area?

Electing councillors

Councillors are elected to serve for four years. The voters in a ward (see diagram below) choose the councillors who serve on the council. Some areas have elections every year to choose part of the council, usually between one-third and one-quarter; some have elections every three or four years to choose a whole new council. Local elections take place on the first Thursday in May.

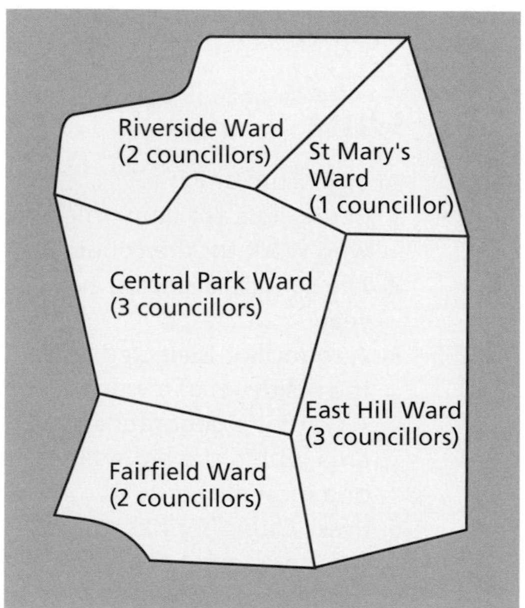

Each council area is divided into wards. In rural areas there is usually one councillor for each ward but in cities and towns there are often two or three councillors for each ward. Elections use the 'first-past-the-post' system. This means the candidate with the highest number of votes wins. In wards which have three councillors to represent them, the three with the highest number of votes are elected.

The council

After the election the political party with the most councillors is in charge of running the council. Sometimes one party does not have a majority, so it has to work with other parties. Not all councillors belong to the big political parties – Labour, Conservative or Liberal Democrats. Some belong to smaller parties like the Greens or may be independent (belong to no party at all). The person who is responsible for running the council is called the council leader.

Meeting local people

Councillors hold 'surgeries' which local people can attend to discuss their problems.

Activity

Find out what type of council runs your local area. Is it a county council, a borough council or something else? All councils have websites. Look up your council's website. Find out about how your council works, what it is doing and any other interesting information that you can share with your class.

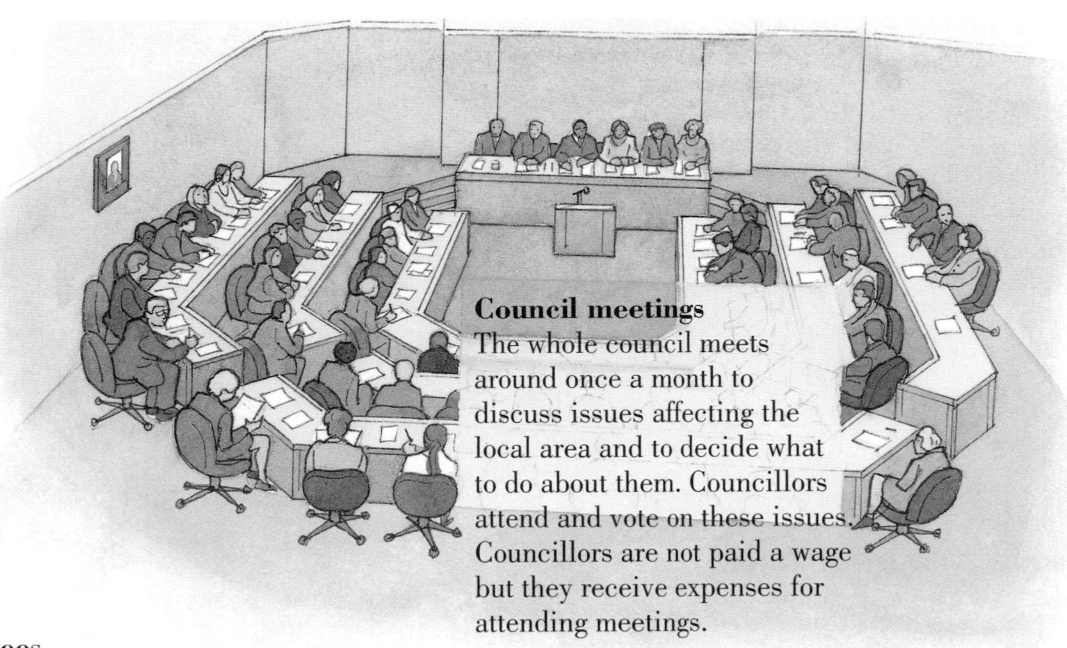

Council meetings
The whole council meets around once a month to discuss issues affecting the local area and to decide what to do about them. Councillors attend and vote on these issues. Councillors are not paid a wage but they receive expenses for attending meetings.

Committees
A small number of councillors sit on committees. Each committee overlooks the work of a particular department and decides the policy of the department. Council officers (full-time council workers) also sit on the committee to give information and advice and play a part in the decisions made. For example, the Planning Committee makes decisions about which housing developments should be allowed to go ahead. Some really big decisions have to go back to the full council.

The town hall
This is where the day-to-day business of running the council is carried out. Council officers organise and run all the services the council provides. You can see these on page 64. Lots of people work for the council doing various jobs, such as sorting out council tax bills, dealing with traffic permits, working in social services, carrying out surveying work, inspecting buildings, checking on the cleanliness of restaurants, etc. The person in overall charge is usually called the Chief Executive.

In a councillor's surgery

Councillors hold 'surgeries' in their wards. On specified days each month people can bring problems that affect them personally or issues that they think are important to the local community as a whole. Quite often, councillors are involved in trying to resolve conflicts between different groups in the ward.

Activity

1 Read cases A–D (below) brought to one councillor's surgery.
   a) Decide what each problem/issue is.
   b) If you were the councillor, which of the following courses of action might you take in each case?

   - Direct them to a department of the council that can help – which one? (See page 64.)
   - Go and see the people involved and try to persuade them to be more reasonable.
   - Arrange mediation between different groups. This means getting people to sit down to discuss matters reasonably.
   - Take the matter to the whole council for discussion because on your own, you can't do anything.
   - Go to the housing department and persuade them to evict the people causing the trouble.

2 Invite a local councillor to come to talk to your class about the work they do.

A. I've come to complain about the Blights. They have just moved onto our council estate. It's only three small blocks of flats with nine families. It used to be really nice and quiet. Now the Blights have moved in with their three teenagers, they are causing havoc. They repair cars in the driveway, throw litter, and swear at anybody who tries to talk to them about it. Mr and Mrs Smith who are now in their eighties feel scared to go out. What can you do about it?

B. We've come with a petition signed by 300 people in our ward. We are against the mobile phone mast that the Blue Company want to put up near our houses. It's a real eyesore and we're worried it might affect our health. We want you to support us and put our objection to the council.

C. My name is Mustapha Kemel. I'm a Muslim. My family has lived on this council estate for nearly 30 years and we've always got on well with our neighbours. Now that there is all this terrorist business we are being continually harassed. Our neighbours won't speak to us and some shout abuse at us. We have had threatening letters and other things pushed through our letter box. We don't believe in violence or terrorism. We just want things to go back to how they were before. Can you help?

D. We're furious. We've lived in this ward for fifteen years and we've just been told that we can't get our daughter into the local secondary school. Apparently, they take 20% of their children from outside the local authority because they select some of their pupils based on their ability.The school is only half a kilometre from us but our daughter will have to take a bus six kilometres to the next school. Other local parents are also very angry. What can you do about it?

3.5 Oldtown

Oldtown Football Club has been doing very well in the Second Division of the Nationwide League. But the shock news is that its stadium has been put up for sale. There is a proposal to knock down the old stadium and in its place build a multiplex cinema, some offices, some shops and some houses. Because of the concern of the local people the club owners, with the agreement of the local council, have decided to call a public meeting.

Oldtown F. C.

Oldtown stadium under threat

Statement by the club director

'The club is losing an enormous amount of money every week and we simply can't afford it. We're already finding it difficult to pay the wages of the players and have had to sell promising young players to bring in the money to carry on. We'll be bankrupt next year if we go on this way. We have found a new site thirty kilometres away where we can build a new stadium. This will include a stunning leisure and sports centre, with a full-size swimming pool and fitness centre. Because it is on the outskirts of town, just north of the ring-road, it will not suffer from the present match-day traffic problems.'

The editor says…

'Oldtown fans are up in arms about the plans to move to a new stadium. Oldtown Football Club puts our town on the map. The move will mean the end of the club which has been at the ground for over 100 years. And what about the loss to our local community – the junior football club, charity sponsorship, and all the other events organised by the supporters' club? That's apart from the fact that thousands of local people go to the matches. This is not just about football – it's about our community!'

Activity

Split the class into groups. Each group will play one of the roles set out on this spread.

Preparing

Look at your role. Then

a) work out what your group's position on the old stadium and the new development is

b) decide what points you intend to raise at the meeting and write down the main points

c) decide who in your group is going to say what.

At the meeting

Your teacher will be the chairperson of the meeting. He or she will ask people to speak in turn and invite others to comment at appropriate times.

a) The meeting will start with the club directors putting the case for why the change of stadium is necessary and how the change will benefit the club.

b) The developers will explain how the new development will benefit the local area.

c) The fans will put the main case against the change.

d) The chairperson will then ask other groups to put their views and ask questions.

e) A general debate will follow.

f) At the end of the meeting the chairperson will take a vote. Everybody must vote in the role they are playing.

Discussion

a) What do you think are the main effects on the local community of losing a football stadium?

b) What sorts of benefits can new developments bring?

c) Do you think that local people can have any real influence over big changes to their community?

d) In some areas fans have mounted campaigns to try to stop their stadium being moved. What sorts of methods could campaigners use to persuade local people to support them?

Club directors

You have to explain your case for moving at the beginning of the meeting. Develop the points below and add more of your own:

- The club is now over a million pounds in debt.
- There is not enough space to expand the existing site.
- The road network in the area and traffic congestion make it very difficult to get large numbers in and out of the ground.
- A new stadium and leisure facilities will bring in a lot more money, will attract more families to games and will allow the club to buy new players and build a better team.
- You might be persuaded to stay if the council is prepared to spend money on the roads around the old stadium and if they allow you to buy some land nearby on which you could build your own leisure centre to earn the club money.

Councillors

Financially, the council cannot pay for the improvements necessary for the stadium to stay, whereas the new development promises to be of great benefit to the area. Work out what you're going to say at the meeting, using the points below to help you:

- If the stadium goes, you will not have to cope with the trouble on match days of crowds, the damage they cause and the cost of clearing up, and for the police needed to control them.
- The club wants you to let it buy land, but you want this land for other purposes.
- With the proposed new development of the Oldtown site the developers will pay for the road developments and the development will raise the standard of the area.

Local shopkeepers and traders

You are very worried about all these proposed changes. Here are some of the things that concern you but you may think of others:

- How your businesses are going to be affected by the closure of the stadium.
- How the new development will affect you; will it improve the area and so be better for you or bring new shops to take your business away?

Developers

You are a business group wanting to redevelop the site of the Oldtown stadium. You know you can get the land cheaply and if you get the development right could make a lot of money out of building shops, offices, a cinema and some houses. So you need to persuade the public that your development will be good for the local community and will provide things they really want. Use these points, and any ideas of your own, to sell the project:

- You will pay for a new road system providing access to the new development.
- Your centre will offer the local people a lot of amenities.
- The whole area will improve – no match day trouble or congestion, new buildings will mean that the property values for all the residents are going to go up significantly.

Long-term residents including families with young children and pensioners

You have all lived in the area for more than ten years. Some of you have lived here your entire lives. You have not made up your minds yet. Points to consider on either side are:

- Concerns about violence at football matches.
- Match days are terrible, it is impossible to go outdoors, there is traffic congestion, huge crowds of people push and shove you on the streets.
- However, some of you have been going to matches for years and a number of community activities, like junior football, are organised around the Oldtown club.
- Will the new development on the stadium site do anything for you; will it provide new amenities which you can afford?

Fans

You are desperate to keep the stadium where it is. You feel it is an important part of your area's history and community. At the meeting you have to say why it is so important and why it should be kept. Develop the points below and use any others you can think of:

- The stadium is part of the area's history and generates a feeling of community.
- It gives the fans pleasure and a sense of belonging; football provides a focus for many people.
- Many activities go on around the club – junior football, charity events, organised trips out for pensioners.
- The club brings a lot of money into the local economy – people going to pubs and restaurants on match days and buying food and drink and other goods in local shops.
- The two plans could be combined. The stadium could stay but the council should put money into a new road system and give extra land for rebuilding the existing stadium and adding new facilities which local people really want.

New residents

You have recently moved into the area and have bought a new apartment near the river. You think that the new development is going to improve the area and your property will increase in value. You bought it because you were sure the old stadium was going to be pulled down. You think:

- The old stadium attracts crowds of troublemakers.
- Getting rid of it will solve some of the terrible traffic congestion in the area.
- A new development might provide extra amenities such as a restaurant, gym and a cinema.
- The area by the river will become very popular and the value of your apartment will go up.

3.6 Regenerate!

How would you regenerate Slighton?

Slighton is an area near the centre of a large city, which has being going downhill for many years. The area has suffered from increasing unemployment as the industries which used to make it prosperous have collapsed. A huge out-of-town shopping centre on the outskirts of the city also took a great deal of trade from the shops in the area.

Slighton has now been made a priority area for regeneration. The government is giving the area a large sum of money – a regeneration budget – to improve the quality of life for the people who live there. Different organisations can 'bid' for some of this money to spend on different projects. A committee has been set up to consider the 'bids' and decide how the money should be spent.

Activity

1 Form groups of five. You are the committee that has been set up to judge the bids. Look at each bid in turn and decide which you are going to support. Remember, you want to get as much value for your money as you can.
   The total money in the regeneration budget is £65 million.
2 Make your decisions and write down the reasons why you have chosen some bids over others.
3 As a whole class, discuss the decisions made by each group. Be prepared, as a group, to argue for your choices.
4 Discuss which of the bids would benefit which groups of people most.
5 What range of bids would provide a good deal for the community as a whole?

Bid 1 **Cost £35 million**

A new library

The Newbook consortium

This bid proposes a very modern library on the site of the old market. A stunning building designed by young architects, it would put Slighton on the map and draw people to it. It would be much more than a place for lending books, CDs and videos. It would also contain an internet section and a space for community meetings, talks and for local clubs and societies to meet.

Bid 2

Total for two years – £4 million

Closed-circuit television (CCTV)

The BeSecure Group

Over the years, the high street has gone downhill. The number of thefts from the shops and street robberies has risen. It is particularly dangerous at night. Some shopkeepers have moved out, leaving empty derelict shops. The BeSecure Group are bidding for money to put CCTV cameras along the high street and in some of the streets nearby which have clubs and pubs. This will make the area safer and encourage people to shop there and come back in the evenings.

Bid 3

Cost £30 million

The Hartington Estate Renewal Plan

The Community Together Association

Hartington Estate, close to the centre of Slighton, is not a pleasant place – mainly grey concrete high rise blocks with dark, dirty, smelly staircases and covered walkways that provide a haven for drug dealers and gangs of young people. The estate has a bad effect on the centre of Slighton. The Association, which comprises several community groups, proposes to remove the walkways, lower two of the blocks, paint the outside, put caretakers in the blocks, build a youth club and employ community wardens to patrol the estate.

Bid 4

Cost £10 million

High Street Redevelopment Plan

Shopkeepers Support Group

This group wants to clean up the high street. The shopkeepers will put in some money if they can get regeneration money for new street lighting, new pavements, new street furniture and road improvements. They also want money for improving shop fronts.

Bid 5

Costs £15 million + £15 million from Leisure United

Leisure centre and swimming pool

Leisure United

This is a group of business people who will match the amount of regeneration money they receive to put in a much needed leisure centre. This will provide jobs for local people and attract people to the centre. The swimming pool will be family oriented with a wave machine, toddlers' pool and sauna.

Bid 6

Cost £8 million

Road safety scheme

Slighton council

The council, with the support of local residents, has put in a bid to introduce traffic calming measures such as road humps, chicanes and raised surfaces. This is designed to improve the quality of the roads and reduce traffic accidents. Some roads will be closed off at one end to stop them being used as short cuts.

Bid 7

Cost £10 million

New training centre

Skills for U group

The Slighton area has a large number of workers who need retraining. They worked in industries that have now ceased to exist. There is a high rate of unemployment, especially amongst young people. The centre would run training courses to equip them with the skills to get jobs in the newer industries which are looking to move into the area, especially computer skills.

Improving your own high street or local centre

Activity

Work in pairs or threes. Think about the high street or area of shops which you and your family use most.

1 Do an assessment sheet for your high street using a chart like the one below with a five-point scale. Add any other categories that you think are helpful.

	1	2	3	4	5	
Very clean and tidy						Dirty, lots of litter
No graffiti						Parts covered in graffiti
Bright, attractive shops						Dull, dingy shops
Good variety of shops						Few shops, some empty and closed up
Pavements easy to walk on						Pavements broken, narrow and dangerous
Lots of trees and plants						No trees and plants
Low traffic congestion						High traffic congestion
Not much air pollution						High levels of air pollution
Good road signs and directions						No road signs or directions

2 Make a list of things that you think would make it a much better place.

3 Take one of the items from your list and prepare a proposal which sets out how you think this could be improved and why public money should be spent on it.

Your proposal should include:

- an assessment of what's there at the present and what's wrong with it
- what you propose in its place or how to improve it
- a drawing or diagram of the proposal
- what your proposal will do for the local area.

4 As a class, put together all the proposals for improving the high street/shopping area and discuss them. Decide which ones are the best. You could invite a councillor or planning officer from the local council to come to discuss your ideas and find out what the council plans for the area.

3.7 What is Local Agenda 21?

Think globally, act locally!

In 1992 at the world conference in Rio de Janeiro in Brazil, there was a meeting of world leaders called the Earth Summit. It was the first time that so many world leaders had met to discuss the future of planet Earth. The aim was to raise awareness of future dangers facing the world if people continue to pollute the planet with waste and harmful gases caused by industrial development. One of the agreements signed was Agenda 21. It was called this because it set out a plan (an agenda) for environmentally friendly development in the twenty-first century.

Local Agenda 21 grew out of that. It is based on the belief that it is only possible to protect the global environment if people take action in their **local** area. People have to think globally (think about what is happening in the wider world), but act locally. It is also about improving the local area in which people live.

Local Agenda 21 focuses on what local authorities, working with their communities, can do to save energy and resources, to cut pollution, and to make the local area a more pleasant place in which to live and work. Local authorities have to devise local action plans for such things as:

- reducing and managing waste
- managing land
- protecting the countryside, the landscape and natural habitats for birds and wild animals
- improving the quality of life for us and those after us
- protecting oceans and coastal areas
- reducing crime
- creating local employment
- raising awareness of environmental issues so that people play their part.

Activity

Contact your local council and find out what the Local Agenda 21 strategies are for your area. Write up a case study of one of these.

A vision for the 21st Century

Lancashire's Local Agenda 21 Strategy, 'A Vision for the 21st Century', sets out 11 goals including:

- producing lower levels of pollution
- encouraging the diversity of wildlife and plants in the environment
- making efficient use of resources and producing less waste
- living without fear of crime
- involving people in the decision-making process

The strategy outlines 54 actions that will contribute towards a more sustainable Lancashire, for example:

- reducing greenhouse gases
- improving the quality of coastal bathing water
- improving the quality of drinking water
- devising travel plans for schools to encourage pupils to walk, cycle, or use buses
- encouraging businesses to be responsible in their use of resources and how they operate in the environment, for example cutting down on any pollution created by their activities
- promoting health in workplaces and schools, for example the healthy schools initiative.

Taking action

There are all sorts of ways in which individuals in the local community can contribute to improving their local environment and 'sustainable development'. Sustainable development means that, while we enjoy a good quality of life today, we make sure that the environment we leave behind supports at least as good a quality of life for the people who come after us. So we should do our best to conserve resources and not pollute the Earth.

THERE ARE LA21 PROJECTS ALL OVER THE WORLD

Case study: *Reducing waste and relieving poverty – Mutare, Zimbabwe*

In Mutare, the local authority, private companies and the community have worked together to reduce waste going to dumpsites at the municipal and household level. People in the community have been persuaded to compost food waste and take paper to recycling depots. This has not only reduced waste but created lots of new jobs for women and young people who run the schemes.

Case study: *Police bicycle patrol – Dayton, USA*

In Dayton, Ohio, the police have left their cars and have taken to riding bicycles to patrol parts of the city. This saves money and reduces the emission of air pollutants and greenhouse gases. But the police have also found that it has improved their relationships with the public and their ability to do their job, serving and protecting the city's citizens.

Activity

Use a chart like this to:

a) record which of these you and your family currently do and which you could do

b) consider how each of these actions can help protect the environment.

	We do this (✓)	**We could do (✓)**	**Impact on the environment**
Recycle: • glass • paper and cardboard • drinks cans • clothes			
Reuse products; hand down children's clothes; take things to charity shops			
Walk or cycle instead of using a car			
Reduce the amount of water and electricity you use (showers instead of baths; turn off appliances, like computers, when not being used)			
Buy locally produced food to reduce food kilometres			
Encourage wildlife by doing things like planting trees and building ponds			
Take a shopping bag instead of using plastic carrier bags at the supermarket			
Buy goods made from recycled products			
Walk to school or take public transport			

section 4

National government – who's running the country?

Key words

- Cabinet
- devolution
- electoral system
- monarchy
- political party
- pressure group
- proportional representation
- republic

In a democracy people choose a government to run the country and make laws. This section looks at how British leaders are elected and how citizens can affect the decisions they make.

You will learn about:

- elections and voting
- government and the role of the Prime Minister
- Parliament – the House of Commons and the House of Lords
- the role of MPs
- pressure groups
- taxation
- the monarchy
- devolution
- the European Union.

You will use the following skills:

- researching political, moral and social issues using information from different sources, including ICT-based sources
- expressing, justifying and defending orally and in writing a personal opinion about such issues, problems or events
- contributing to class discussions and debates
- understanding, explaining and evaluating critically views that are not your own.

4.1 Who should run a country?

Who used to rule Britain?

Through the greater part of British history, British monarchs claimed that they were appointed to the throne by God and therefore had a 'divine right' to rule. They were supported by rich lords and knights who made sure that ordinary people obeyed the monarch.

In the extract below from the comedy film *Monty Python and the Holy Grail*, King Arthur meets a peasant who does not understand this system of government.

Narrator: King Arthur is riding through Britain in his quest for the legendary Holy Grail. He encounters a peasant called Dennis and an old woman working in a field near a castle.

Arthur: Please, please, good people, I am in haste. What knight lives in that castle?

Old woman: No one lives there.

Arthur: Well, who is your lord?

Old woman: We don't have a lord.

Arthur: What?

Dennis: I told you, we're an anarcho-syndicalist* commune, we take it in turns to act as a sort of executive officer for the week.

Arthur: Yes...

Dennis: But all decisions of that officer...

Arthur: Yes, I see.

Dennis: ...must be approved at a bi-weekly meeting by a simple majority in the case of purely internal affairs.

Arthur: Be quiet.

Dennis: ...but a two-thirds majority...

Arthur: Be quiet! I order you to shut up.

Old woman: Order, eh? Who does he think he is?

Arthur: I am your King.

Old woman: Well, I didn't vote for you.

Arthur: You don't vote for kings.

Old woman: Well, how did you become king then?

Arthur: The Lady of the Lake, her arm clad in shimmering samite,* held Excalibur aloft from the bosom of the waters to signify that by Divine Providence ... I, Arthur, was to carry Excalibur ... that is why I am your King.

Dennis: Look, strange women lying on their backs in ponds handing over swords ... that's no basis for a system of government. Supreme executive power derives from a mandate from the masses not from some farcical aquatic* ceremony.

Arthur: Be quiet.

Dennis: You can't expect to wield supreme executive power just because some watery tart threw a sword at you.

* anarcho-syndicalist – no government, workers run their own affairs

* samite – golden medieval dress material

* aquatic – in or on water

Activity

1 Where did King Arthur get his right to become king?
2 In the past, from what source have monarchs claimed that they got their right to be ruler of the country?
3 What did Dennis and the old woman think was the best way of choosing the rulers of a country?
4 What two points of view about who should rule a country are represented here?

Discuss

1 What is your view on the monarchy? (Find out more about the role of the monarchy in Britain on pages 120–23.)

2 What reasons do you have for supporting, or not supporting, the monarchy?

Who runs the UK now?

Although the UK still has a monarch who plays an important part in the British system of government, the real power lies with a government that is chosen by the people. The important point is that this government can be changed every five years in general elections, so no group of people can become too powerful and rule without the support of the British people.

The diagram on pages 88–89 shows the main parts of the British parliamentary system. In the rest of this section, you will find out more about it. But first, try this quiz.

Quiz

Answer true or false.

a) The Prime Minister is the head of the armed forces.
b) The queen or king is in charge of running the government and making laws.
c) The Cabinet is a collection of powerful ministers who work with the Prime Minister to decide the main government policies.
d) Collective responsibility means that all Cabinet ministers share the responsibility for the results of the government's policies.
e) Civil servants are elected to Parliament to make laws.
f) The job of the second chamber, the House of Lords, is to check laws being passed and to scrutinise the government.
g) The Opposition is formed from the second largest party in the House of Commons.
h) The job of the Opposition is to agree with the government and help it as much as possible.
i) The government is formed by the party with the largest number of MPs in the House of Commons.
j) The Prime Minister is chosen by the people in a separate election.

You can check your answers on pages 88–89.

The monarch

The king or queen is the head of state but is no longer very powerful. The monarch's main jobs are to:

- open and close parliament
- ask the leader of the party with the most MPs after an election to become Prime Minister and form a government
- give the royal assent (agreement) to new laws
- meet leaders and heads of state from other countries
- give out honours to people who have given noteworthy public service.

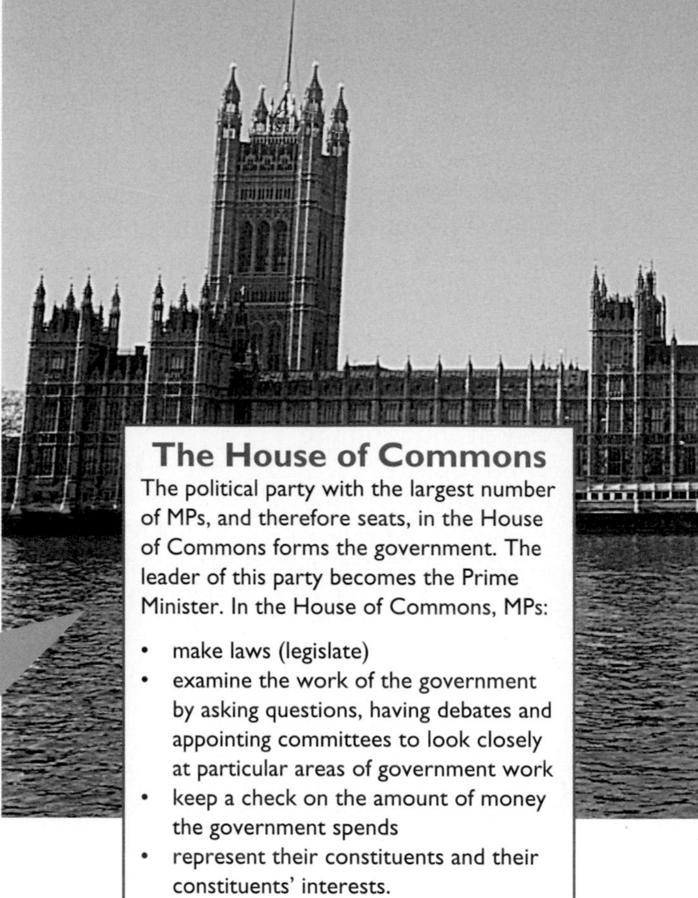

The House of Commons

The political party with the largest number of MPs, and therefore seats, in the House of Commons forms the government. The leader of this party becomes the Prime Minister. In the House of Commons, MPs:

- make laws (legislate)
- examine the work of the government by asking questions, having debates and appointing committees to look closely at particular areas of government work
- keep a check on the amount of money the government spends
- represent their constituents and their constituents' interests.

Members of Parliament

All the elected MPs – 659 of them in all – get a seat in the House of Commons in the Houses of Parliament at Westminster, London.

General Elections

Elections to choose a new government must be held at least every five years. But a Prime Minister can call an election at any time during those five years.

The United Kingdom is divided up into areas called constituencies, with around 67 000 people living in each one. At election time political parties put forward a number of candidates and each voter has to choose one to represent them in Parliament – a Member of Parliament (MP).

Any British citizen over twenty-one can stand as a candidate in a general election except: members of the House of Lords, clergy, bankrupts, certain offenders, people in certain jobs, e.g. judges and police officers.

The electorate/citizens

Every British citizen aged eighteen and over can vote, except for members of the House of Lords, some people in prison and patients held under mental health laws. Voting is not compulsory.

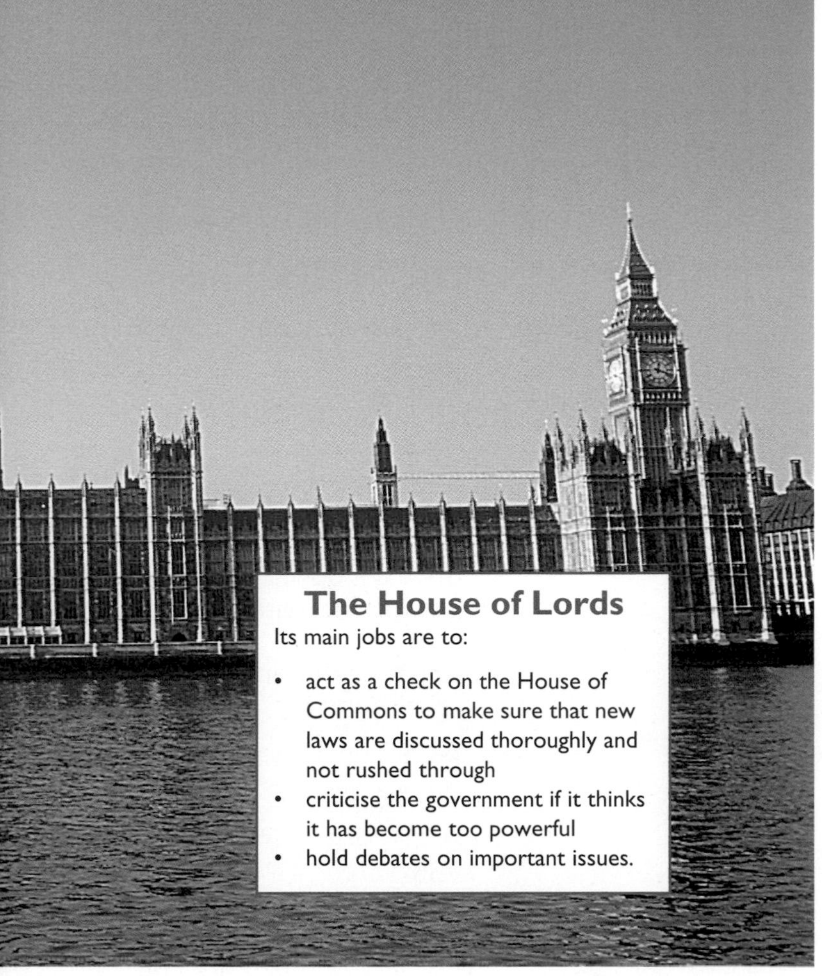

The House of Lords

Its main jobs are to:

- act as a check on the House of Commons to make sure that new laws are discussed thoroughly and not rushed through
- criticise the government if it thinks it has become too powerful
- hold debates on important issues.

The Opposition

The political party with the second largest number of MPs in the House of Commons forms the official Opposition. The job of the Opposition is to criticise and challenge the government to ensure it does a good job, is not corrupt and does not do things that harm the citizens. The Opposition forms a Shadow Cabinet. Its members 'shadow' the jobs of government ministers, for example the Minister of Health, to scrutinise what the minister does.

The government

The Prime Minister

- leads the government and directs government policy
- chooses Cabinet ministers and chairs the Cabinet
- is the head of the armed forces
- appoints senior judges and archbishops in the Church of England
- represents the nation in international affairs.

The Cabinet

The Prime Minister chooses a group of people to help run the country, called the Cabinet. They are the most important ministers in the government who are in charge of the big departments such as:

- the Foreign Office (relations with other countries)
- the Home Office (law and order, police and courts)
- Health (hospitals, doctors and nurses)
- Employment (jobs) and Education (schools and colleges).

The Cabinet works with the Prime Minister to decide the government's major policies, for example what it intends to do to cut crime. Once they have agreed the policies they all take **collective responsibility** for them, that is they have to support the policies and not disagree with them in public.

Civil servants

There are a number of government departments run by ministers with the help of other government members in over 100 posts. The people who work in these departments – many thousands of them – are called civil servants. Their job is to carry out the government's policies. For instance, if the government decides to build more hospitals or more roads, the civil servants have to make sure that this is done.

The duties of government are:

- to protect citizens and keep them safe
- to look after their welfare
- to watch over the employment of citizens
- to look after the environment
- to run the economy.

Activity

Draw your own chart or diagram to show how the British system of government works. Use icons and illustrations to make your diagram interesting.

4.2 Would you give the vote to a sixteen-year-old?

The UK is a democracy. The voters or 'electorate' choose politicians to run the country on their behalf. This means that politicians who want to be elected have to present the voters with their policies – what they will do if they are elected. They will usually present policies which they expect most people to support, such as improving public transport. In other words, they have to take the wishes of the voters into account in preparing their policies. In the UK at present you must be eighteen to vote in general, local or European elections. There is a debate over whether the voting age should be lowered to sixteen. Do you think this is a good idea?

How does the law affect young people?

At 16 you can:

Agree to sex
Buy alcohol with a meal
Buy cigarettes
Drive a moped under 50 ccs
Get married with parental consent
Join the army and fight for your country

At 17 you can:

Drive a car

At 18 you can:

Vote
Buy alcohol in a bar
Get a tattoo
View an 18 certificate film

At 21 you can:

Stand as an MP or MEP

Activity

1 Read statements **a)** to **n)** opposite and decide which are for and which are against lowering the voting age to sixteen.
2 Discuss this in class, and have a vote to find out what people in your class think.
3 Choose to do one of the following:
   - Devise a questionnaire to ask other students in your school about the issue. Ask a sample of other adults and friends as well. How do opinions differ between the generations?
   - Imagine there is to be a referendum (the chance to vote for or against a particular idea) on the reduction of the voting age to sixteen. Devise a small poster either supporting or rejecting this idea.
   - Imagine that the voting age has been reduced to sixteen. You are in a team of young people who are going to encourage others to vote. How would you go about persuading people in your school to vote? What methods would you use? What arguments might persuade them to take an interest and to vote in a General Election?

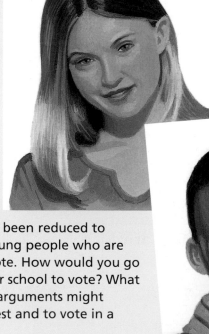

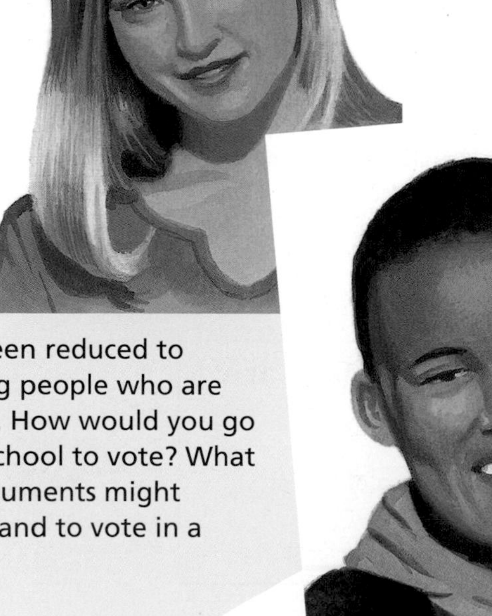

a) If young people are responsible enough to get married and to join the army, then they should be mature enough to vote.

b) How can we give the vote to people who are not mature enough to drink or see a horror film?

c) Young people have a lot of economic (spending) power but not political power – this is wrong.

d) It is undemocratic for young people who can pay tax to be denied a say in how their tax money is spent.

e) The minimum wage affects young people and they should have a say in it.

f) People should not have a say just because a policy affects them – otherwise nursery kids would have the vote.

g) Today's sixteen-year-olds are more mature than ever before and there is not much difference between sixteen and eighteen.

h) The arguments against young people are the same as those used in the last century against women having the vote.

i) Several countries have reduced the voting age to sixteen. Iranian young people have the vote at fifteen.

j) Young people already feel excluded from the adult world and reducing the voting age would help to include them.

k) Many sixteen-year-olds are still immature children.

l) Why stop at sixteen? Why not fifteen or fourteen? The line should be drawn at eighteen.

m) Maturity and responsibility are not requirements for becoming a voter – there are many irresponsible older people who can vote.

n) Most sixteen-year-olds would just either copy their parents or do the opposite of their parents – this would not be an informed decision.

4.3 How does someone become an MP?

In the General Election, the UK is divided up into 659 constituencies. Each has around 67 000 voters. The voters in each constituency choose one Member of Parliament (MP) to represent them in Parliament. The MP chosen has to represent the interests of all the people living in their constituency, not just those who voted for them.

Activity

Design a flow chart to show how someone becomes an MP.

1 John Blincoe joins a political party. He works for the party for a number of years: attending meetings, canvassing, raising funds for the party. He serves as a councillor in his local authority.

2 John decides that he wants to be an MP. He puts his name forward for an interview with the selection committee of the Brightsea constituency. Several other people are also interviewed. He is chosen to be his party's candidate at the next election.

3 An election is called. John has an agent to run his campaign; she organises posters, leaflets and public meetings. Party volunteers canvass for him; this means they knock on doors asking the voters to vote for John and his party, explaining the party's policies.

4 On election day the voters go to a polling station. They are given a ballot paper with the names of the candidates on it, which they take to a polling booth where no one can see what they are doing. They put an 'X' next to the candidate they are voting for and put their ballot paper in a box which is sealed after all the votes have been cast.

5 After the voting has closed, the ballot box is taken to a hall with all the other ballot boxes in the constituency. The ballot papers are counted. The returning officer then announces which candidate has the most votes. John has won. He is now the MP for Brightsea and will sit in the House of Commons.

Activity

Work in groups of four.

Who will you choose as your candidate?
In your constituency you need to select a candidate for the General Election.

Stage 1: Agree a specification
Most jobs have a 'specification' stating the knowledge, skills, experience and personal qualities a person needs to do the job. Look at these four lists and put each in rank order – the most important quality an MP should have at the top and the least important at the bottom.

You can add any other items to each list, but your group should still agree on the final order.

Knowledge of:	Skills
– the local area – local issues – national issues – international issues – how Parliament works – how the party works	– public speaking – putting across a particular message – being interviewed for television – chairing committees – fund raising – managing a business – negotiating
Experience	**Personal qualities**
– married with children – lived in local area for several years – running a business or organisation – worked in a profession – high-level qualifications – worked on campaigns for a pressure group – been a candidate before – served as a local councillor	– honesty – straightforwardness – able to be positive at all times – empathetic – sociable – loyal to family – cheerful and amusing – strong – dedicated – hard working – ability to get on with all kinds of people

Stage 2: Write some interview questions
You want your candidate to represent the interests of young people.

a) Plan five questions to ask at the interview to reveal whether this candidate understands what is important for young people. Questions can cover any topic, such as:

- education
- health
- money
- sport
- music
- jobs
- environment
- global issues
- public transport

b) When you have written your questions, note down the main points you would want to hear in the answers to each question.

Stage 3: Role play a selection panel
Split your group in two. Two of you will be candidates and two of you will be a selection panel, who will interview candidates from another group. First, prepare:

Interviewers: Choose at least three questions to ask the candidates and decide who will ask each one and in what order. You might also add some questions about the candidate's knowledge, skills, qualities and experience. You should ask each candidate the same questions so that you can compare them fairly.
Candidates: Spend some time thinking about the answers you would give to the questions you designed in Stage 2. But be careful – the selection panel you visit may ask you different questions. Try to think what they might be and have an answer ready.

a) Lay out the room for an interview like this:

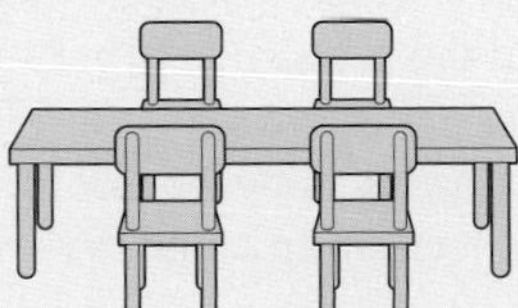

b) Your teacher will match candidates with panels from different groups. Now start the interviews.

4.4 Meet Oona King MP

Oona King is only the second black woman to become an MP in the UK Parliament.

Profile

- Born in 1967. Mother from working-class Jewish family in Newcastle; father, Professor Preston King, African-American who played a significant role in the American civil rights movement
- School – Haverstock Comprehensive, North London
- Joined Labour Party aged fourteen
- 1990 – graduated from York University
- Worked as a research and political assistant to members of the Labour Party in Europe and at Westminster
- 1995 – became full-time worker for the GMB, Britain's general trade union, as a regional organiser
- 1997 – aged 29, elected MP for Bethnal Green and Bow in London.

In the constituency

Surgeries

Oona holds surgeries in her constituency every Friday. People come to see her about everything – housing, car clamping, even plumbing problems! She can't do something about all of these but she likes to help out with real problems if she can. Sometimes she can persuade council officials to take action, for instance keeping families together who might otherwise be separated when they are rehoused. But her power is limited. 'A lot of people think that MPs have a magic wand and of course the reality is very, very different,' she says. But MPs can get things moving and make sure things are being done in the right way.

In the House of Commons

Making laws and debating

One of the most important jobs of the House of Commons is making new laws or changing old ones. Oona takes a full part in this process (see page 104) and also in the debates which are held on important issues.

Working on committees

Oona has been on several Select Committees that scrutinise the work of the government. 'It is our job to check what ministers are doing and to consider new policy or changes in policy that we want the government to look at. We can call ministers before us. When I was on the Select Committee for International Development, we called Gordon Brown, the Chancellor, and asked him what he was doing about debt problems facing poorer countries. We asked him to introduce some measures and he did.'

Travelling and fact finding

MPs go on trips around the UK and abroad to find out about people's concerns and difficulties at first hand. This can help in providing information to the government in making policies and new laws. Oona has travelled to developing countries where there is conflict, debt problems and issues about women's rights.

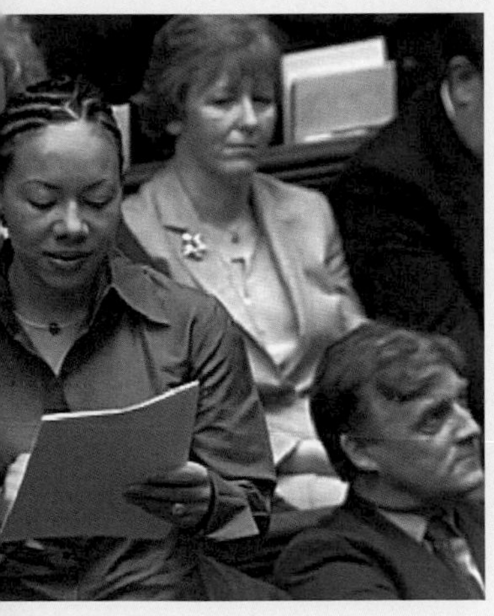

Bringing people together

An MP can help different groups in the community to work together. For example, on one occasion the government had offered £56 million towards improving an estate in Oona's constituency but different groups could not agree on how it should be done. Oona chaired the programme and helped the groups agree on a plan to get the project going.

Activity

1 Read the information on these two pages. Copy and complete this table – put one example of Oona King's work in each column.

In the constituency	In the House of Commons	Outside the House of Commons

2 Which of the categories of work do you think is the most important aspect of Oona King's work as an MP? Explain your answer.

3 Find out about your local MP's surgeries:

a) What issues are local residents invited to discuss with their MP?

b) How useful do you think residents might find the surgeries?

Passionate about . . .

Oona is passionate about many issues, such as:

Electoral reform – a crucial area because this is about who forms the government and makes the decisions that affect all our lives. Oona favours proportional representation because it would more fairly represent the votes people cast for different parties (see page 101). It would mean that every vote cast would count. 'If young people are to get involved in politics, they have to feel that their vote is going to count.'

Europe – Oona thinks the issue is not about giving away sovereignty. Events in Europe and the world affect the UK economy whether we want them to or not. It is better to be fully involved in Europe so that we have real influence in shaping the rules and the policies that will affect our jobs and our lives. As 60% of our trade is in Europe, this is where our interest lies. Oona wants us to join the euro as soon as possible. She thinks this is the best way to achieve economic prosperity in the future.

Experience as a young black woman in Parliament

Oona has not really had problems as a black woman in Parliament. However, because she is one of only two black women MPs – there are also ten black or Asian male MPs – she gets thousands of letters from people in minority ethnic groups, or from organisations trying to help minority ethnic women, asking for her support or help. It is hard to deal with all the issues these raise. Oona feels it is essential to have more MPs from minority ethnic groups to make our democracy more representative.

Most embarrassing moment

Having waited a long time to speak in a debate, she was finally called by the Speaker – and had forgotten what she wanted to say!

Experience representing a multi-cultural constituency

Oona King has a black father and a white mother. This gives her some insight into the experiences that people from different cultures have in her constituency. She feels that white, black, Asian or people from other minority ethnic groups have different experiences and the only way for people to live together is to 'respect' those experiences and be sensitive to each other – and this applies to everybody. Black and Asian groups have to acknowledge that changes have had a big impact on white communities; white people need to be sensitive to the needs of minority ethnic groups and support moves to promote equal opportunities and end discrimination. Oona feels it is no good people and communities barricading themselves off from each other; they have to work together if Britain is going to flourish.

Loves about being an MP . . .

'Bringing people into the House of Commons who would normally never go there to see what goes on.'
'Being able to initiate things.'
'The honour and privilege of being able to sit in the British Parliament taking part in debates where we decide how to run our country.'

Hates about being an MP

'The way the House of Commons runs is stuck in the Stone Age. The working practices are diabolical, for instance:

- nothing is modern, for example you can't vote electronically
- we often legislate in the middle of the night
- you have to virtually give up your family; this almost makes me want to resign.'

'I hate how unrepresentative it is.'

One final piece of advice

'I would encourage young people reading this to join a political party and try to become an MP too.'

Activity

1 Write down two things that you feel passionately about – things that if you were an MP you would try to do something about.
2 Do some research into the MP for your area. Many MPs have a page on the House of Commons website (www.parliament.uk/about_commons/about_commons.cfm). You could write a 100-word profile giving:
   a) some bullet points about their background and achievements
   b) one or two of their main policies – what they would like to achieve.

   You could interview them to find out similar things to what we have learned about Oona King.
3 Write to your MP asking for their view on a local issue that your class is interested in.
4 Look at Oona's final piece of advice. Why do you think she is so keen that people reading this book join a political party or try to become MPs?

4.5 What do political parties stand for?

A political party is an organised group of people with a leader and members. They have a set of views about how the country should be run. They have policies that they think will make the country a better place. The party prepares a manifesto at election time saying what they will do if they are elected. People support a party because they agree with its ideas.

political party | aims of the party | policies | manifesto

what the party wants to achieve

a group of people who stand for a set of ideas

the party's statement before an election about what it will do if it is elected

the things it will do to achieve its aims and honour its manifesto

Activity

1 Match the words in the panel (left) with their meanings.
2 Look at the logos and party names below.
   a) Which have you heard of?
   b) Which are the biggest?
   c) Which party forms the government?
   d) Which party is the official Opposition?
   e) Who are the leaders of the parties you have heard of?
3 Choose two that you have never heard of and discuss what you think they stand for.

Political parties which have had Members of Parliament

Sinn Fein

Scottish National Party

Scottish Conservative and Unionist Party

Democratic Unionist Party

Social Democratic and Labour Party

Plaid Cymru
The Party of Wales

Plaid Cymru

SCOTTISH LIBERAL DEMOCRATS

Scottish Liberal Democrats

Liberal Democrats

Labour Party

Ulster Unionist Party

Conservative Party

Parties which have no Members of Parliament. The British Register of Political Parties has 110 organisations listed!

Green Party of England and Wales

UK Independence Party

Pro Life Alliance

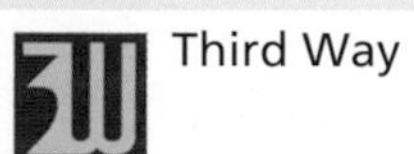

Third Way

Monster Raving Loony Party

The three main parties

You probably hear about the main political parties all the time because they are in the news. They are the Labour Party, the Conservative Party and the Liberal Democrats.

Party 1

This party is sometimes called the 'Tory' party, which derives from a word meaning 'robber'. It was in government for much of the twentieth century. It is often associated with big business and landowners and has always supported the right of individuals to run their own affairs. It tries to reduce the role of government in people's lives. In recent times its most famous leader was Margaret Thatcher, who in the 1980s reduced the power of the trade unions and encouraged business enterprise.

Party 2

This party has been growing in recent years. In the nineteenth century the Liberal Party was very powerful and often in government. For much of the twentieth century it was a relatively small party which could not compete with the two big ones. In 1989 it joined with another party, the Social Democrats. It believes strongly in civil liberties and human rights. It also wants to see a different way of electing MPs – called proportional representation – so that smaller parties will have more MPs in Parliament to represent the views of the voters.

Party 3

This party was formed in 1906. It emerged from the trade union movement. Its main aim was to represent workers and try to improve the quality of their lives. It believed in the ideas of socialism – sharing out the wealth of a country amongst all the people and redistributing wealth from the rich to the poor. After the Second World War this party was elected to government and nationalised a number of big industries including the railways, coal and steel. It also started the National Health Service. In recent years it has reinvented itself after losing several elections.

Research

Split the class into groups or pairs. Each group should choose one of the parties on these pages and find out more about it at www.uk-p.org/Parties/. Make a two-minute presentation to the rest of the class about your chosen party.

Activity

1. Look at the three descriptions on the left. Which description fits:
   a) Labour
   b) Conservatives
   c) Liberal Democrats?
2. What do you know about the three main parties? Work in groups. Make three lists, one for each of the political parties. Brainstorm and write down words and names that describe each party for you.
3. Write to or e-mail the three biggest political parties and ask them for information about their policies. You could invite local MPs to speak to your class. Prepare questions to ask them and decide who will ask which questions. You can also look at their websites:
   www.labour.org.uk
   www.conservatives.com
   www.libdems.org.uk

4.6 Is 'first past the post' a good system?

The system of elections used in the UK for parliamentary and local elections is called **first past the post**. The candidate with the most votes takes the prize (a seat in Parliament) and the runners-up get nothing. This policy has led to a predominantly two-party system.

The map shows the results of an election in the City of Townside. Townside has six constituencies (voting areas) and each contains 10 000 voters. This means that six MPs represent the people of Townside. See if you can work out who won the election and whether you think the electoral system was fair.

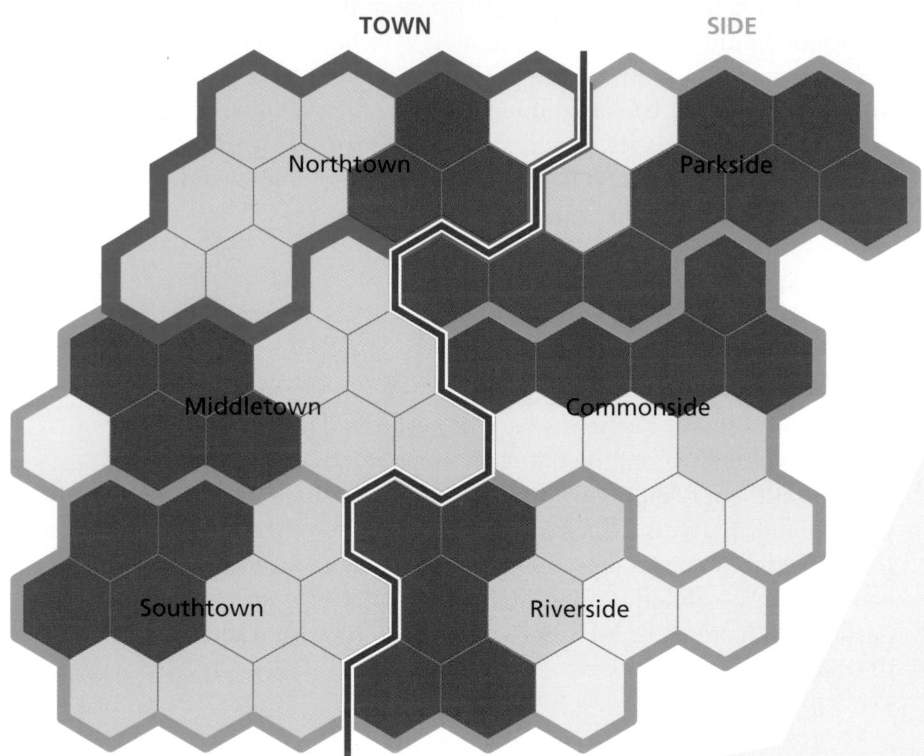

Activity

Stage 1

Make a team of four people. You have been asked to study the election results for Townside and report on the pros and cons of the first-past-the-post system.

1 First of all you need to work out the results for each constituency like this:

Northtown constituency

Result

Blue – 6 000 votes

Red – 3 000 votes

Yellow – 1 000 votes

So Blue wins!

Analysis

- *Blue has a majority of 3 000 over Red who came second.*
- *Blue has an overall majority (over all other parties combined) of 2 000.*
- *4 000 people voted for parties (Red and Yellow) not elected.*

2 Answer these questions.
   a) How many MPs were elected for each party?
   b) How many people in Townside as a whole voted for Reds, Blues and Yellows?
   c) On average how many votes did the winning candidate get? (Add up the six winners' votes then divide by six to get the average.)
   d) In which constituency did the winning candidate have no overall majority?
   e) How many votes in total were cast for the winning party?
   f) How many votes in total were cast for the losing parties?

Stage 2

The City of Townside is to change its voting system. Instead of six constituencies, each electing one MP, there will now be two larger constituencies – the Town and Side constituencies with 30 000 registered voters in each. Each constituency elects three MPs. The new boundary is shown on the map.

NB At this election assume each party receives exactly the same number of votes as in the first election.

1 In the new system you must make sure that the proportion of seats each party gets reflects *as far as possible* the proportion of the total votes they received. In your groups, devise a proportional representation method to ensure this.
2 How does the outcome compare to the previous situation?
3 Which party gains and which loses?

Stage 3

Debate: 'This house believes the UK should introduce proportional representation for the next General Election.'

Arguments for and against the 'first-past-the-post' system

For	Against
It is simple to understand	All those people who did not vote for the winner feel their vote was wasted
People know that they have one MP for their constituency whom they have chosen to represent them	They are discouraged from voting because they feel their votes don't count
It is fair that the person with the majority wins	In 1997, nearly half of the votes cast were for people who lost
The MP represents all constituents, not just those voting for him/her	Often there is little difference between the two big parties, so alternative views are not heard
It supports a two-party system	Proportional representation is fairer as more MPs from smaller parties are more likely to be elected.
British democracy has stood the test of time – why change it?	

Proportional representation

One of the main arguments against the first-past-the-post system is that some parties get a lot of votes but not many seats. One way to solve this problem is called the proportional representation (PR) system. This means that the number of MPs elected depends on the number of votes for each party.

Does first past the post lead to strong government?

First past the post has led to strong governments in Britain. In 1997, although Labour got only 43% of votes they got 65% of MPs in Parliament. This meant that they could pass the laws they wanted to. If the number of MPs had been based on the votes given to all the parties then 57% of MPs would be from other parties. This would mean Labour would need to join with another party to get laws passed in Parliament. This is called a coalition government. Coalitions mean both parties have to compromise, but if they fall out the government fails and there has to be another election. Many European countries have coalition governments because they use proportional representation in their general elections. Labour and the Liberal Democrats have formed a coalition in the Scottish Parliament. Many local councils have a coalition because no party has overall control.

4.7 House of Commons virtual visit

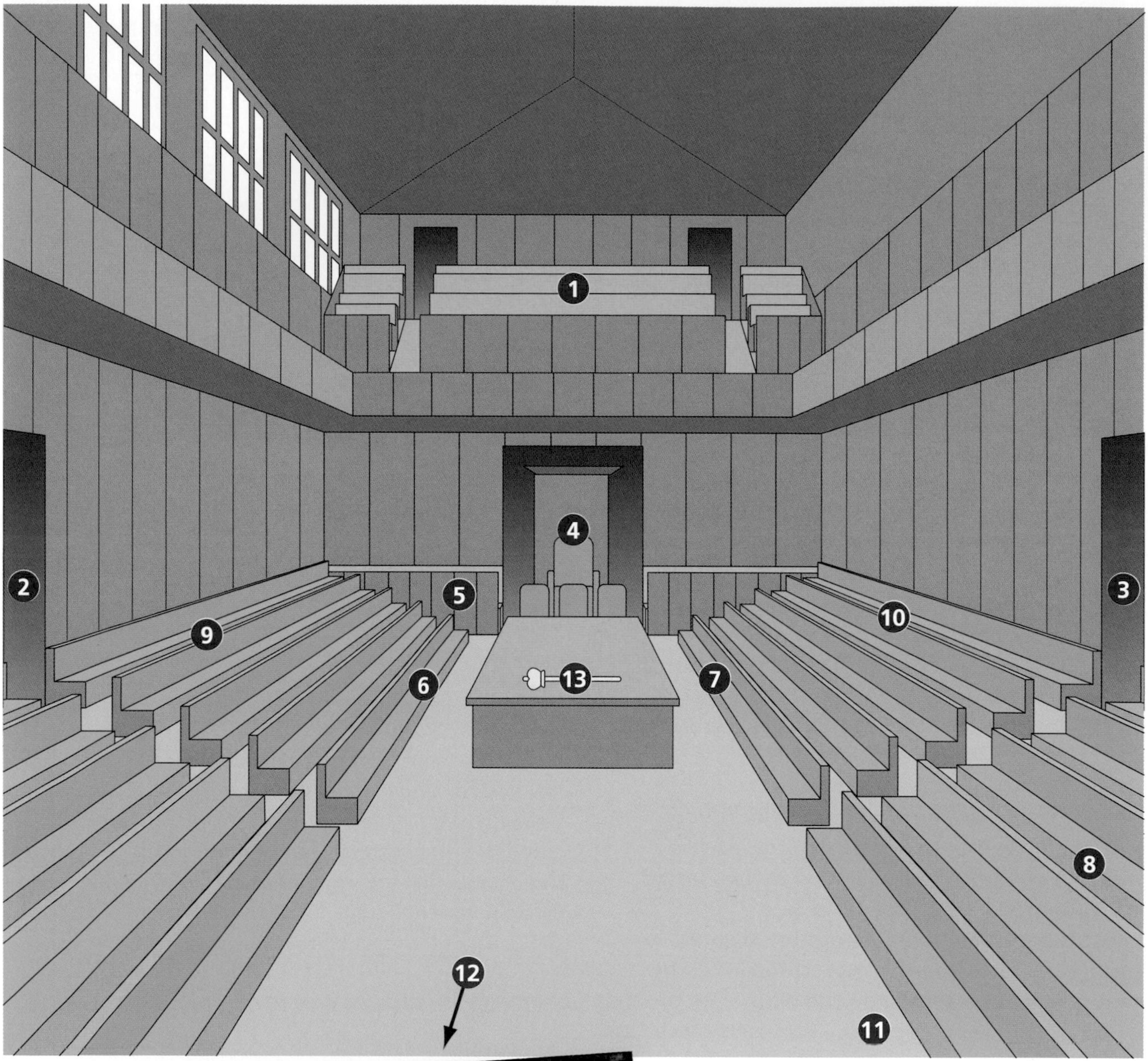

MPs are elected to serve in the House of Commons. The illustration above is the view you would get if you were sitting in the public gallery. This is where voters and foreign visitors can sit to see Parliament in action.

Debates and question times in the House of Commons are often shown on television. It might look like chaos to you, so here is our rough guide to who's who in the House of Commons.

Activity

The diagram on page 102 illustrates the seating plan for the House of Commons. The numbered labels on the diagram and below show people and different parts of the House. The letters explain who or what they are. Match each number to the appropriate letter.

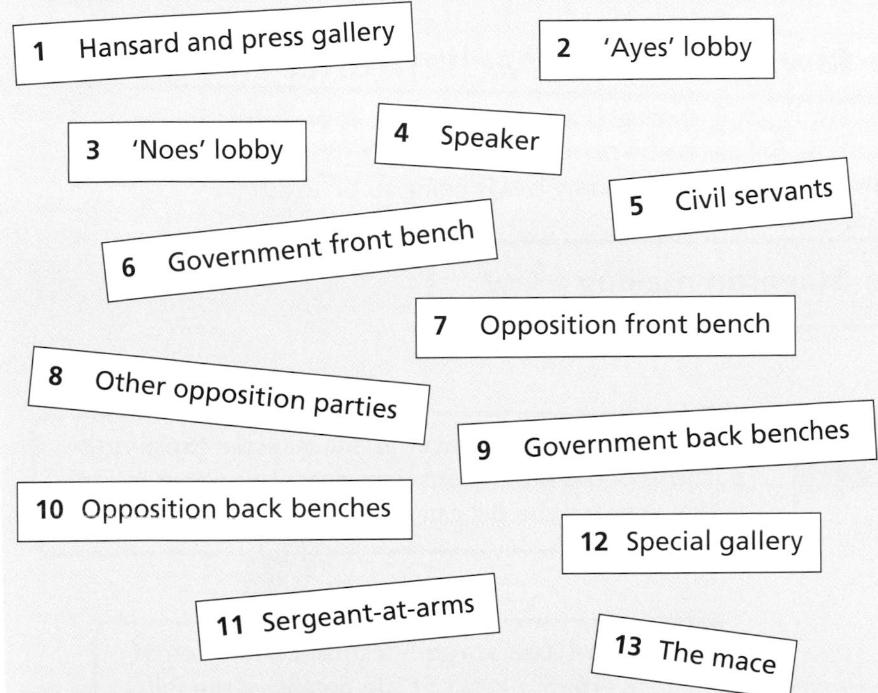

A Where government ministers sit during debates
B Place where MPs walk to vote No in a debate
C Officials who can provide answers to tricky questions for ministers during a debate
D The person who handles security in the House
E Journalists and people keeping a record of all that is said in the House
F Where ordinary MPs from the political party which forms the government sit
G Symbol used to show Parliament is sitting
H Place where MPs walk to vote Yes in a debate
I MPs' guests can sit here to listen to debates
J The person who keeps order in a debate
K Where Shadow ministers (Opposition MPs) sit during debates
L Where MPs not in the Shadow Cabinet (backbenchers) sit in debates
M Where MPs belonging to the parties which are not in government or the official Opposition sit

You can make a virtual visit to the House of Commons on the internet at www.explore.parliament.uk . There are also other activities on the site that help you learn about how Parliament works.

Making laws

One of the most important jobs of the House of Commons is to pass new laws or improve existing ones. There is a well-developed process (see diagram below) which Parliament uses to make sure that the laws are thoroughly checked before they are put into action. This process gives MPs the opportunity to include changes that they feel are necessary.

How are laws made in Parliament?

While a proposed new law is going through Parliament, before it becomes a law, it is called a Bill. The Bill has to be properly written out (drafted), explaining carefully how and when the new law is going to be used.

Stages in making a law

1. **First reading** – the Bill is published for MPs to read. There is no discussion or vote.
2. **Second reading** – a government minister explains the purpose of the Bill and answers questions about it. Only if MPs vote for the Bill can it go on to the next stage.
3. **Committee stage** – a small committee of MPs (16–60) looks at the details of the Bill and discusses them. It suggests changes or amendments to the Bill and votes on these.
4. **Report stage** – the committee reports to the House of Commons on what it has done to the Bill. MPs can suggest further changes.
5. **Third reading** – gives the House of Commons a chance to look at the whole Bill again with all its amendments. After a debate, MPs vote for it or reject it.
6. **House of Lords** – the Bill goes to the House of Lords. The Lords check it and can suggest changes to the Bill; there may be some discussion with the House of Commons about these. But the House of Lords cannot stop a Bill becoming law.
7. **The Royal Assent** – once the Bill has been passed by both Houses, it goes to the monarch who gives the Royal Assent (agreement).
8. **Act of Parliament** – the Bill is now a law.

Activity

Make a law

Working in groups of three, you are going to make a new law about the legalisation of cannabis. You have to follow the rules below.

1. The new Bill proposes that cannabis should be legalised.
2. You are going to debate this in class. The class must divide in half, one half supporting the Bill and the other half against. This means that you may have to argue for something you do not believe in. It is important to do this sometimes.
3. First, work in your small group. Use some of the arguments set out below as well as your own ideas to develop your argument. You could also look at arguments on the internet if you have time to prepare. Choose which one of your group is going to speak in the debate. This means there should be three or four speakers for each side.
4. Hold the debate.
5. One amendment has already been suggested. Each group can suggest one amendment (change) to the Bill that they think is fair and good. The whole class discuss and vote on the amendments. If there is a majority in favour, the amendment is 'passed'.
6. The class now vote on the whole Bill with the agreed amendments. If the majority vote for it, it becomes 'law'.

Amendment that has already been suggested

Cannabis should be decriminalised but not legalised. This means that people will not be criminals if they smoke it, but it cannot be sold legally in shops, so the sellers would still be criminals and liable for punishment.

Arguments

Using cannabis leads on to harder drugs, so we should not encourage people to start on the slippery slope.

So many people smoke cannabis that keeping it illegal makes lots of people criminals when they really are not.

It creates an illegal trade. If it were legal you would not get any criminals involved.

It's no worse than alcohol and probably not as bad for you. It's hypocritical to allow people to drink alcohol but not to smoke cannabis.

Many people smoke cannabis all their lives and don't go on to harder drugs.

It would bring a lot of relief to people with certain medical conditions.

Cannabis takes away all your drive and makes you lazy and complacent.

Cannabis is very harmful to our health, it kills brain cells over a long period of time. People have to be protected from harming themselves.

Decriminalising cannabis would cut crime, and the time police spend on it could be spent on serious offences.

The present law isn't working, it doesn't stop people getting hold of cannabis.

4.8 How should MPs behave?

MPs can have a lot of influence. Sometimes it is very helpful to have an MP on your side, pushing your interests. For instance, you might be a businessman who wants to get a government contract worth millions of pounds or you might be a person who wants to get your voice heard in Parliament or in government circles. So you might offer the MP something – a luxury holiday on one of your yachts in the Caribbean, for example. You might be prepared to donate money to the party funds of the MP even though you might not give it to him or her directly. There are all sorts of ways to try to get influence over an MP.

During the 1990s there were several scandals involving MPs and ministers. The name given to this by the media was sleaze. In 1994 the Committee on Standards in Public Life was formed. It has published the Seven Principles of Public Life as a guide to all people involved in public affairs.

'Yes, I think this government is sleazy, but a tenner could persuade me to change my mind'

Activity

Form a group of three or four. You are members of the Committee.

1 Read through the Seven Principles (below).
2 Look at each of the incidents on page 107 in turn and decide if any principle was broken. Return one of the following verdicts:

- No principle broken
- Principle broken (say which principle and how it was broken)
- More information needed.

THE SEVEN PRINCIPLES OF PUBLIC LIFE

People who hold public offices, such as MPs and civil servants, should:

1 take decisions solely in terms of the public interest. They should not do so in order to gain financial or other benefits for themselves, their family or their friends
2 not place themselves under any financial or other obligation to outside individuals or organisations that might influence them in their work
3 make choices on merit in carrying out public business, including making public appointments, awarding contracts, or recommending individuals for rewards and benefits
4 be accountable for their decisions and actions to the public and must submit themselves to whatever scrutiny is appropriate to their office
5 be as open as possible about all the decisions and actions that they take. They should give reasons for their decisions
6 have a duty to declare any private interests relating to their public duties (honesty)
7 promote and support these principles by leadership and example.

Incidents

Cash for questions

An MP accepted money from an oil company in return for putting questions to ministers in the House of Commons.

Passport

An MP promised to talk to the Home Office about obtaining a passport for a relative of a millionaire constituent.

Wife and secretary

An MP used his secretarial allowance (money from Parliament to pay for an MP's secretarial support) to employ his wife as his secretary.

Football or diplomacy

A sports minister combined going on a visit to a foreign country, paid for by the taxpayers, with going to a football match in that country involving the team she supported.

Insider knowledge

An MP, who knew about change in government policy that might affect share prices, tipped off a relative so they could sell their shares and make a big profit.

Mortgage loan

The minister at the head of the department for fraud accepted a secret loan, to buy a house, from an MP who was being investigated by the minister's department at the time for dodgy financial dealings.

Discuss

How strict should the rules for MPs be? Which of the two statements below do you agree with?

a) Ministers and MPs should never be allowed to take gifts or favours like free accommodation for themselves and their families. The people who give them will want something in return.

b) MPs and ministers are public figures. They are bound to be offered gifts. It does not matter too much as long as the gifts are not too big and they don't use their position to get special advantages for the giver.

4.9 How do pressure groups try to influence MPs?

People who have strong opinions on a particular issue often try to influence what happens by putting pressure on MPs and people who make decisions. They are called 'pressure groups' or sometimes 'lobby groups' or 'protest groups'. Some pressure groups work to protect the interests of their members, such as the trade unions or the CBI (Confederation of British Industry). Others work to promote a cause, such as animal welfare, or fight for the rights of others, such as SPUC (Society for the Protection of the Unborn Child).

Here are some examples of pressure groups.

Royal Society for the Prevention of Cruelty to Animals (RSPCA)

The National Union of Teachers (NUT)

Campaign for Nuclear Disarmament (CND)

NACRO - the crime reduction charity

British Medical Association (BMA)

National Society for the Prevention of Cruelty to Children (NSPCC)

Amnesty International

Help the Aged

Road Haulage Association (RHA)

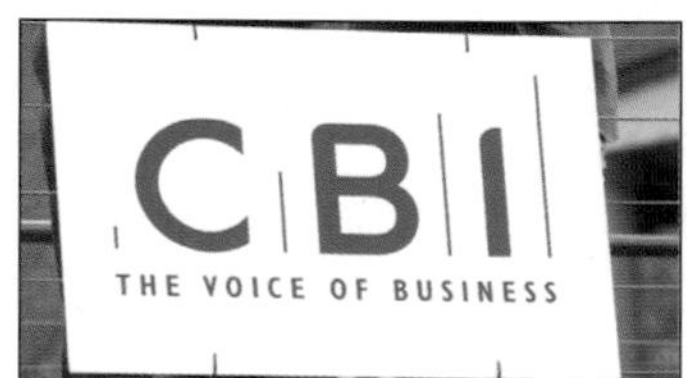

Confederation of British Industry (CBI)

Activity

1. How many pressure groups can you identify from their logos? Write a sentence for each one to explain what it stands for.
2. Which pressure group activities can you see in the photographs on page 109?
3. Choose three of the pressure groups above. Which of the activities on page 109 do you think it would be appropriate for them to use to be most effective?
4. Which activities do you think would be most effective in influencing:
   a) public opinion
   b) politicians?
5. Which of the activities are extreme and illegal? Do you think violent tactics can ever be justified?

Methods

Pressure groups try to influence the government by affecting what politicians think. They can do this by traditional methods, such as getting people to write to their MP, or they can stage demonstrations or protests. The internet has made it easier for people to form pressure groups and to organise protests such as the anti-capitalist demonstrations in London and around the world.

Pressure group activities

- * Marches to the House of Commons
- * Demonstrations
- * Fly-posting campaign
- * Staging stunts to attract the media (for example climbing high buildings)
- * Petitions
- * Meeting government ministers
- * Targeted violence against property
- * Putting case on national television
- * Letter-writing campaign to newspapers
- * Direct action such as setting animals free from farms/labs
- * Advertising campaign in the national press
- * Writing letters or e-mails to MPs
- * Phone-in campaign to local radio stations
- * Meeting MPs and councillors
- * Violence against people

Are pressure groups good for democracy?

The aim of pressure groups is to promote their cause so that the government and people in power take notice. When this is a group like the National Society for the Prevention of Cruelty to Children, this does not seem a problem because most people would support the aims of the group. But when it is the tobacco industry trying to promote the sale of cigarettes, or the Countryside Alliance supporting fox-hunting, then some people would not be so happy if these groups gained influence over the way the government acts. Pressure groups are often in conflict with one another and struggling for influence over MPs and the government. For example, here are some of the pressure groups that try to influence government policy on transport.

Activity

1 Do you think the way Greenpeace acted against Shell in the Brent Spar case study, below, was:
   a) effective
   b) reasonable?
2 Look at the diagram showing the different pressure groups for transport. How would the different groups try to influence MPs, and what would their arguments be about the following policies?
   a) Congestion charges to be applied in cities to ease traffic-flow problems.
   b) A cut in road building programmes along with more taxes on fuel and heavy lorries, in order to protect the environment.

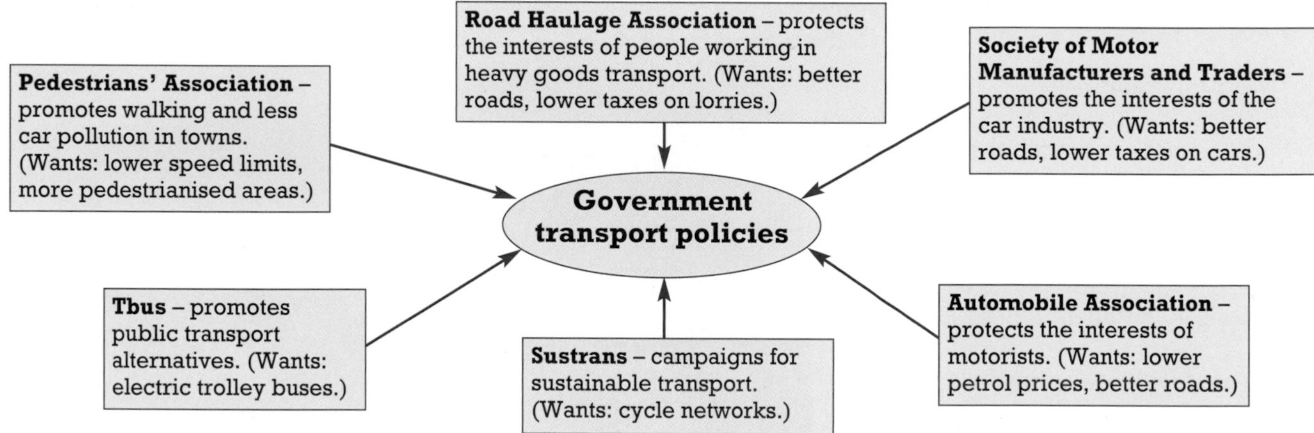

Road Haulage Association – protects the interests of people working in heavy goods transport. (Wants: better roads, lower taxes on lorries.)
Pedestrians' Association – promotes walking and less car pollution in towns. (Wants: lower speed limits, more pedestrianised areas.)
Society of Motor Manufacturers and Traders – promotes the interests of the car industry. (Wants: better roads, lower taxes on cars.)
Government transport policies
Tbus – promotes public transport alternatives. (Wants: electric trolley buses.)
Sustrans – campaigns for sustainable transport. (Wants: cycle networks.)
Automobile Association – protects the interests of motorists. (Wants: lower petrol prices, better roads.)

Case study: *Successful pressure group campaign – Brent Spar*

In 1995, the multinational oil company, Shell, planned to sink the Brent Spar oil platform at sea. The platform contained some radioactive and industrial waste. Greenpeace, the environmental pressure group, objected to the damage this would cause to sea life. The alternative was to tow the platform to shore and to break it up. The attention of the world's media was focused on Brent Spar when Greenpeace landed two of its members on the platform. In addition tens of thousands of consumers across Europe joined Greenpeace's call for a boycott of Shell products. In Germany alone petrol sales at Shell garages fell by 50%. Although Shell was supported by the British government, the company relented under this pressure and announced that it would not sink the platform.

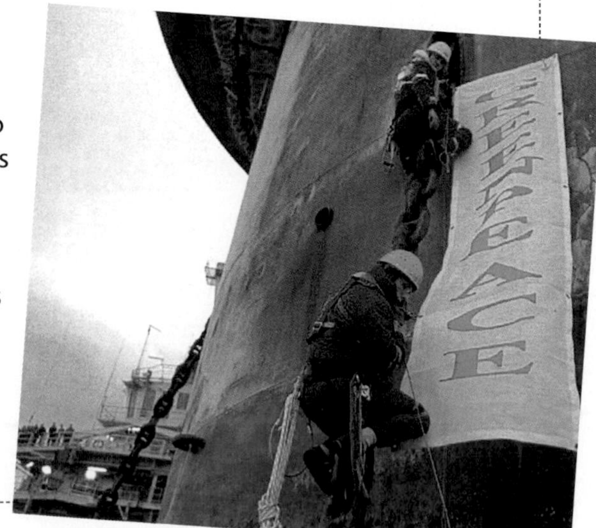

Activity

1 Look at the arguments below. Decide which of them support the argument that pressure groups are good for democracy and which do not.
2 Debate the issue in class.
3 Are there any restrictions you would want to place on the activities of pressure groups?

A Pressure groups make sure that governments are aware of what people think on an issue.

B They provide a lot of useful information for the public.

C They get the public involved in issues that affect their lives.

D Rich and powerful pressure groups, for example big business groups, can get more influence.

E They might use bribery or corruption to gain influence.

F They can gain undue influence over MPs and the government and so the interests of a few people might win out over the interests of the majority.

G They challenge the government on significant issues and can act as a check on what the government does.

H They stand up for people who are weak and powerless, like children and farmers in developing countries.

I Pressure groups can be undemocratic because they reduce the importance of individual voters and even of MPs in Parliament.

J Some pressure groups take extreme action to make their case, damaging property and even hurting people.

Activity

Either:
Choose one of the pressure groups mentioned here, such as Greenpeace, or find one of your own. Find out what it stands for, its history, what campaigns it is running and what methods it uses. Present your findings to the rest of the class.

Or:
Choose an issue – it could be a local issue important to your community or a national/ international issue, like animal rights (see pages 112–13). Plan a campaign to put over the arguments for this issue. Think about:

- what you would call your pressure group
- how you would let people know what you think to try to get them to support you
- who you would write to
- what other pressure group activities you might use to attract attention.

Animal rights

One issue that concerns many people is that of animal rights. Do non-human animals have rights? And if so, what are they and how should they be protected? Various animal rights pressure groups have developed in Europe and America to fight for animal rights. These groups have used a range of methods to get their message across. Where do you stand on animal rights? How far should people be allowed to go in support of their cause?

A squalid puppy farm in Wales

Activity

Stage 1

Where do you stand on animal rights? Look at the questionnaire and decide whether you agree or disagree with the statements. Then use the scoring system on page 113. There are no right or wrong answers.

	Animal rights questionnaire	**Disagree**	**Don't know**	**Agree**
1	Animals are able to think and feel pain like us so they should have rights.	○	○	○
2	Humans are much more complex than non-human animals, which do not deserve rights.	○	○	○
3	Human beings who are part of society have rights and responsibilities – animals live by instinct and are irrational so cannot have rights.	○	○	○
4	A society that rejects cruelty to animals and gives them rights is truly civilised.	○	○	○
5	Some animal rights activists are terrorists who do not respect human life.	○	○	○
6	Human beings are related to other animals and so animals should be given similar rights to us.	○	○	○
7	Denying that animals have rights is a short step away from denying rights to infants or people with disabilities.	○	○	○
8	It is natural for humans to use animals for food as happens in the wild when animals prey on others.	○	○	○
9	We need to test new medicines on animals before they are tried on people.	○	○	○
10	It is wrong to test cosmetics on animals.	○	○	○
11	Blood sports are using animals' suffering for our pleasure and this must be wrong.	○	○	○
12	Bullfighting is a part of Spanish culture and fox-hunting is part of English culture.	○	○	○

Stage 2

1 Some animal rights groups have taken very strong direct action. For example, they have:

- released animals from cages
- targeted individuals who work in laboratories using animals in experiments, by damaging their cars or even attacking them
- sent letter bombs.

Do you think this sort of action is ever justified?

PeTA
Here's the rest of your fur coat.
www.furisdead.com

2 Work in a group of four and choose an issue from the following list:

- fox-hunting
- fishing
- zoos
- shooting, (say, grouse or pheasant).

Design the front page of a leaflet campaigning for or against the continuance of the activity. Write 100 words to explain your case.

You can find a lot more information about animal rights on the internet.

When you have finished, display your leaflet and be prepared to talk about it to the rest of the class.

Scoring

- If you agreed with statements 1, 4, 6, 7, 10 and 11, score +1 for each
- If you disagreed with statements 1, 4, 6, 7, 10 and 11, score −1 for each
- If you agreed with statements 2, 3, 5, 8, 9 and 12, score −1 for each
- If you disagreed with statements 2, 3, 5, 8, 9 and 12, score +1 for each

Add up your total score

+5 to +12: You are an animal rights enthusiast.
+1 to +4: You are a moderate supporter of animal rights.
0: You are probably confused and need to sort out your thinking.
−1 to −4: You are moderately against the idea of animal rights.
−5 to −12: You think that the idea of animal rights does not make sense.

Discuss

Hold a class debate on the subject: 'We believe that zoos, circuses and horse-racing should be banned as they exploit animals.'

4.10 You the taxpayer

Tax makes some people very angry. You have to pay tax on what you earn and the goods that you buy. The government also makes businesses pay taxes. Taxpayers' money goes to the government, but why is it needed?

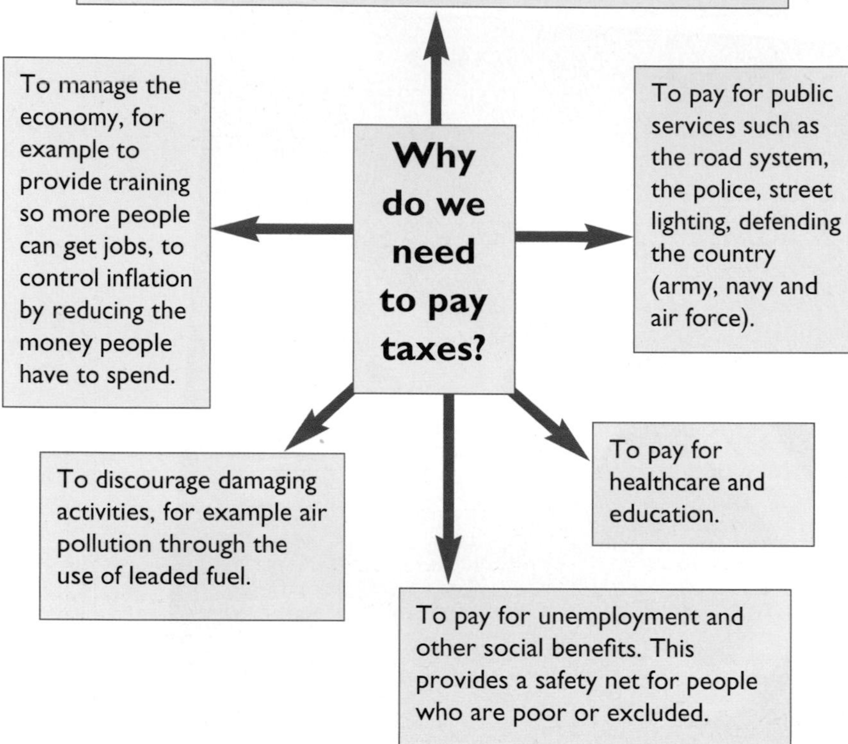

Why do we need to pay taxes?
To redistribute income. Our economy tends to produce extremes of rich and poor; taxation can be used to take some money from better off people in order to help poorer families.
To pay for public services such as the road system, the police, street lighting, defending the country (army, navy and air force).
To pay for healthcare and education.
To pay for unemployment and other social benefits. This provides a safety net for people who are poor or excluded.
To discourage damaging activities, for example air pollution through the use of leaded fuel.
To manage the economy, for example to provide training so more people can get jobs, to control inflation by reducing the money people have to spend.

Activity

You are a taxpayer, and the government has asked you to pay more tax to fund the following programmes. Which would you agree was a good use of your money? Which would you disagree with?

- A pay rise for teachers
- Smaller class sizes in primary schools
- An increase in the state pension
- A programme of increased road building in major cities
- An increase in weapons for the army and planes for the airforce
- An increase in prisons for young offenders.

The two main types of tax

Direct tax

A direct tax is one paid directly to the government or local council.

Income tax is the most important direct tax. It is taken from people's wages and salaries. It is said to be a **progressive** tax because the higher your income the higher the amount of tax you pay. The table below shows the three rates of tax.

Rate 2003–4	Income (£)	Tax (£)
Personal allowance	First 4615	No tax
Starting rate	The next: 0–1960	10% (you pay £10 tax in every £100 you earn)
Basic rate	1961–30 500	22% (you pay £22 tax in every £100 you earn)
Higher rate	Over 30 500	40% (you pay £40 tax in every £100 you earn)

There is also tax on business. Every business has to pay Corporation tax on its profits.

Indirect tax

Indirect taxes are charged on the goods and services we use. They are paid by businesses, which get their money back by increasing the price that we pay. The most well-known indirect tax is value added tax (VAT) which is charged at a rate of 17.5% on most goods and services we buy. This means we have to pay £117.50 for something worth £100. Other indirect taxes are the tax or duty on tobacco, alcohol and fuel. So people who are non-smoking, teetotal pedestrians pay none of these taxes. Indirect taxes are said to be **regressive** as everyone pays the same whether they are rich or poor.

Government spending

The government has to decide how to spend the money it receives from taxation. This is also called 'public spending'. There are lots of things on which to spend the money collected from taxes, but never enough money to go around. The most important decisions about spending are made by a special committee called the Cabinet. The Cabinet is chaired by the Prime Minister and is the main decision-making body. It is made up of ministers who are in charge of running all the main government departments.

Each year the Chancellor of the Exchequer has to draw up the **Budget**. This states how the government is going to raise the money – **revenue** – it needs and how it is going to spend it.

Minister for Social Security
Minister for Defence
Minister for Transport
Minister for Health
Foreign Secretary
Home Secretary
Prime Minister
Minister for the Environment
Chancellor of the Exchequer

The Cabinet

Activity

The government has to make difficult decisions about what to do and how to pay for it. In this activity you will be members of a Cabinet Committee set up to plan government spending for the coming year. Work in groups of five or six.

Stage 1 – Public spending

The economy is successful at the moment so you think you will be able to increase public spending by £6 billion or more. Each department has put in its bid for increased spending – see column 4.

Government department	Main responsibilities	Spending in current year (billions)	What each department plans to do next year and the extra money needed to fund it (billions)	Your decision
Education and Skills	schools, colleges, universities, training	£22	big expansion of university places – £1 school buildings – £2	
Health	National Health Service, hospitals, doctors	£50	large hospital building programme – £3 pay increases for NHS staff – £1	
Environment, Food and Rural Affairs	countryside, farming	£5	support for rural areas – £0.5	
Transport, Local Government and Regions	public transport, local councils, regional development	£42	increased spending on railways – £2 increased repairs on major roads – £1	
Home Office	police, courts, prisons	£10	new prison building programme – £1.5	
Defence	army, navy, airforce	£24	new aircraft for the RAF – £2 more peacekeeping roles in the world's trouble spots – £1	
Trade and Industry	businesses, exporters	£5	support for exporters – 0.5	
International Development	overseas aid	£3	more aid for Africa – £0.5	
Work and Pensions	unemployment benefits, state pensions	£5	increase in state pension – £2	
		Total = £166		Total =

1 For each of the departments' plans decide if you think it is:
   - top priority – vital
   - mid priority – a good idea but not vital
   - low priority – not important.
2 Work out how many of your top priority projects you can pay for from £6 billion.
3 Decide whether to increase spending above £6 billion. Going for a higher figure will mean you can satisfy more of the demands of the spending departments but you will have to raise more money in taxes in Stage 2.
4 In this activity the smallest increase you can give is half a billion and the maximum increase you can give to one department is £2 billion.
5 When you have made your decisions record them on your own copy of the table and note down the thinking behind them.

Stage 2 – Government revenue

Of course any increase in public spending must be paid for by an increase in the government's income (revenue). These increases will be paid for by increasing one of the following taxes. (Governments can also borrow money if they wish but in this activity you don't have that option.)

Tax	What is it?	Who pays it?	Current revenue (billions)	Increase (billions)
Direct taxes Income tax	tax on people's income	everybody working or receiving income from property, shares etc.	£100	
National insurance	tax on employment	employers and employees	£60	
Corporation tax	tax on business profits	businesses that are making profits	£40	
Business rate	tax on companies	businesses that have premises	£18	
Indirect taxes Value added tax (VAT)	tax on goods and services	people and businesses when they buy something	£61	
Petrol duty	tax on fuel	anyone who drives cars, motorbikes, vans, lorries, etc.	£23	
Tobacco duty	tax on tobacco	people who smoke	£8	
Alcohol duty	tax on alcohol	people who drink alcohol	£7	
Vehicle excise duty (Road tax)	tax on cars and other vehicles	anyone who drives cars, motorbikes, vans, lorries, etc.	£5	
			Total = £322	Total =

Out of this figure the government has to pay back borrowing and spend money on other projects.

1 Decide how you will pay for your increased spending. Which taxes will you raise? Will you increase several taxes by a small amount or go for one large increase?

2 When you have made your decisions you must be prepared to explain and justify them. Who would benefit most from your changes and who would lose the most? You must consider how your tax decisions will affect:
   - people and families
   - businesses
   - the economy

3 Consider how the news media might react to your proposed tax changes. Draft some headlines in support of, and against your tax plan.

4.11 How would you reform the House of Lords?

Design your own second chamber

The British Parliament has long been a two-chamber system – the two 'chambers' are the House of Commons and the House of Lords. But the most powerful house is the House of Commons. This is because the Commons is directly elected by the British people and represents them. The government is formed by the political party that wins the General Election and has the most MPs in the House of Commons. It is in the Commons that laws are made. However, it is still thought that a second house is a good idea because it acts as a check on the power of the Commons. It can stop laws going through quickly and can raise questions about them. It can also criticise the government.

Until recently the members of the House of Lords included many hereditary lords or peers – people who were there because one of their ancestors had been made a lord, perhaps several hundred years ago. This was declared undemocratic and many of these hereditary lords recently lost their right to sit in the Lords. In 2003, the Lords is still undergoing reform. There is now a big debate about who should be in the second house.

There are lots of issues to think about:

- How do you think members should be chosen to serve in the Lords – elected or appointed?
- How will you ensure that a wide range of people, with expertise in all aspects of life, is included?
- How will you ensure a fair representation of women and people from minority ethnic groups?
- What power should the second house have?

Activity

You can design your own second chamber by choosing from the options set out below. Work in a group of three to discuss each set of options and make a choice. When you have finished be prepared to explain your second house to the rest of the class. You may need to look out for contradictions in your decisions. For example, if 100% of members are to be elected and you have said 50% should be women – how would this work?

1. The name of our second chamber would be:
   a) the House of Lords
   b) the Second House
   c) the Senate
   d) some other name – you decide
2. The members of the second house would be:
   a) 100% elected by the voters
   b) 75% elected and 25% appointed
   c) 50% elected and 50% appointed
   d) 25% elected and 75% appointed
   e) 100% appointed
3. If members are to be appointed who should have this power?
   a) a body independent of the government
   b) the Prime Minister
   c) half of those appointed should be chosen by the government and half by the Opposition
   d) half of those appointed should be chosen by an independent commission and half by the government
   e) some other method – you decide
4. If there are to be elections, should they be held:
   a) at the same time as the General Election (at least every five years when the government decides)
   b) every four years at a set time
   c) every two years at a set time
   d) some other period – you decide
5. The members of the second house should be largely made up of (you can choose more than one option):
   a) older, experienced people from different careers – scientists, lawyers, doctors, teachers, religious leaders, business people and trade unionists
   b) a minimum percentage of women and ethnic minorities (you decide what percentage)
   c) a mix of young and older people
   d) representatives from the three main political parties
   e) representatives from the English regions
6. What power should the second house have?
   a) the power to reject Bills passed in the Commons
   b) the power to delay Bills passed in the Commons
   c) the power to advise and suggest changes to Bills passed in the Commons
   d) some other powers – you decide.

Research task

Compare your own second house with the current set-up of the House of Lords. What are the main similarities and differences?

4.12 What is the future of the monarchy in the UK?

Monarchy – being ruled by a king or queen – is one of the oldest forms of government. Traditionally, monarchs claimed that their right to rule came directly from God. In the past 200 years many countries in Europe have got rid of their monarchies altogether and become republics. Others, like Britain, have become constitutional monarchies. This means that the country has kept a monarch but the monarch has given up most of their power to parliaments elected by the people. The monarch has to obey the law just as other citizens do.

What role does the monarch play in British politics and society?

Activity

All of these pictures show different roles that the monarch plays in British politics and society. See if you can identify them.

a) Which show the monarch playing a role in the British political system?
b) Which show the monarch as a symbol and figurehead?

If you can't work them all out, look back at page 88 for help.

4
5
13
6
12
1ST
11
10
ELIZABETH·II·D·G·REG·F·D·2001
THE QUEEN'S AWARDS
FOR ENTERPRISE
9
Onslow
Chilworth
7
8

The future of the monarchy

What do you think about the monarchy?

Are you a republican – someone who wants to get rid of the monarchy in Britain?

Or are you a traditionalist – someone who wants to leave things as they are?

Or are you a moderniser – someone who believes in monarchy but wants to update it?

Decide whether you agree or disagree with the statements in the opinion survey. Then use the scoring system at the bottom of page 123.

Opinion survey

		Disagree	Agree
1	It would be good if the royal family did ordinary jobs and lived in normal houses.	○	○
2	We should replace the monarch with an elected President.	○	○
3	The monarchy has been there for a thousand years and it has served the country well.	○	○
4	We should change the law so that the eldest child inherits the crown, not the eldest male.	○	○
5	The monarchy brings lots of tourists and their money to Britain.	○	○
6	We should not give the royal family public money to support their lavish lifestyle.	○	○
7	The monarch, through the Commonwealth, contributes to Britain's role in the world.	○	○
8	The monarch should no longer be Head of the Church of England, as we live in a country with lots of religions.	○	○
9	The monarchy is a symbol of the class system.	○	○
10	The monarchy should be kept, but its role should be limited to ceremonial duties only.	○	○
11	The monarchy is undemocratic and should have no role in Parliament.	○	○
12	The monarchy has a key role in the British system and should be left alone.	○	○

Activity

Now that we are in the twenty-first century, how should the monarchy change?

Work in pairs to draft a job description for a future king or queen in 2010. Set out your job description using the template below. State the main purpose of the job and all the major tasks or roles.

Title: King or Queen
Main purpose:
Key tasks:

Debate

Organise a class debate on one of the following topics:
'This house believes that in the twenty-first century the UK should no longer be a monarchy.'

or

'This house believes that the British monarchy is a key part of British culture and our system of government.'

Monarchists say:

The monarch has little real power.

The monarchy acts as a symbol of national unity, particularly in time of war.

Monarchs are part of Britain's history and heritage and part of what makes us British.

Royal palaces and ceremonies attract millions of tourists who spend a lot of money in Britain.

Monarchs are more popular than elected presidents.

Monarchs are politically neutral whereas presidents are usually linked to political parties.

A constitutional monarch brings stability to the political system of a country because they are there year after year.

Republicans say:

Many members of the royal family have become an embarrassment. Their failed marriages and squabbles are constantly in the press and set a bad example for the public.

The monarch is the head of the Church of England, which is divisive in multi-cultural and multi-faith Britain.

The cost of the royal family to the public cannot be justified.

They do exercise some influence, which is often hidden from the public.

Their existence supports the class system and inequality in Britain.

Monarchy is undemocratic – nobody voted for them.

The system of giving honours (medals and knighthoods) creates divisions in society and mostly helps the already rich and powerful.

Score only if you agreed with statements.

- Score 5 each for 2, 6, 9 and 11: you want to end the monarchy (*High Republican*)
- Score 5 for 3, 5, 7 and 12: you are a strong supporter of the royal family (*High Traditional*)
- Score 5 for 1, 4, 8 and 10: you are a strong supporter of change (*High Moderniser*)
- Score less than 20: you are a monarchist in favour of change (*Medium Traditional* and *Moderniser*)

4.13 Devolution

Devolution means giving powers to regional and local assemblies. After many years of debate, referendums in Wales and Scotland were held in 1997. People voted in favour of devolution. There are now three devolved assemblies – the Scottish Parliament, the National Assembly for Wales and the Northern Ireland Assembly. The map gives you more information about these assemblies.

Northern Ireland Assembly

- Set up in 1998 after the 'Good Friday' (Belfast) Agreement
- 108 members were elected in 1998
- Can make laws and variations in laws passed at Westminster
- Has power over a range of policies using money provided by the Treasury

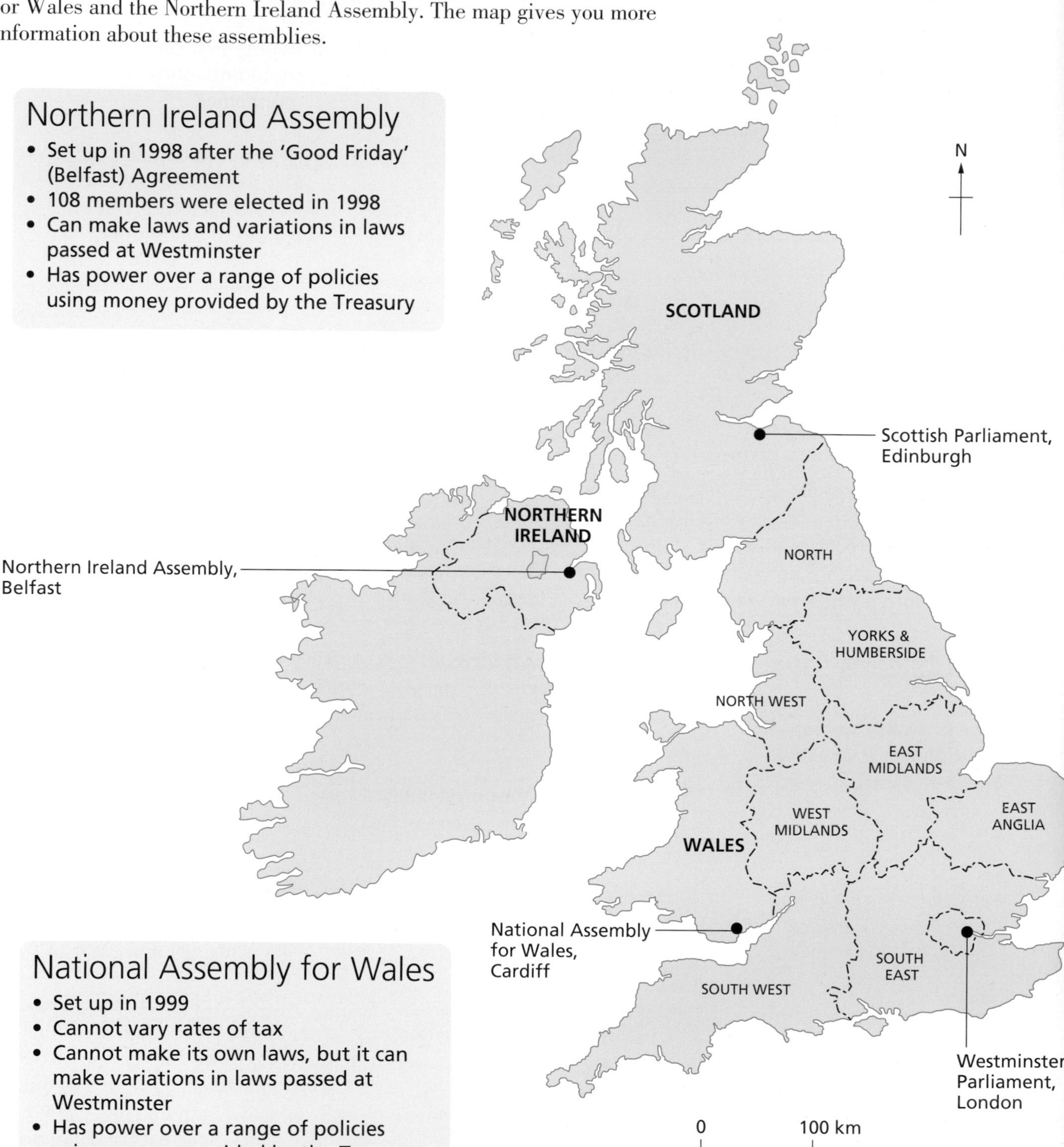

National Assembly for Wales

- Set up in 1999
- Cannot vary rates of tax
- Cannot make its own laws, but it can make variations in laws passed at Westminster
- Has power over a range of policies using money provided by the Treasury, for example can decide National Curriculum for Wales

The United Kingdom and English regions

Scottish Parliament

- Set up in 1999 after referendum voted Yes to devolved parliament
- Can vary rates of tax
- Run by Labour and Liberal Democrats
- Scotland can make its own laws – banning hunting with dogs, scrapping student fees and paying for care for the elderly
- Cannot vote for a referendum on independence

English regional assemblies

- There are nine English regions (see map)
- There is a London Assembly and Mayor that have certain devolved powers in the capital
- Each region has a Regional Development Agency that supports the regional economy and a government office
- There are discussions about whether there should be regional assemblies in England (similar to that in Wales)

Westminster Parliament

- Still the sovereign Parliament – its laws come before laws passed by the devolved assemblies
- The monarch is still the Head of State for Northern Ireland, Wales and Scotland
- The UK government has control of foreign policy including on Europe
- The most important issues are 'reserved', that is only the Westminster Parliament can make decisions on these
- A set of agreements or concordats have been made between Whitehall government departments and departments in Scotland, Wales and Northern Ireland

Activity

1 Where do you stand on devolution? Discuss the following questions and for each one choose one of the two options.

- Should Scotland become an independent country?
  - **a)** Scotland should be allowed to vote for independence, if its people want it.
  - **b)** Scotland should remain part of the United Kingdom; there must be no referendum on independence.
- Does the Scottish Parliament have too much power?
  - **a)** The Scottish Parliament has too much power to make decisions that embarrass the UK government – this should be stopped.
  - **b)** The UK government should follow the lead of the Scottish Parliament, for example paying for care for the elderly, scrapping student fees
- Should there be an English Parliament?
  - **a)** There should be an English Parliament separate from Westminster so the English can have power in their own country.
  - **b)** We do not need an English Parliament when we have Westminster already.

2 How should regional assemblies involve young people? One idea is for a Young People's Parliament in each location. These Parliaments would debate issues coming up in the main assemblies. Do you think this is a good idea? How would Young Members (YMs) be chosen? What powers would a Young People's Parliament have? Prepare your ideas and be ready to explain them to the rest of the class.

4.14 The European Union

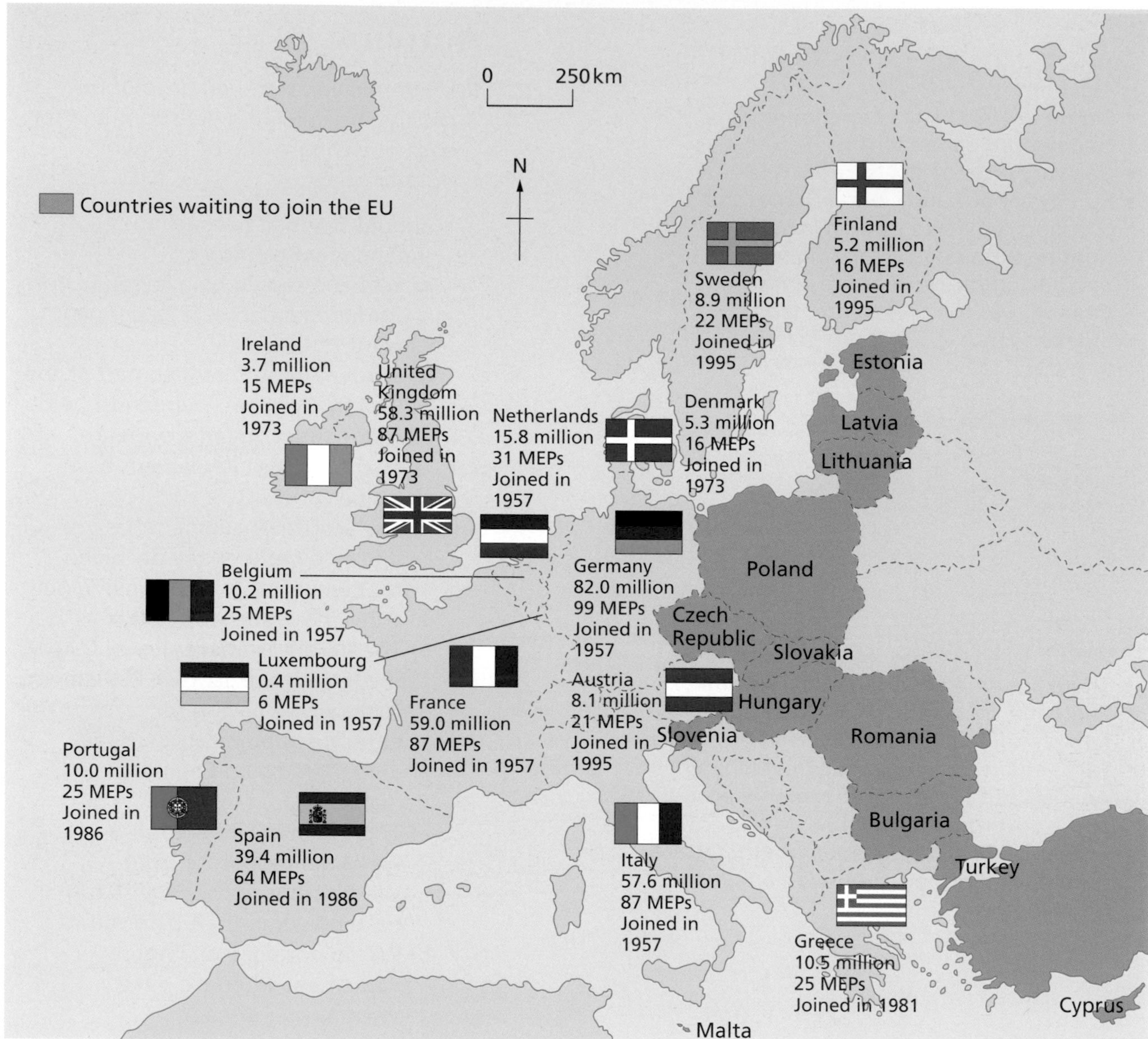

The UK has a close relationship with mainland Europe. We are more likely to travel there for holidays or to work than to other countries in the world. The UK has a long history of trade with other European countries. But there has also been a history of disagreements and wars. In the twentieth century, two world wars showed how great the destruction and devastation could be when European countries fought each other.

After the Second World War, European countries, particularly Germany, France and Italy, were very anxious to forge links that would bind countries in Europe together and make war less likely. In 1957, six countries signed the Treaty of Rome which brought the European Economic Community, or Common Market as it was then called, into being. The aim of this market was to increase trade between member countries so that they would become more prosperous. Britain joined in 1973 because it could see the advantages of being part of a large trade bloc. By 1993 several other countries had joined.

There have been some major developments in the way the union is organised, particularly in 1987 when the Single European Act was agreed by members and in 1993 when the Maastricht Treaty was signed, binding member countries even closer together with a tighter set of rules. It was after this that it changed its name to the European Union.

The main organisations of the European Union

The Commission

- Commissioners (chosen by member countries) organise the day-to-day work of the EU.
- They develop policies (courses of action).
- They draw up new regulations.
- They make sure that regulations are carried out by members.

The Council of Ministers

- Each member state sends one minister.
- The ministers discuss the policies and regulations the Commissioners are proposing and agree or disagree with them. If they disagree then the policies may be changed or abandoned.
- Ministers take the key decisions.

The European Parliament

- The member countries elect Members of the European Parliament (MEPs). The European Parliament has 626 members representing around 370 million people.
- The MEPs debate the policies of the EU and the work of the Commission. Their discussions can result in things being changed or new ideas being put into practice.

The European Court of Justice

- Settles disputes between member countries, particularly when some countries think others are breaking regulations.
- Gives rulings on European law.

Activity

1. On an outline map of the European Union:
   a) mark the original six countries in one colour
   b) mark the three countries including the UK which joined in 1973 in another colour
   c) mark the remaining six countries which joined after this in a third colour.
2. Name two differences between the European Parliament and the British Parliament in Westminster.
3. Which organisation has the most power in the European Union? Why do you think this?

The headquarters of the EU (where the Commission is) is in Brussels, Belgium. The European Parliament meets both in Brussels and in Strasbourg, in France.

What are the advantages of the EU?

The EU aims to protect the **environment**. There are rules and regulations about pollution and cutting down on waste. Many rivers and coastal areas are now cleaner because of EU rules.

The EU **helps poorer countries and regions** in Europe to develop by giving them large sums of money.

The EU is a **huge market** of nearly 400 000 million people. Companies find it easier to sell their goods and services in other EU countries because there are no barriers to trade. Goods that come in from outside the EU are taxed, which make them more expensive.

The regulations make sure that **trade is fair** and protect consumers from being exploited.

The EU provides **security** for its members. Other countries are not likely to attack or threaten an EU member state. It is highly unlikely that member countries would fight each other.

People are **able to move around more easily** and get jobs in the other member countries.

EU citizens have a much **wider choice of goods and services**, which are often cheaper because of competition.

The **standard of goods** is guaranteed.

What do people say against the EU?

The EU **wastes a lot of money**, particularly on its agricultural policies.

The EU is **not democratic** because the decisions are taken a long way away from the people; people who are affected by the decisions have little chance to protest.

Some countries **break the rules** and get away with it.

There are **too many rules** and regulations, some of which are not sensible.

The EU **organisations have too much power** and have taken away the right of the individual countries to make their own decisions about economic and other matters.

Enlargement

Since 1989, the collapse of the Soviet Union has led to many countries in Central and Eastern Europe becoming democratic. Now there is a queue of countries wanting to join the European Union. Supporters of enlargement believe that allowing these countries to join will protect democracy and lead to the end of European conflict. They think that bringing in ex-Communist countries will bring more stability to Eastern Europe as well as creating a larger trading market. Critics think that it will be difficult to make decisions with so many countries involved. Others think that allowing poorer countries to join will soak up the money in Europe as richer countries will have to help them.

Profile: *Latvia*

Population: 2.37 million
Capital: Riga (population around 800 000)
Currency: lats
Type of government: parliamentary democracy
Main trading partner: the EU
Economic factors: Latvia is situated at an intersection of trade routes and has been a bridge for centuries between Western Europe and Russia. It has three major ports, one of which is the largest port on the Baltic Sea and one of the fifteen leading European ports in cargo turnover. Its main industries are in electronics, mechanical engineering, chemicals, wood processing, textiles and information technologies.
Recent history: Founded as an independent state in 1918, it was swallowed up by the Soviet Union after the Second World War. It was dominated by the Russians until the collapse of Communism in 1991. Its neighbour, Russia, still makes it anxious. It wants to protect its independence and become a prosperous modern state.

Activity

1 Latvia is a small country that wants to join the EU. You can find it on the map on page 126. Look at its profile above and work out why you think it wants to join.
2 Give three reasons why so many countries are queuing up to join the EU.
3 Why are some people worried about the EU becoming much larger?

The following thirteen countries are waiting to join the EU:

Bulgaria
Cyprus
Czech Republic
Estonia
Hungary
Latvia
Lithuania
Malta
Poland
Romania
Slovakia
Slovenia
Turkey

The EU is negotiating with these countries. It is unlikely that Turkey will join for some time because of its human rights record, but some of the other countries are getting close to becoming members.

How far should the UK get involved?

Since the UK joined the European Union, British citizens have been able to travel freely, live and work in the countries of Europe and sell goods and services to them. But people still disagree about how far the affairs of the UK should be decided by other countries which are members of the European Union. Some people are worried about the loss of sovereignty of the British national government. There are many rules and regulations that the UK and other European countries have to obey with regards to food and farming, how businesses are run, fair competition, the rights of workers, European human rights and many other areas. The newspaper headlines on the right show some of the complaints of those opposed to EU regulations.

British fishermen lose their jobs as European fish quotas cut amount of fish they are able to catch

EU regulations bury businesses in red tape

New European human rights laws mean that the Home Secretary will not be able to add to the sentences of criminals. Murderers will go free earlier than expected

'I'll stick to pounds and ounces, not kilos,' says Yorkshire butcher

The euro

In February 2002, twelve EU countries gave up their own currency and adopted the euro. They believe it will help their economies grow because they will all be using the same currency. It will make it easier for people and businesses to work and travel within the EU. There is no need to exchange currency – the euro in Germany is the same value as the euro in Italy. This makes it easier to compare the value of goods, such as cars, in different countries and be able to get the best deal. Critics say that joining the euro is a big step towards a United States of Europe. They believe that countries are losing control of their own affairs.

Activity

Some people think it is good for the UK to be part of the European Union and want to be even more closely connected. For instance, they want the UK to use the euro rather than the pound. Others think it is not a good idea and want our level of involvement to remain as it is. There are even quite a few people who would like to see the UK leave the EU altogether.

Look at the statements on page 131. Decide, in pairs, which speakers support the UK being a member of the European Union and would want more involvement, and which would like to see the EU having less control over people in the UK. Make two lists.

a) We don't want to be told what to do by other countries, particularly Germany, which is the strongest and largest of the European countries.

b) Mainland Europe, for example Italy and France, is lovely to visit and it is good to feel that we are all working together for a better future.

c) Over 60% of our trade is with EU countries. If we withdraw from the EU it could cost us thousands of jobs. We should get more involved and become a major force in deciding the future of the EU.

d) Many big companies, like the Japanese companies Sony and Nissan, invest in this country – building factories and offices here – because that is a way for them to get a market in the EU. If we got less involved with Europe, they might pull out.

e) Our relationships with the United States of America and countries like Australia and New Zealand are more important to us than our membership of Europe. We should develop them as trading partners rather than European countries.

f) The European Union is a democracy. Everyone has a chance to vote for a Member of the European Parliament and all countries are represented on the Council of Ministers. It is better to be in Europe having a say, than outside it with no say in how our neighbours behave towards us.

g) Being in the EU is fine if you are a poor country. You get lots of help from the richer countries. But richer countries, like Britain, have to pay to provide that help. It costs too much money.

h) There have been too many wars in Europe in the past. The countries of Europe must work closely together so that war would be completely impossible because everyone would have too much to lose. It provides security for all countries in Europe.

i) People of Britain, being on an island, have always been independent. They like to drive on the left, use pounds and ounces as measures of weight, and miles for distance. They don't like being told to be like the rest of Europe.

j) Many companies now operate Europe-wide. They take on staff who are expected to live and work for some periods of time in Europe. These companies need consistent rules in dealing with staff.

k) Membership of the European Union has brought many rights for workers, such as paid holiday and better working conditions.

l) Europe creates mountains of 'red tape' – rules and regulations – which we would be better off without.

m) If we don't join the euro, British businesses will be at a disadvantage compared with the businesses which are in the euro zone. We still have to exchange currencies which makes trade harder.

n) If we join the euro we will have no control over our own money. It will be controlled by a European central bank.

Activity

Now compare your lists with another pair. As a group decide whether you are in favour of the UK being more involved in the EU or not. Using these arguments and others that you can find (you can do some research in the library or on the internet), plan a short speech to give to the whole class. Your teacher will choose one group to speak in favour and one to speak against. The whole class can then join in a general discussion.

Are you a good European?

Answer these questions to find out what sort of European you are.

Questionnaire

A B C

1 Do you or would you:
- **a)** like going to Spain, France or Italy for your holidays
- **b)** prefer to stay in England or Wales because the countryside is just as beautiful here
- **c)** be happy to holiday in the UK or any European country?

2 Would you be:
- **a)** happy for the euro to replace the pound sterling in this country
- **b)** very angry if the pound sterling was replaced
- **c)** not really concerned?

3 Would you:
- **a)** be happy to see all weights and measures in metric – kilometres, grams, kilograms, etc.
- **b)** want to keep miles, pounds and ounces
- **c)** be happy to use both systems as at present?

4 Do you:
- **a)** love to try different foods from European countries, like pasta or paella
- **b)** stick to food popular in Britain – fish and chips, sausage and mash, and curry
- **c)** eat whatever you're given?

5 Do you feel that:
- **a)** the rules and regulations from the EU make the UK a fairer place and it gains as much as it loses
- **b)** the UK should have total control over its own affairs and not give up its sovereignty to any other country
- **c)** there is no real problem in having rules and regulations which all EU countries, including the UK, have to follow?

6 Do you think:
- **a)** popular music from countries like France and Germany is okay
- **b)** British groups are far better and are the only ones worth listening to
- **c)** it's okay to listen to different types of music wherever you are?

7 Do you like:
- **a)** French and Italian films
- **b)** British and American films
- **c)** any films from any country?

8 Do you:
- **a)** enjoy speaking a foreign language in other countries
- **b)** think that everybody should speak English wherever you go
- **c)** not worry about it too much and use sign language?

If you chose mainly **a)** as your answer, you're a good European.
If you chose mainly **b)** you are not very happy about more involvement in Europe.
If you chose mainly **c)** you're prepared to accept whatever happens.

section 5

Money and work

Key words
- consumer rights
- credit
- the economy
- employment rights
- low pay
- market
- National Minimum Wage
- price
- trade union
- workfare

Everyone needs money to survive and most of you will need to work to earn it. You can't all win the lottery! So this section is about you and your future as a consumer and as a worker.

You will learn about:

- personal finance
- consumer rights
- the economy
- rights and responsibilities of employers and employees
- pay and working conditions
- trade unions.

You will use the following skills:

- researching political, moral and social issues using information from different sources, including ICT-based sources
- expressing, justifying and defending orally and in writing a personal opinion about such issues, problems or events
- contributing to class discussions or debates
- understanding, explaining and evaluating critically views that are not your own.

5.1 What should Chris do?

Activity

You may have seen programmes on television where experts give people tips on how to manage their money. Work with a partner to offer some advice to Chris.

Chris is aged eighteen. She is in her final year of college. She finds her studies difficult but expects to pass all her exams.

Chris is undecided about whether to go to university after college or to look for a full-time job in an office or in a retail shop.

Chris has:

- £500 savings in a bank deposit account
- a current account with £43 in it and a Switch card with which she can make payments from her account electronically or take cash from a bank machine
- one credit card with a £1000 credit limit. It is charged at 12% per annum (this means she pays 1% per month, which is £1 for every hundred she borrows).
- earnings from her Saturday job, where she earns £3.50 an hour for a seven-hour day.

Decision 1

Chris lives with her mother in a terraced house. Her mother has asked her to pay £10 a week towards her upkeep. What would you advise Chris to do and why?

a) Extend her hours with the shop so that she works after college during the week
b) Offer to do more chores around the house instead of paying the £10
c) Use the £500 savings to cover the payments.

Decision 2

Chris wants to replace her old hi-fi system. She has seen a new mini hi-fi in the sale. There is £50 off so it will cost £250. What would you advise Chris to do and why?

a) Use half her savings to buy the system
b) Take advantage of the store's interest free credit to pay it off at £25 per month
c) Use her credit card to buy it.

Decision 3

Chris is out one day and sees a watch that she would like to buy for her mother. It will cost £50. What would you advise Chris to do and why?

a) Use her debit Switch card
b) Use her credit card
c) Use the store's credit scheme (charged at 30% per annum).

Decision 4

Chris decides she wants to go to university. She would like to experience life in another part of the country, but is worried about the cost of renting a room. What would you advise Chris to do and why?

a) Save on accommodation costs by living at home and going to a local university
b) Take a gap year, work and save enough money to afford live-in student accommodation
c) Take out a student loan and pay it off after leaving university, once she gets a job.

Activity

Chris is affected in several ways by other economic factors. Match up Chris's experience to the factors that affected her.

Chris's experience

1 The amount of interest she gets on the money she keeps in her deposit account

2 The price she paid for the hi-fi system

3 Her hourly rate of pay

4 Student fees

5 Her part-time job

6 The rent on her student flat

Is affected by . . . (economic factors)

a) How low the government sets the minimum wage

b) How much money the government raises in taxes and is prepared to give to students

c) How much accommodation is available for rent

d) How much money retailers are making and whether they want people to work for them

e) How cheap imported goods are

f) The level of interest rates set by the bank

5.2 'Money makes the world go around'

Almost every day you make economic decisions that affect other people. This is because you are a consumer – you consume goods and services in order to survive – and what you choose to consume affects other people. To consume means to buy and use things, like food, lighting, heating and entertainment. Products are things you can see and touch, such as a CD or an apple, whereas services are things that people provide for you, such as a haircut or internet access.

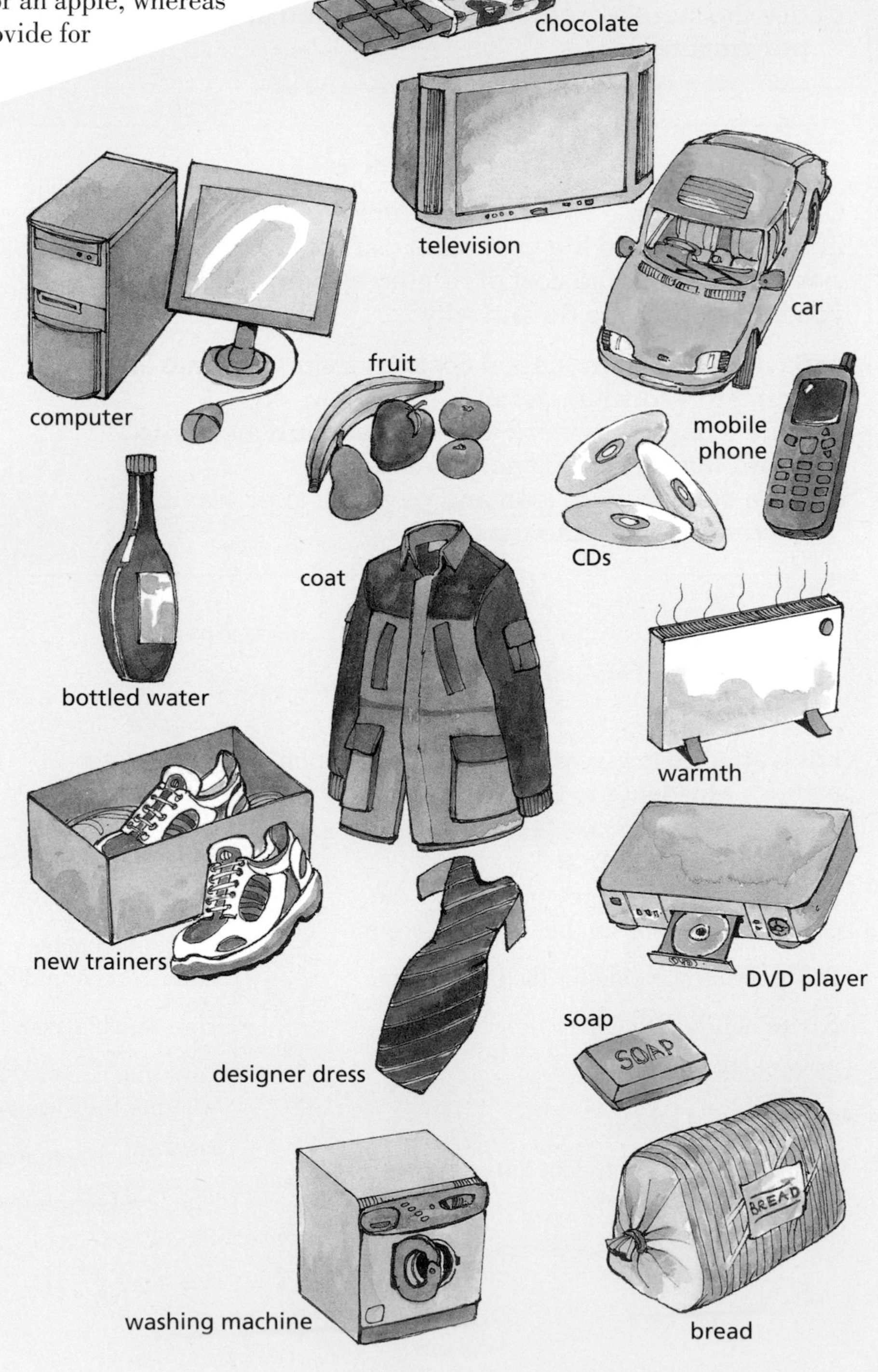

Activity

1 People choose to spend their money in a variety of ways. You can spend your money on:

- needs – things you must have to survive – also called necessities
- wants – things that are not essential but which you want to own – sometimes called luxuries.

a) Look at the collection of items shown here and decide which are needs and which are wants. Then write them out as separate lists.

b) Compare your lists with those of a partner. Do you agree about which items are necessities and which are luxuries?

2 Here are some economic decisions you might make in the next four years.

Whether to:

- Take a Saturday job in a supermarket
- Sell old belongings at a car boot sale
- Put money in a bank account for a trip to France
- Buy some jewellery for a friend
- Do some odd jobs for a neighbour for £3 an hour
- Ask parents for £100 to pay for driving lessons
- Take out a student loan to cover living expenses at college
- Buy some new clothes.

a) Which of these decisions would you expect to make in the next four years?

b) Draw up a table with four headings like the one below. Put each of your chosen decisions under the right heading.

c) Now add some more items to the table from your experience. Try to put something in each column.

d) Compare your lists with those of a partner.

Spending	Saving	Earning	Borrowing

3 Look at the diary entries below. In a group, discuss how realistic the entries are. Who is going to be in financial trouble and why?

4 Now think about your own situation in four years' time. What will your spending, saving, earning and borrowing be like? Write your own diary entry for a day four years from now.

Jo's diary August 2003

My financial position is looking up. I have managed to save £2000 during my gap year. I am earning £200 per week after tax but aim to give up my job in the sports shop. I need to buy a plane ticket to Australia for a two-month backpacking tour. I think this will cost about £700, but I also need to budget £100 for when I get there. I will need to sort out a student loan before I go to college.

Jason's diary August 2003

My finances are great. I'm earning £350 a week as a trainee plumber. I give my mum £50 a week for my keep. I'm going to get a flat soon with two friends. No money to save, too many things to buy! I will get a car soon. I'll need to borrow some money for that – £2000 should get me something really good. Somebody said that car insurance will cost me another £1000 but I don't believe them. I owe £400 on my credit card but that should not take too long to pay off.

5.3 What is the economy?

The economy

Government

The government is also a major employer of people. Local and national government, nationalised industries and public bodies make up the public sector. The government gets money through taxes on households, businesses and on goods and services. It spends this money on services, such as refuse collection, schools and the emergency services and on providing pensions, unemployment benefit and child benefit.

Other countries

Payments, e.g. pensions, benefits

Taxes, e.g. income tax

Spending

Taxes, e.g. VAT

Imports

Exports

Households

These are people living in or outside of families. They are active in the economy if they are working. They are inactive if they are too old or too young to work or are unemployed. Most individuals are involved in buying and selling. As consumers they buy goods and services and as workers they sell their labour to businesses.

Work

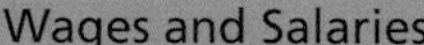

Wages and Salaries

Spending

Goods and Services

Businesses

Most people are employed in businesses, which are run for a profit. This is called the private sector. Businesses are also involved in buying and selling. They sell goods and services. They buy labour, raw materials, energy, land – anything they need to make their products or services. Many businesses buy raw materials they need and products to sell (such as clothes) from abroad.

Savings

Savings

Interest, loans

Investment

Financial organisations

These include banks, insurance companies, building societies and pension funds. They all accept savings from households and businesses. They also invest in businesses through stock, shares and loans; and they give credit and loans to individuals.

You can see from the diagram opposite how the four parts of the economy are interdependent. A change in one part affects the other parts of the system.

The state of the economy affects the lives of everyone in a country. The more money, goods and labour there is flowing around the cycle, the better the economy is doing. Everyone can benefit from a successful economy.

If the flow slows down then the economy is doing badly. When that happens everyone can suffer. People might lose their jobs or not be able to find a job. Prices might go up very quickly and the numbers of people living in poverty might grow. If the economy is in a poor state the government is not able to spend as much to provide adequate public services.

Activity

Consequences

Get into a group of four to play this game of consequences. In the game each of you will represent one of the four parts of the economy: Households, Businesses, Government or Financial organisations. Look at the headlines A–D below and decide how each would affect you. Here is an example:

Example

250 000 people lost their jobs in the last two months

so . . .

Households	Businesses	Government	Financial organisations
250 000 households will have a big reduction in their income. They will stop spending so much money in the shops. Some will also withdraw some of their savings from banks to use for necessities like food shopping.	250 000 people will stop spending so much money on clothes, food, electrical goods, so the income of businesses will fall. The businesses will make less profit.	250 000 people will not be paying income tax so the government will get poorer. They will also have to pay out extra state benefits to the people who have lost their jobs.	People will start taking money out of their accounts. Savings will fall and less money will be paid into current accounts.

A

Best employment news for 10 years

Over a million new jobs have been created in businesses over the last year as the economy booms.

B

Income Tax Shock!

The government has announced a huge rise in income tax for everybody earning over £20 000 per year. People will be giving more money in tax to the government to pay for a big improvement in the health service.

C

Pound collapses

Prices of imported goods rise as the pound loses value against the euro and the dollar! Because the British pound won't buy so many dollars and euros, goods coming into this country from abroad are much more expensive.

D

New Government Plan to Support 100 000 New Small Businesses

The government plans to give large sums of money to help people start new businesses all over the country.

5.4 Are you a confident consumer?

We are all consumers – we all buy goods and services, whether this is buying shoes and CDs or going to the cinema. There are times when we don't always get what we pay for. Sometimes this is the result of a genuine mistake or unfortunate circumstances. But sometimes it is because the goods are shoddy or the services are not run properly. When this happens you are entitled to complain and get some redress (compensation).

When we do buy things, two laws protect our rights – the Sale of Goods Act 1979 and the Sale and Supply of Goods Act 1994.

Guide to consumer rights

The Sale of Goods Act 1979 and the Sale and Supply of Goods Act 1994 say that goods should be 'of satisfactory quality, fit for all intended purposes and as described'. When you buy something a contract is formed between the consumer and the shop. Money is exchanged for the goods and the receipt is proof of the contract. What does the law mean in practice?

Satisfactory quality

If goods are faulty or damaged when purchased and this was not pointed out to you at the time, then you should have a full refund. This is because the contract was broken. Retailers cannot blame manufacturers. It is the retailers who have the contract with you. However, if the fault was pointed out at the time (for example, shop soiled, A/F – as found, seconds), then the fault was obvious at the time of purchase.

Fit for purpose

If a product is unfit for its intended use or develops a fault very rapidly, then you have a right to a refund or damages. If some time has passed since the product was bought, but the fault is unreasonable, then you have the right to damages. Damages means that the shop might offer to repair the item or to give some money back – taking some off to allow for the use already made of the item.

As described

Goods must fit any description or claim made on the packaging or display in the shop. You will be entitled to a full refund if, when you open the packaging, you find the goods do not match the description.

Sale goods

When goods are marked as sale goods (£19.95, now £15) then they should have been sold at the higher price for 28 consecutive days in the last six months. Your rights on sale goods are the same as for non-sale goods.

Presents

If you get an unwanted present, you have no rights to get money back or to exchange it for something you want.

What can you do to ensure your rights?

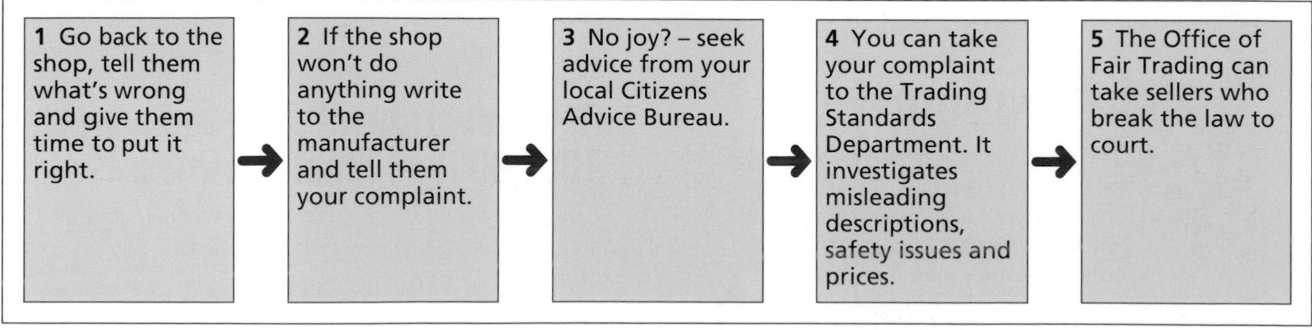

1 Go back to the shop, tell them what's wrong and give them time to put it right.
2 If the shop won't do anything write to the manufacturer and tell them your complaint.
3 No joy? – seek advice from your local Citizens Advice Bureau.
4 You can take your complaint to the Trading Standards Department. It investigates misleading descriptions, safety issues and prices.
5 The Office of Fair Trading can take sellers who break the law to court.

Activity

Can I get a refund?

Role play in groups of three. One of you will play the customer and one will play the shop assistant. The third person will be the local trading standards officer – an expert in consumer rights. Study the roles and decide who will play which role. You will find four situations on page 142 which you should act out. The person playing the trading standards officer should carefully read the guide to consumer rights (opposite), so that they know the law, and should then watch the other two act out the scene. For each new scene the customer and the shop assistant should swap roles. After each role play, the trading standards officer should explain the consumer's rights and what the shop should have done.

Roles

Trading standards officer

You work for the local council and your job is to advise consumers on their rights. You also have powers to visit businesses that are breaking the consumer laws. You need to be an 'expert' in consumer law so you must study the guide to the law opposite. Listen to the conversations between the customer and the shop assistant. Decide whether any rights have been ignored. Explain the position clearly to the shop assistant and the customer.

Customer

You are a young person who has bought an item from a local high street shop. But there is a problem and you have to decide what to do about it. This involves your returning to where you bought it. Decide what you want to happen and explain this to the shop assistant. Do you want a refund of your money or a replacement? Try to keep calm.

Shop assistant

You work in a local high street shop. The shop is not very well run and your manager does not like taking goods back. It is the shop that likes to say 'No'. You are working in the shop when a customer comes in to speak to you. Try not to let the customer bully you into doing what they want. Here is a list of things you could say to put the customer off:

- 'You must have damaged the goods.'
- 'You need to get in touch with the manufacturer.'
- 'Did you not see the sign that says no refunds?'
- 'The fault was pointed out to you at the time.'
- 'Sorry, can't do anything without a receipt.'
- 'I am sure it didn't come from this shop.'
- 'I am afraid you bought it too long ago for me to be able to do anything.'
- 'I think you are exaggerating – it's only a small problem.'
- 'Sorry, the law says that we only have to give you a replacement not a refund.'

Discuss

When you have finished the four role plays, discuss with the whole class what happened in each one (see page 142).

a) How good were the customers at complaining?
b) How difficult was it to keep making the case? Did some give up?
c) Did the shop assistants find it easy/difficult to put people off?
d) What judgement did the trading standards officer come to in each case?
e) What do you think about the rights and wrongs of each case – should the customer have got a refund?

Situation 1: Hi Fidelity

You have just bought a music CD when your uncle sends you the same CD as a gift. You return to the Hi Fidelity music shop with your CD and receipt.

Situation 2: Toni's Toys

You bought a wind-up racing car for a young relative. After a week of playing with it the winder has fallen off and now the car does not work. You return to the shop to complain.

Situation 3: Doubleday Department Store

You bought a 100% cotton shirt in the store, but when you got it home and tried it on you realised it was a cotton/polyester mix. You don't like these kinds of shirts as they affect your skin. You repackage it as best you can and take it back to the shop.

Situation 4: Lucy's Lighting

You purchased a table lamp as a present for your mother. When you switched it on you noticed that the fittings became very hot. She burnt her hand when trying to switch it off and the plastic fitting is beginning to turn yellow. You decide to return it to the shop.

Are you a credit-oholic?

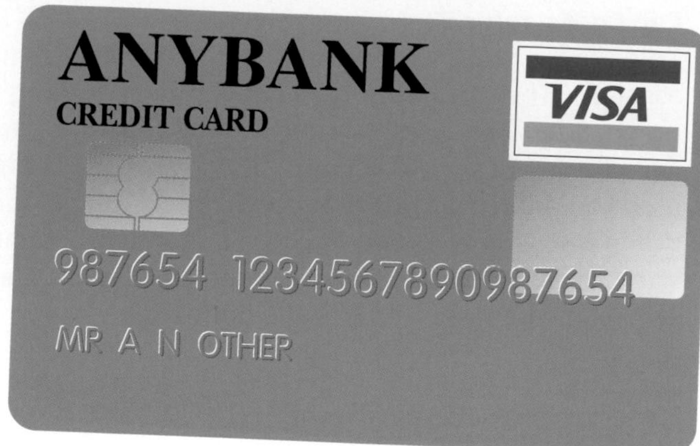

Today there are huge opportunities to buy things we want on credit. Young people are bombarded with messages in the media and through the post about credit cards. Students going to college and young people starting work find it all too easy to obtain credit. Getting into debt and not being able to pay can have all kinds of bad consequences. The most obvious is your name appearing on a blacklist used by finance companies and banks. This may mean you cannot get credit when you really need it, for example, to buy a house or car. You can have goods or your home repossessed for repayment.

It is usually better for young people to stick to a debit card. This can only be used when there is money in the account to cover the purchases. Credit cards all have credit limits beyond which you are not supposed to go. But there is a temptation to have several credit cards and store cards. All of these have high rates of interest if you do not pay them off immediately. Store cards are particularly expensive. This means they are a very expensive way of borrowing money.

White's Department Store
Shopping Street
1234567890987654
MR A N OTHER

Credit cards are **good** when you:

- need to be identified, for example when hiring a car
- do not want to carry cash
- want to take advantage of a low price, for example in the sales
- want to order something by phone or on the internet
- want insurance in case something goes wrong, for example when paying for a holiday.

Credit cards are **bad** when you:

- are constantly tempted to overspend
- buy non-essential items, such as take-aways, CDs, new trainers
- increase spending on impulse
- do not pay off the debt straight away.

Activity

How likely is it that you could become a credit-oholic – a person addicted to using credit cards? Read the following statements and decide whether you agree or disagree.

	Statement	Disagree	Agree
1	A store card helps me to buy more things easily from those shops which give me one.	○	○
2	A credit card helps to impress my friends by paying for presents, drinks or meals.	○	○
3	I often can't remember what money I have spent during the day.	○	○
4	Having credit cards will help me to improve my lifestyle.	○	○
5	I like to be able to buy things on impulse whenever I feel like it.	○	○
6	It's okay to be in debt for spending money you don't have.	○	○
7	I borrow money from relatives and friends, but don't always pay it back straight away.	○	○
8	It's not necessary to save up to buy things you want.	○	○
9	It doesn't matter if my credit bill mounts up as I will be able to pay it off when I earn more.	○	○
10	Credit cards make me feel better as I can buy whatever I want, whenever I want.	○	○

If you agreed with the following number of statements:

0–1 You are financially responsible and not likely to get into debt.

2–5 You are at risk of getting addicted to credit and should think three times about getting a credit card.

6–10 You are likely to become a plastic-spending addict. Best not to get a credit card at all.

Discuss

1. What do you think about credit cards for young people? Do you think that banks and stores are irresponsible in offering these cards to young people?
2. Choose to do one of the following:
   - Write a letter to a bank or credit card company or shop protesting against credit or store cards being made freely available to eighteen-year-olds.
   - Design a poster to put up in the school or community centre warning of the dangers of credit card debt.
   - Write a letter to a newspaper explaining why credit is a good thing if used sensibly.

5.5 Working life: is it fair?

All workers have a right to be treated fairly by their employers. This is not only good for the workers, it is also good for the employer. Treating employees fairly:

- makes people feel better at work
- helps to keep valuable staff
- reduces time off sick
- improves work performance
- helps the company to have better relations with its customers.

Workers' rights are protected by law. Many of these laws are about equal opportunities. The Equal Opportunities Commission is responsible for enforcing equal opportunities. They hear complaints against employers at industrial tribunals. They may ask employers who break these laws to pay damages or back pay or else to reinstate, or promote unfairly treated workers.

The Laws

Sex Discrimination Act 1975

Bans discrimination against people because of their sex or because they are married or single. It also protects against sexual harassment. This includes offensive remarks, requests, touching, staring – all of these can badly affect people's work.

Race Relations Act 1976

Forbids discrimination against people based on race, colour, ethnic or national origin.

Equal Pay Act 1970 and Equal Pay (Amendment) Regulations 1983

Bans unequal pay or other benefits for people doing the same job or work of equal value.

Disability Discrimination Act 1995

Bans discrimination against people with disabilities.

Health and Safety at Work Act 1974

This could protect people from bullying at work as it affects workers' health and safety.

Employment Rights Act 1996

This covers the right to return to work after a period of maternity leave.

Your rights

As soon as you start a new job your employer is responsible for providing or ensuring:

- a pay slip setting out all stoppages (deductions), for example tax, and national insurance
- equal pay for people doing the same work or work of equal value
- no discrimination against staff on the grounds of sex, race or disability
- time off for public duties such as sitting on a jury
- time off for antenatal care and eighteen weeks' maternity leave
- no more than a 48-hour working week
- twenty days' paid leave each year.

After one month's service with your employer you must be given:

- one week's advance notice if you are to be dismissed, that is sacked
- payment if you cannot work for medical reasons
- some guaranteed payment if you are laid off, that is if there is not enough work for you to do.

After two months you must be given a written statement of your terms of employment. But most people get this before they start work.

After one year with your employer, you have the following rights:

- to go back to work after forty weeks' maternity leave
- to have thirteen weeks' unpaid paternity leave
- to be protected against unfair dismissal by your employer.

After two years' working for the same employer, you are entitled to a payment if you are made redundant.

Activity

Work in groups of three. You represent an employment tribunal looking at a number of cases. One of you is an employer, one a trade union representative and the other a neutral chairperson. The role of the chairperson is to have the deciding vote. The employer should look at the case from the employer's point of view, but should decide what is lawful and fair. The trade unionist should take the employee's side, but again decide based on what is lawful and fair. Try to make a decision on the case, explaining why you have made your decision. Where the employer is in the wrong, say what they should do to put things right.

Use these questions to guide you in looking at each case:

a) Is this fair?
b) What does the law say about this case?
c) What is your ruling on what the company should do?

Case 1: *Thomson Bus Company*

Jenny Brown has made a complaint against the Thomson Bus Company. She attended an interview for the position of bus driver where she was asked about her family circumstances – she is married with two children at primary school. This was because the bus driver's job involves shift work with some late shifts. When talking to a male candidate she learned that the interviewers did not ask him about family responsibilities.

Case 2: *Chocobox Plc*

Anita Fallon is a machine operator at Chocobox, a confectionery manufacturer. She works from 5.30p.m. to 10.30p.m. for five days a week. A male operator working in another department on a different sweet works on two different shifts which change every week. He is paid more because of a 'shift premium' payment. They are both paid the same basic pay rate. Mrs Fallon is claiming that she should get the same as the male worker, equal pay for work of equal value. She says that she also works in the evening and should get a premium for 'unsocial hours'.

Case 3: *Philips Wine Store*

Nita Kumar works as a manager of a wine shop, working 39 hours a week. As a manager her contract says that she must work 'such hours as are necessary to carry out her duties'. She argues that flexible hours discriminate unfairly against women. After maternity leave she asked the company if she could work fixed hours. This was because she could not arrange childcare if she did not know in advance what hours she would need to work. The company claim that they would need to appoint a second manager on a jobshare, but that jobshare would not work as the manager needs to lead staff, manage stock control and run the business.

Discuss

1 Compare the decisions you reached with the rest of the class.
- **a)** Does everybody agree about the cases – whether they were unfair and whether the law had something to say about them?
- **b)** What rulings did the group tribunals make? How similar/different were they?

2 Discuss the issue of fairness at work.
- **a)** Do you agree with the laws?
- **b)** Do you think employees have too many rights?
- **c)** Does anybody know of any experiences from family and friends similar to the cases discussed?

5.6 Who gets the job?

Discrimination can happen in lots of different areas of life: housing, benefits, schools, hospitals, and particularly at work.

- The 1975 Sex Discrimination Act makes it illegal for people to be discriminated against because of their sex.
- The 1976 Race Relations Act makes it illegal to discriminate against someone because of colour, race, nationality or ethnic origin.

Both **direct** and **indirect** discrimination under these Acts are against the law.

Direct discrimination happens when someone is treated badly simply because of their sex, colour, race, nationality or ethnic origin – for example, if a company refuses to give a woman a job because she has children but does employ men with children.

Indirect discrimination happens when certain conditions are unfair for some people – for example, if a job involves wearing clothes that cannot be worn by people of a particular religion.

- The 1995 Disability Discrimination Act makes it illegal for an employer to treat a disabled person less favourably for a reason which relates to that person's disability.

Activity

Work in groups. You are going to decide who should be appointed to some jobs on a construction site. There are three jobs and three applicants for each job. Your task is to decide which of the applicants to appoint for each job.

1 Read the job descriptions carefully.
2 Read all the letters of application (pages 147–49). Discuss them and agree on the three people you would appoint. Be prepared to give reasons for your choices.

Job description 1

Electrician

A skilled electrician is required for one year's work on the construction of a large hotel. The work will involve all aspects of electrical installation including lighting and high voltage cabling. The person appointed must have qualifications and experience. He/she will need their own tools and must wear safety gear at all times, including hard hat and boots.

The job will involve shift work and there will be overtime payments for night work. Some heavy lifting of electrical gear will be required.

Reply to Mr Jones,
Recruitment,
Beauchamp Construction Ltd,
Fairview Avenue,
Billinston

Job description 2

Site manager

A site manager is required for a year-long hotel construction project. He/she must have experience in managing construction workers and working closely with architects, surveyors and suppliers. The work will involve working early in the morning and taking on shifts for some night work.

Reply to Mr Jones, Recruitment,
Beauchamp Construction Ltd, Fairview Avenue, Billinston

Job description 3

Accounts clerk

An accounts clerk is required to maintain records and orders for a project involving the construction of a large hotel. You must have good accounting qualifications and be confident in the use of spreadsheets and other computer software. You will be working closely with the site manager and the architect, but will also make up weekly wage packets for the construction workers.

Reply to Mr Jones, Recruitment,
Beauchamp Construction Ltd, Fairview Avenue, Billinston

Letter 1: Electrician

Beauchamp Construction Ltd
Fairview Avenue
Billinston

Dear Sir,

I am replying to your job advertisement which I saw today in the *Billinston Argus*. I have recently qualified as an electrical engineer from Billinston College, where I gained my NVQ at level 3. I have worked for short periods of time in the previous six months as an electrician, carrying out rewiring etc. for a renovation company in the town.

I am now looking for a longer contract, since my daughter has started secondary school and no longer needs me to collect her every day. I hope you will consider appointing me. I can provide you with the names and addresses of referees both from the college and from the renovation company.

Yours faithfully,

Janet Johnson

Janet Johnson

Letter 2: Electrician

Beauchamp Construction Ltd
Fairview Avenue
Billinston

Dear Mr Jones,

I am looking for work as an electrician. I have been an electrician all my life, although I have been unemployed for a little while since I was made redundant from the South Billinston Electricity Board. Before then I did the full range of electrical work.

Although South Billinston Electricity Board closed a year ago, I can give you details of people who would write references.

I look forward to hearing from you.

Yours truly,

James Harris

James Harris

Letter 3: Electrician

Beauchamp Construction Ltd
Fairview Avenue
Billinston

Dear Mr Jones,

I am a qualified electrician who has recently moved to this country to live. I have joined my family and have all the necessary documentation that permits me to work.

In India, I worked on numerous housing development projects, some funded by development aid and some private development companies. I have qualifications equivalent to your NVQ level 4 and have also been studying, until recently, for a management course.

I have not yet worked in this country, but I am hard-working and enthusiastic.

Yours sincerely,

P.J. Desai

P.J. Desai

Letter A: Site Manager

Beauchamp Construction Ltd
Fairview Avenue
Billinston

Dear Mr Jones,

I have recently gained a degree in architecture from Billinston University. During my degree course, I worked on a number of real projects and gained work experience on three construction sites around the country, job-shadowing the site architects.

Before studying for the degree, I worked as a supervisor in a supermarket.

I have been appointed to a post in Canada which will begin in one year's time, and I am looking for a post during the year's gap. The post of site manager would suit me ideally, and I hope that you will give my application serious attention.

Yours sincerely,

Elizabeth Ogone

Elizabeth Ogone

Letter B: Site Manager

Beauchamp Construction Ltd
Fairview Avenue
Billinston

Dear Sir,

I saw your advert today for a site manager for the Fairview development. Although I have no experience of site management, I have supervised workers in a biscuit factory for four years. Before that I worked as a bricklayer, just after I left school.

I have three GCSEs, including Maths and English, and I know about managing people.

I hope to hear from you soon.

Yours faithfully,

Nick Smith

Nick Smith

Letter C: Site Manager

Beauchamp Construction Ltd
Fairview Avenue
Billinston

Dear Mr Jones,

I wish to apply for the post of site manager, which was today advertised in the *Billinston Argus*.

I have many years' experience of managing sites and have worked for national companies like Wampey Building Co. and Bevis Construction, as well as Wallington's, the local building firm. I can obtain references for you from all of these companies.

I am a qualified carpenter by trade, but moved into management three years ago, when I developed arthritis in my legs. I am able to walk short distances, but can no longer bend and lift.

I hope you will give my application serious attention.

Yours sincerely,

Charles McKenzie

Charles McKenzie

Letter X: Accounts Clerk

Beauchamp Construction Ltd
Fairview Avenue
Billinston

Dear Mr Jones,

I am a qualified and experienced secretary, with accounting skills. I have worked for a wide range of different organisations including a large local hotel, a school and a hospital. In all of these posts, I was responsible for budgeting and in one, I was wages clerk. I have little experience in the use of spreadsheets, but I am willing to learn any new system you may have. I am very quick and will attend evening classes if necessary. I am looking for re-employment after a long illness, which has left me with some loss of hearing. However, medical advice is that I am fit for work.

Yours sincerely,

Alice Goodman

Alice Goodman

Letter Y: Accounts Clerk

Beauchamp Construction Ltd
Fairview Avenue
Billinston

Dear Mr Jones,

I am responding to your job advertisement in the *Billinston Argus*. I have recently obtained an AS level qualification in Business Studies and I have attended and passed a Potmans' secretarial course, which included accounts. I have enclosed photocopies of my qualifications.

I spent last summer working for a temping agency and worked in a wide variety of offices and organisations, using many different IT systems and spreadsheets. My main experience is with Microsoft Excel.

I think I would be well suited to the job you describe.

Yours sincerely,

Davis Jones

Davis Jones

Letter Z: Accounts Clerk

Beauchamp Construction Ltd
Fairview Avenue
Billinston

Dear Mr Jones,
I have just left school with four GCSEs and I want to be a secretary. I took IT at school and know a bit about spreadsheets. I have had a few Saturday jobs, working on the till in supermarkets and once in a clothes shop.

I am sure I would be a good accounts clerk.

Yours truly,

Sally Notal

Sally Notal

Activity

1 When your group has decided who gets which job, announce your decisions to the whole class. Did all the groups agree?

2 Now discuss the following questions:

   a) What sorts of things affected your decisions about who should get each job?

   b) Were there any times when your decisions were affected by a person's age, sex, race, disability or family circumstances? If so, why?

   c) In the real world, do you think people's attitudes about these things affect their decisions about who gets a job?

5.7 High pay – low pay

We usually think of fruit and vegetables when people use the word 'market'. But there are also markets for skills and workers. People with very scarce skills tend to be paid lots of money. For example, Premier League footballers earn thousands of pounds each week. That is because there are very few 'quality' players who can compete at the highest level and lots of clubs all over the world are prepared to pay large sums of money. Premier League footballers' average pay is £400 000 per year.

At the other end of the scale many more people are low paid. That is because there are lots of people with the required skills to do those low-paid jobs. Supply exceeds demand.

In Britain there is a National Minimum Wage. It is illegal for an employer to pay less than this. However this minimum wage is a low wage and families who are paid at that rate often live in poverty (see factfile on page 151).

Activity

1 Look at comments A and B (below). Do you agree with Abiodun or Simon?

2 Give four reasons why Premier League footballers are paid so much more than players from lower divisions of the football league.

3 **a)** List five other jobs that you think are highly paid in this country. For each one explain why those jobs are highly paid.
   b) Do you think these jobs *should* be highly paid?

4 Look at the list of low-paid jobs on page 151.
   a) Why do you think these jobs are low paid?
   b) Are there any of them that you think should be paid a lot more? Why do you think that?

5 Young people aged sixteen to seventeen do not qualify for the minimum wage. Do you think they should? Give your reasons why or why not.

The entire Manchester United football team ... have all scored on this year's [2002] *Sunday Times* Pay List. None of its top players earned less than £1.6 million last year. The team's combined earnings are calculated to have topped £80 million.

It is not just Manchester United players who are doing well. There are now as many footballers in the league of Britain's top 500 best-paid people as there are City financiers ...

David Beckham, 27, is the highest paid footballer with earnings of £15.5 million this year ... (He) has now nudged ahead of the Queen for the first time, taking £300 000 more than her back to Beckingham Palace. Already Beckham's £90 000-a-week salary is eclipsed by deals that cover him from head (£1m a year from Brylcreem) to toe (£3m a year from Adidas to wear its boots). Last week he was signed up to promote Vodaphone's new camera phone in a £1m deal.

Beckham made £1.75m more than the City's highest flyer, Bob Diamond, 51, chief executive of Barclay's Capital, who made £13.75 million.

Beckham is also the biggest earner under the age of 30, just pipping Robbie Williams, 28.

From the *Sunday Times*, 3 November 2002

DO PLAYERS' WAGES DISGUST YOU? – WHAT THE FANS SAY

A

Let's face it; we live in a market economy where prices are fixed by market forces and not the whims of producers or consumers. Football players' salaries are no exception. If doctors don't earn as much, it's because we the public don't think they deserve that much. Limiting footballers' wages is detrimental to the football business, the market economy, and to democracy as a whole.

Abiodun, USA

B

It truly sickens me to think that you can earn £50 000 a week for kicking a piece of leather around a pitch and yet scientists researching cures for cancer and other deadly diseases start on around £14 000 per year. Surely these people are more important than a footballer – we can live without footballers but we can't live without these guys – they never get any credit!

Simon, UK

Low pay factfile

- From 1999 the National Minimum Wage has guaranteed a basic minimum income for people. It is illegal for employers to pay less than this rate. The National Minimum Wage is £4.50 an hour for employees over 22, and for 18- to 21- year olds it is £3.80 an hour (as of October 2003).
- Part-time and casual workers are entitled to the minimum wage but not children or young workers aged sixteen and seventeen.
- 1.3 million adults and 140 000 18- to 21- year olds across the UK earn the minimum wage.
- In the past twenty years privatisation has reduced pay in many low-paid jobs. For instance, workers (such as cleaners and security staff) employed by private companies in the health service, local government and education are paid lower wages than if they were employed directly by the hospitals and councils.
- Many workers on the minimum wage don't have rights to paid holidays, sick pay, a pension or compassionate leave.
- Many low-paid workers work long hours and do several jobs. Family life can be harmed by people working long hours.
- There is a difference between the minimum wage and a living wage. It is estimated that a single parent with two children living in East London needs a disposable income (gross) of £272 per week to have 'a low but acceptable' standard of living. Without benefits the parent would need £6.30 an hour.
- One group who are campaigning against low pay are the trade unions. The unions have set £6.30 an hour as the living wage target in their campaign to improve wages in East London.

Top ten low-paid jobs

Average hourly pay for those in full-time work, April 2000

Women

	£
Bar staff	4.41
Launderer, dry cleaner	4.50
Kitchen porter, hand	4.51
Waiter	4.67
Petrol pump attendant	4.74
Hairdresser	4.79
Checkout operator	4.84
Catering assistant	4.85
Cleaner	4.85
Childcare assistant	4.91

Men

	£
Bar staff	4.62
Kitchen porter, hand	4.63
Counter hand	4.91
Hotel porter	4.99
Waiter	5.01
Launderer, dry cleaner	5.15
Cleaner	5.35
Agricultural machinery driver	5.35
Fishmonger	5.44
Farm worker	5.50

Case study: *Surviving on the minimum wage*

Fran Abrams, a journalist, spent a month trying to live on the minimum wage. She worked as a night cleaner at the Savoy Hotel in London. At the end of the month she calculated her income and spending as follows.

Income

Hours worked: 120.75 (excluding breaks)
Minus six hours' unpaid training: 114.75
Total pay at £4 an hour: £459
Employer deducted £10 payroll charge: £449
Minus £45.90 income tax: £403.10
Minus £20 National Insurance: £383.10
Plus £89.83 housing benefit
Total income: £472.93

Spending

One room bedsit: £260
Transport: £76.90
Food: £137.24
Total spending: £474.14

She concludes:

'Can people survive on the minimum wage in London? Not if my experience was in any way representative. Not if their employers knock bits off the edges of their pay cheques. Not if they don't already have some savings to keep them going to pay day. Not if they want to buy shoes and get their hair cut occasionally. Or have a life. And yet there are countless thousands of them doing just that.'

From the *Guardian*, 29 January 2002

5.8 Would you join a trade union?

One of the questions you might face when you start work is whether or not to join a trade union. When you have worked through the activities in this section you will be in a better position to make this decision.

What do unions do?

Trade unions developed during the nineteenth century. Workers formed unions to try to improve the conditions they worked in and the pay they received. The unions gave workers more power to bargain with employers for improvements. Pay negotiations are an important part of trade union work. Many employers prefer to talk to one trade union about pay and conditions rather than all the employees individually. This is known as collective bargaining and such agreements cover about half the workforce of Britain.

In addition to pay, today's trade unions:

- give information, support, legal and other advice
- represent people with problems at work such as redundancy, discipline and legal action
- keep an eye on health and safety through trained representatives in the workplace
- campaign for equal pay for women and fair pay for all
- support workers in discrimination cases
- offer a range of financial and other services – credit cards, special discounts, good insurance deals
- provide further opportunities for education and training.

Activity

1 Working in pairs, discuss the following questions. You will have to do some research to discover the answers to some of them.

- How many trade unions can you name?
- Which types of employment do they cover?
- Do you have any relatives who have joined a union? Which union did they join and what do they see as the benefits of joining the union?
- Do you know any relatives who decided not to join a union? What were their reasons?

2 Again working in pairs, study the headlines on page 153 from some trade union papers.

a) What issues at work are raised in these articles?
b) How has the trade union tried to help the employees in each example?
c) Are you more or less likely to join a trade union as a result of learning more about what they do?
d) If you would join a union what would be your main reasons? If you would not join a union what would be your reasons?

Flying High at BAe

Pay rises of £25 a week and an introduction of the four-day week have been won recently for union members at the British Aerospace factory in Filton, Bristol.

Senior T&G shop steward Shem Hogan has no doubt that this is because of the decision by lay members to get involved positively in changing management techniques. 'When new management techniques were proposed two years ago the trade unions made a presentation to management stressing the need for trade union involvement,' said Shem.

Adapted from *T&G Record*, May 1997– Transport and General Workers' Union

HARASSMENT? LEAVE IT OUT!

If you're having trouble fending off unwanted advances at work, the CWU is here to help.

The joke is the same in most workplaces around Britain and even the world. Sexual harassment – and how to get it.

The trouble is, sexual harassment is no joke for thousands of women at work every day. And yes, it can happen to men, too.

The CWU recognises that branch officials have an important role in providing support for those suffering harassment at work. Our education service can play a vital part in creating a culture which helps prevent harassment in the first place.

Adapted from *CWU Voice*, February 1997 – Communication Workers' Union

Occupational asthma: £91719 for AEEU member

Following a two-day trial at Cardiff County Court, AEEU member Allan Baber has been awarded £91 719 for occupational asthma.

The court heard that Allan contracted the disease as a result of exposure to oil mists in his work as a toolroom grinder with Chubb Fire Limited, where he worked for 25 years.

John Allen, who has responsibility for the Union's legal department, said: 'This is a very important win for Allan, and a very significant victory for the AEEU. Despite Chubb Fire's denials, we were able to prove not only that the company was at fault, but that exposure to oil mists has led to occupational asthma.'

Adapted from AEEU newspaper – Amalgamated Electrical Engineering Union

Time to put an end to low pay in the theatre

Theatre managers have been put on warning – actors and stage management will no longer subsidise theatres by taking low salaries and small subsistence allowances when touring.

The union has put in claims for a minimum rate of £250 a week together with much more realistic allowances.

Adapted from *Equity Journal,* December 1996 – actors' union

Stop the Bullying
This could happen to you

Member X suffered over two years of systematic bullying by a group of his colleagues, led by his immediate superior.

The group isolated him, his work was closely monitored and he had difficulty getting leave. He took action through BIFU, and the bank eventually moved him after three years. But this left the bully free to bully other staff who are also taking out grievances.

BIFU is a member of the Campaign Against Bullying. It negotiates policies on bullying with employers and provides advice and support for members.

Adapted from BIFU report, February 1997 – banking union

5.9 Workfare

In most developed countries, it is common for unemployed people to be given state benefits – a payment to go towards rent, food bills, clothes, and so on. To be eligible for this money, they have to be looking for work. But political parties have raised the issue of whether taxpayers should pay for people to be unemployed and expect nothing in return.

The idea of workfare began in some US states – unemployed people have to work on government-approved schemes or risk losing their benefits. Usually this would be after they had been unemployed for some time and not been able to find work. Similar schemes, being considered in many countries, are very controversial. Some people say they are the same as forced labour and they are anti-women as they hit single mothers particularly hard. Others say some unemployed people are lazy and could work if they wanted to. What do you think?

Activity

Decide which of the following arguments support and which oppose workfare.

Workfare – the arguments

A Getting benefits for doing nothing makes people dependent on the state and makes them apathetic and lazy.

B The city government has the right to expect something in return for taxpayers' money.

C Workfare schemes treat people like slave labour.

D The schemes mainly involve manual work and do not use the talents and skills of unemployed workers.

E Employers want higher level and IT skills which workfare schemes do not provide, so they do not help people on workfare get jobs.

F Doing productive work will increase the self-esteem and confidence of the unemployed, making it easier for them to get a job.

G High unemployment is the result of economic changes and declining industries such as steel. It is not the fault of individuals. Workfare blames the victims.

H People claiming benefits for being out of work often have cash-in-hand jobs in the black economy. They are defrauding the taxpayer. Workfare stops them doing this.

I Many long-term unemployed are older workers who cannot find work because employers prefer young workers.

J Workfare schemes stop people looking for work and attending interviews.

K Workfare will push some people into crime rather than having to do menial jobs.

L The local community benefits from the work done, for example on environmental improvements or for local charities.

M People doing workfare jobs will not care about what they are doing and so the job will be poorly done. Would you trust someone on workfare to do a good job?

N Workfare harms people in low-paid jobs and may force more people out of work.

O Many workforce schemes have a bad effect on the families of single mothers. Childcare is not usually provided.

Activity

1 You are a group of councillors in the city of Greenville. Study the arguments for and against workfare and decide whether or not you want to introduce a scheme in your city. You are aware that many voters and taxpayers are in favour of such a scheme because they do not want to pay more taxes and they think that people should not be paid to be idle. On the other hand, the closure of the steel plant has led to the long-term unemployment of older male workers. These men are desperate to find new manual jobs, but these types of jobs are no longer available.

2 Assume your council has decided to introduce a scheme. What would it be like? Make decisions on the following points.

- For how many months would people have to be unemployed before they went on workfare?
- What kinds of work would they be required to do?
- How many hours would they be required to work?
- How would they be helped to get off workfare into work?

3 Now that you have planned your scheme, think how it would affect the people it is aimed at. Consider the position of the four people in the case studies on the right.
 a) Describe what they might say about the workfare programme.
 b) How might it affect their lives?
 c) What would the benefits be?
 d) What problems would the scheme bring?

4 What would the newspapers say about your scheme? Write two short paragraphs as if from a local newspaper – one for and one anti-workfare.

5 Hold a class debate on the subject: 'This house believes that unemployed people should have to work for their benefits.'

Workfare case studies

Joe Green, aged 53

Joe worked for Greenville Steel for 30 years before being made redundant a year ago. His skills as a steel worker are not required in the Greenville economy, which has many jobs in offices and services, such as shops and building societies. He has four children aged thirteen, fifteen, sixteen and nineteen. His wife has a part-time job. He has been on benefits for one year. He has been on IT training but left before the end of the course. He is still looking for manual work in a factory setting, but there are few vacancies.

Jane Smith, aged 22

Jane has been unemployed since leaving school four years ago. She has two children aged three and four and lives in her mother's house. She is separated from her husband who has disappeared and pays no maintenance. She would be interested in working with children but has no qualifications.

John Jenk, aged 29

John has been unemployed for eighteen months following a spell in Greenville prison for burglary. After leaving school he had a few unskilled jobs as a labourer on building sites. He was convicted of benefit fraud five years ago and was fined. He is a single man living in a rented flat. John would like regular work in the building trade, but thinks he is discriminated against by employers because of his criminal record.

Wilfreda Johnston, aged 45

Wilfreda has special needs and has had a succession of jobs, mostly in the fast food sector as a cleaner. She has been unemployed for six months and has no qualifications. She is unmarried and has two children aged ten and eight. She would like a full-time job as a cleaner.

5.10 Special assignments – work experience

Most young people have one or two weeks of work experience during years 10 and 11. This is an opportunity to develop your understanding of work. At the placement you can carry out a special assignment. On pages 156–58 we give you five examples of assignments that link citizenship to the world of work.

If, whilst on work experience, you want to interview people or write an assignment, you have to ask permission. This is best done in a meeting with your employer before the placement starts. Then any interviews and time to write up the assignment and make a presentation can be built into your schedule of work.

Any assignment will follow the same pattern.

QUESTIONS → RESEARCH → ANALYSIS + REPORT → PRESENTATION → EVALUATION

Assignment 1: Rights and responsibilities of employers and employees

As you know from this section people have many rights at work. These are matched by responsibilities. Understanding those rights and responsibilities is an important function in any business or organisation.

Questions

- What are the rights of employers in managing employees?
- What are the responsibilities of employers in managing employees?
- What role does the human resource (usually called HR) or personnel department play?
- What rights do employees have at work? What responsibilities do employees have at work?
- What changes to legal rights and responsibilities would employers and employees like to see?

Research

- ➜ Ask for a copy of the induction pack for new staff.
- ➜ Ask to read documents on the company intranet.
- ➜ Read notices posted on boards around the workplace.
- ➜ Interview an HR manager.
- ➜ Interview a trade union or staff representative.

Assignment 2: Employer–employee relations

Today most organisations and companies try to have good relations with their employees. This makes for a happy and more productive workforce. The fact that it is difficult to talk to all staff means that discussions are held between representatives of staff and the employer. Trade unions or staff associations are often involved in this.

Questions

- How are representatives of staff chosen?
- Are trade unions recognised? Which unions are recognised? What is the relationship between the branch of the union at the workplace and the national union?
- Are there people who represent employees? Who are they? How were they chosen? Why did they want to take on this role?
- How, when and where do representatives of the employers and employees meet?
- What kinds of issues are discussed? What problems occur and how are they solved?

Research

- ➔ Visit the TUC website (www.tuc.org.uk) to find out more about trade unions and employer–employee relations.
- ➔ Interview someone from HR or a manager.
- ➔ Interview a trade union representative or member of the employee forum or association.

Assignment 3: Work–life balance

Increasingly it is recognised that people are more than just workers. Stress at work can lead to time off sick. People have friends and family and lives outside work. They value employers who are flexible so that working arrangements can suit their own circumstances. In this way they can strike a better balance between work and life.

Questions

- What does work–life balance mean?
- How flexible is the employer over issues like working hours, holiday times, part-time work, working from home, and childcare?
- What do employees think about work–life balance?
- What does the employer think about work–life balance?
- How might things be improved so that people could have a better balance between their working life and their lives outside work?

Research

- ➔ Visit the TUC website (www.tuc.org.uk) to find out more about flexible working and work–life balance.
- ➔ Interview someone from HR or a manager.
- ➔ Interview a trade union representative or member of the employee forum or association.

Assignment 4: Health and safety

It is very important that everyone is safe and healthy at work. Employers and employees have a legal responsibility for health and safety. Risks and hazards must be identified and steps taken to make sure that accidents do not happen.

Questions

- What responsibilities do employers have over health and safety?
- What are the main risks or hazards present in the workplace? How are those risks managed?
- What health and safety briefing were you given when starting your work experience? What responsibilities do employees have to their own, and other people's, health and safety?
- What happens if there is an accident at work?
- How might health and safety in the workplace be improved?

Research

- ➔ Make notes on your health and safety briefing.
- ➔ Read health and safety notices and posters.
- ➔ Interview the health and safety representative and a 'first aider'.
- ➔ Interview your supervisor.

Assignment 5: Equality and diversity

Equality of opportunity means making sure that people are treated in the same way at work and that no one receives different treatment because of their gender, ethnicity or disability. Diversity is about celebrating the range of cultures, genders and ages of people at the workplace and not valuing one group over another.

Questions

- What is the gender balance at the workplace?
- Are there any patterns to the work roles of men and women? How can any differences be explained?
- What is the ethnic diversity of the workplace?
- What training have staff had in working in an ethnically diverse workplace?
- What training do staff get in equal opportunities?
- What kinds of equal opportunities issues arise at the workplace? How are these issues handled?

Research

➜ Interview someone from HR or a manager.
➜ Interview a trade union or staff representative.
➜ Ask for a copy of the organisation's equal opportunities policy.
➜ Read information about equal opportunities in the induction pack for new staff or on the intranet.

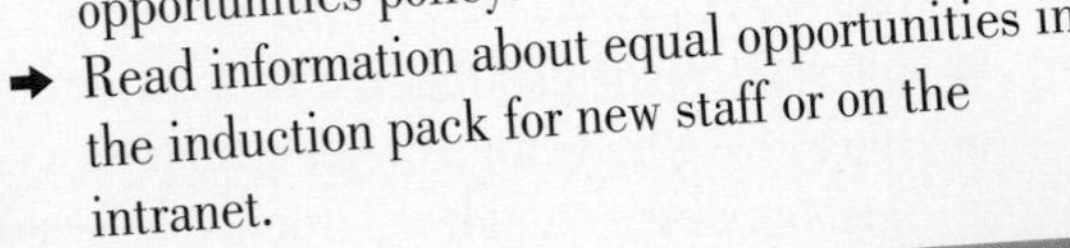

Analyse, report and present

When you have completed the research for your assignment, you need to analyse the data you have collected:

- Make notes around your questions.
- Write a short report and highlight any further questions, issues or problem areas you have found.

And then:

- Prepare a five-minute presentation (if you have access to PowerPoint try to write one slide for each question).
- Make your presentation to your supervisor or the manager.
- Ask them for some feedback on your presentation – did you make any points they had not thought about? Will they take any action as a result of your report – even if this is only to discuss further the points made?

Evaluate your assignment

- Make a presentation to the class and ask for their feedback.
- Listen to what other students found out in similar assignments and any recommendations that they made.
- Did your research and report make a difference:
  a) to the organisation
  b) to the way your supervisor or employer will deal with other students
  c) to you personally?

section 6

The media

Key words
- censorship
- images
- freedom of information
- freedom of the press
- misinformation

How do we get information about what's going on?

We all use mass media. Newspapers, the TV, the internet, keep us informed and help us to communicate. But they also influence our lives in ways we might not expect. In this section you will examine how mass media affect your life for better or for worse.

In this section, you will learn about:

- the role of the media in society
- the impact of the media in forming opinions
- a free press
- freedom of information
- censorship in the media.

You will use the following skills:

- finding out about how the media are used
- discussing the media in small groups and with the whole class
- making decisions
- giving your opinion and explaining it to others
- listening to other people's opinions.

6.1 How do the media affect you?

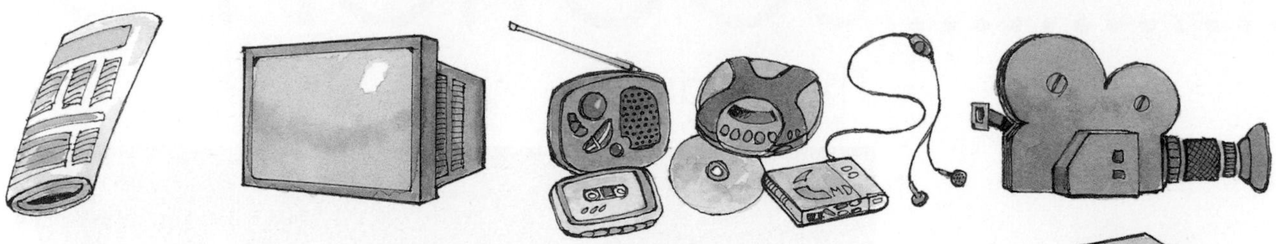

The mass media – television, radio, newspapers, magazines, films, advertising, popular music, the internet – influence every part of our lives. Most of us have grown up surrounded by the mass media. We are used to being entertained by television and radio. Advertisements are a common part of our lives and we expect regular news bulletins and daily newspapers to keep us abreast of what is happening in the world. Knowledge and opinions are formed by what we hear, read and see in the media.

The technology is developing rapidly. Until recently, the media sent messages one way – from the writers and producers to us, the viewers, listeners and readers. Now people use the media to communicate with others, use the internet to find things out, book holidays, shop, send messages and chat to people all over the world. Digital television makes it possible for us to choose what we watch and when we watch it. We are encouraged to vote on a variety of broadcast topics, to e-mail and phone in to programmes. And the media will become more and more interactive in the future.

This makes the media very influential but also, possibly, very dangerous. People who control the media can control us. They can persuade us to buy their products, they can influence what we think, they can control the things we know about. So it is important to be sceptical about the media, to decide what we trust and what we don't. Just because something is on TV does not mean it is true.

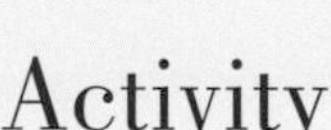

Activity

1 Work in pairs and interview each other about your exposure to the mass media on one typical day. Use the pictures above of different forms of mass media to find out:

- which of the mass media you have heard, seen or read during a day
- for how long you have listened, viewed or read since you woke up in the morning
- why you chose these forms of mass media.

2 Suppose you had to pick one of the forms of media that you could not live without. Which one would it be and why is it so important to you?

Activity

1 a) Look at the illustrations below. Where do you get your information about the things shown? Draw up a chart like the one started here:

Information about:	**Which media**
Music	Magazines, CDs and minidiscs, internet, TV programmes, radio
Sport	
Celebrities and pop stars	

b) How far can you trust the media? Work through the chart above and say how much you trust the media to tell you the truth. Do it on a five-point scale where 1 means 'I hardly trust the media at all' and 5 means 'I trust everything the media tell me'.

Discuss

In the whole class, discuss how important you think the media are in determining how you run your life – the things you do, wear, listen to, etc.

products

politics

fashion

music

entertainment

celebrities and pop stars

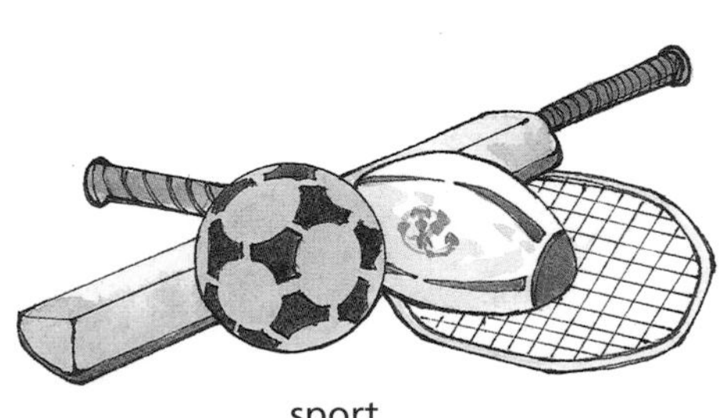

sport

news and current affairs

6.2 How do images influence us?

The media have many influences on us. The most important is influencing the opinions and attitudes we form. They do this partly through the images they present of people, events, news or products. Some of the images are positive and some are negative, and can be expressed through words as well as pictures. Sometimes an image makes us feel envious and leaves us wanting to be like the person portrayed. Another image can make us feel angry with the people shown. Images are central to the mass media – advertisements, news bulletins, newspapers, magazines, television programmes.

Yobs caught on CCTV

Activity

1. Look at the following images. Describe the emotions that each picture and caption are likely to evoke.
2. Explain how the image encourages these emotions.
3. In a group of three, look through a collection of magazines. Find several photographs (and captions) which have been used to put across particular images. Stick them on a piece of paper and explain what image they are trying to convey.

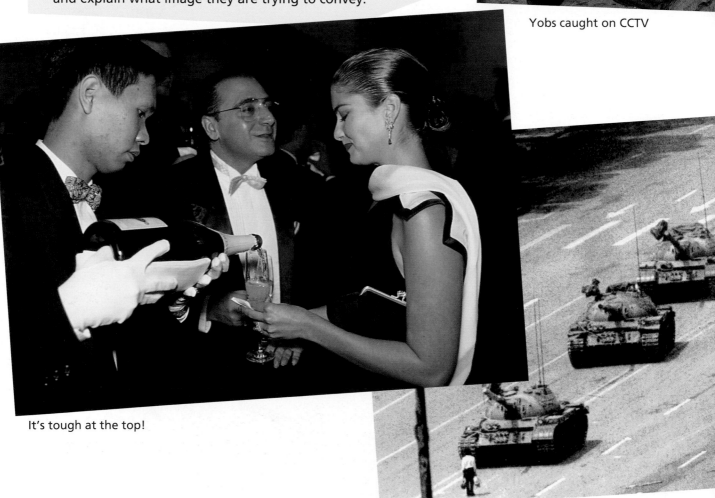

It's tough at the top!

What price freedom?

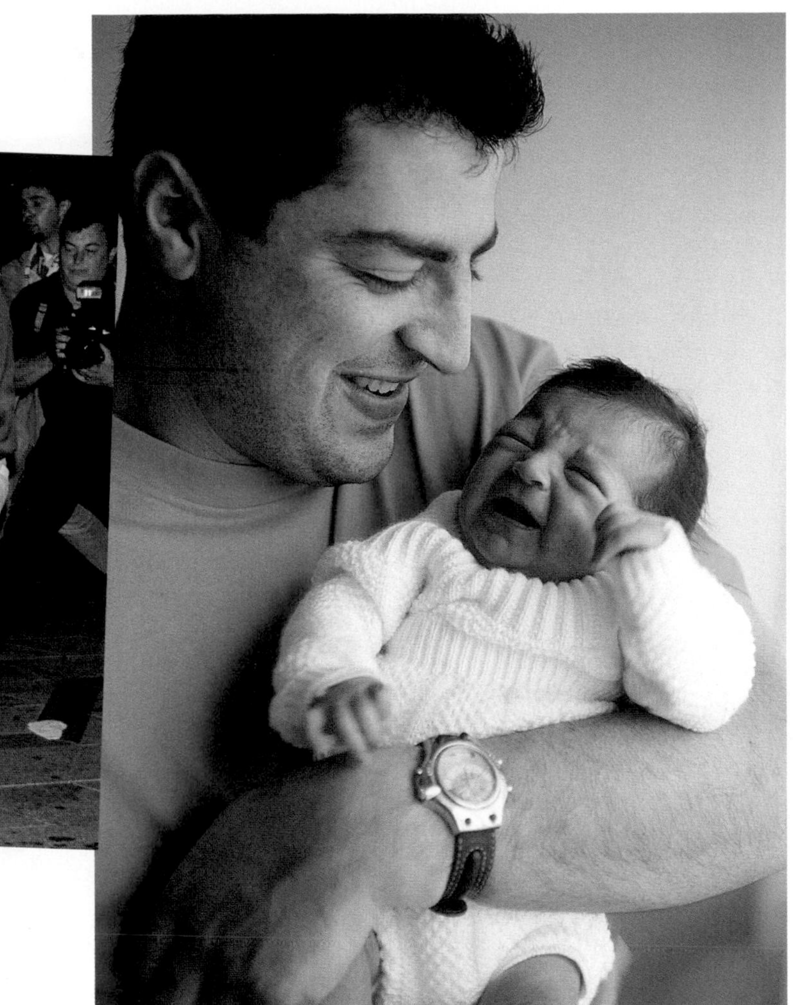

The most important person in the world

Spoil yourself!
Why not?

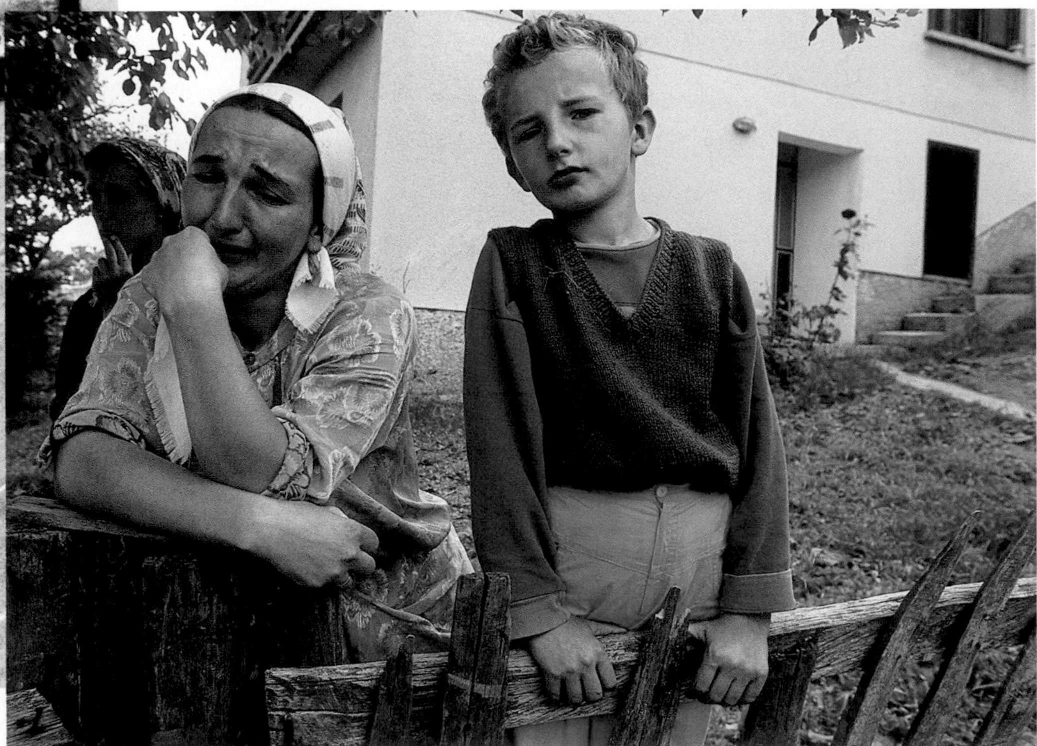

Help us!

How do advertisers use images?

Advertising is a huge industry that uses images to persuade us to buy products and services. It uses a range of techniques, some of which are listed on page 165. Advertisers are trying to make us focus on the **brand name** of a particular product. They use techniques to draw this brand name to our attention or to make sure we always link it with the product. For instance, when we think of breakfast cereal, we immediately think of Kellogg's. Advertisers also want us to identify with particular brands so that we feel these brands say something about us.

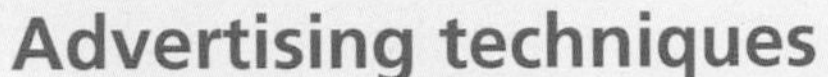

Advertising techniques

- **Appeal to snobbery – If rich and important people buy it, so should I. It shows I have good taste.**
- **Sex appeal – If I buy this product, it will make me sexy like the people in the advert.**
- **Use of celebrities – If a person like this uses this product it must be good.**
- **Use of humour – This makes me feel good about the product.**
- **Use of guilt – If I don't use this product I may not be doing the right thing.**
- **Quirky images or words – This is intriguing. I wonder what this advert is all about and what the name of the product is?**
- **Shock tactics – This has grabbed my attention. The name of the product really sticks in my mind.**

Activity

1 Which techniques are being used in the adverts shown here? Put your answers in a chart like the one below. An example of a different advert has been done for you.

What product is being advertised?	What is being shown in the advert?	What technique is being used?	Who is the advert aimed at?	Explain how the images are used.
Sunglasses	David Beckham looking 'cool' in sunglasses	Use of celebrities	Young people from 18 to 30	People admire and want to be like David Beckham. So they might want to buy these sunglasses.

2 Choose different adverts from magazines or TV and describe the techniques they use. Add these to your chart.

6.3 Who decides what's in the news?

The media control our knowledge of the news. Most people follow the news every day, even if they just listen to the headlines on the radio between their favourite music programmes. Important items such as train crashes, political scandals, serious crimes or terrorist attacks are covered first and everyone knows about them soon after they happen.

But big stories don't happen every day, and broadcasters and newspaper journalists still have to fill their news slots. Thousands of events happen in the world, but most people hear about only the few stories which are chosen to fill the half-hour news bulletin on TV or the front page of a newspaper. So who decides what to cover and how do they decide?

The stories chosen are the ones thought to have the most **news value**. Newspapers and broadcasters decide what they think people will find interesting and important.

Stories are thought to have news value if they:

- **are dramatic or terrible**
- **have pictures available**
- **involve 'human interest'**
- **affect a lot of people**
- **are interesting to the target audience (the people who usually read the paper, or watch/listen to the programme)**
- **can be told simply and quickly**
- **are up to date and topical**
- **involve powerful or famous people.**

Activity

Look at examples A–D of stories from the media and decide which of the listed news values they have.

A

Sandra Hose, the actress, was photographed coming out of a rest and drugs rehabilitation centre. She said she had needed a rest after working non-stop for months and denied that she was there for drug abuse treatment. This follows her well publicised appearance on a TV show where she had laughed uncontrollably and screamed at other guests.

B

The latest news to come out of 10 Downing Street from the Prime Minister is that an announcement about the General Election is imminent...

C

Heavy rain storms last night hit homes in York once again. Martha Preston, who owns a house near the river, was in tears as she spoke to reporters: 'This is the third time in two years that we have been flooded. We have lost everything – carpets, furniture, our record collection and the photographs of our children when they were young . . .'

D

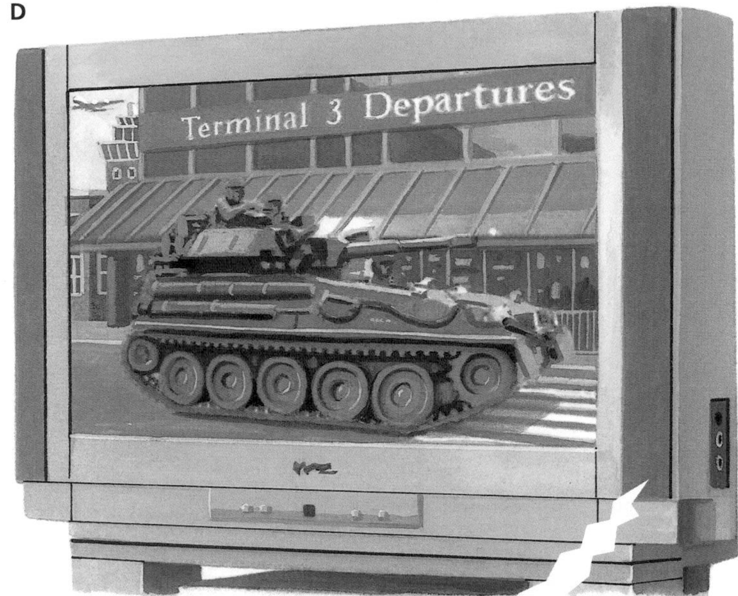

Dramatic pictures have just reached us of tanks and soldiers surrounding Heathrow airport. They have been deployed to counter a possible terrorist attack. Thousands of people are trapped in airport terminals as flights have had to be cancelled.

Activity

1 Work in a group of three or four. Bring in to the class the front pages of two different papers, published on the same day. One should be a tabloid and one a broadsheet. Compare the front pages.

a) Decide why the front-page stories were chosen. In what ways do they have 'news value'?

b) What is the difference between the stories chosen by the two newspapers?

c) Who do you think the stories in the tabloid are aimed at and why were they chosen?

d) Who do you think the stories in the broadsheet are aimed at and why were they chosen?

2 Watch a news broadcast on TV. Make a list of the stories/news items in the broadcast and the news values of each story.

Time given to news item	What the story was about	What news values it contained
1.		
2.		
3.		
4.		

Tabloid newspapers
The Sun
Daily Mirror
Daily Mail
Daily Express
Daily Star
Evening Standard

Broadsheets
The Times
The Independent
The Guardian
The Daily Telegraph
Financial Times

Hold the front page!

Local newspapers are usually published once a week, so the editors have time to collect a range of stories that have local interest. They have to decide which stories have news value, how much space each should have and which order they should follow in the newspaper. Local newspaper journalists seek out news from a variety of sources. These can be:

- press releases from different groups
- tips phoned in by the public
- information from the police or a local council
- items from press agencies
- other newspaper reports
- stories researched by their own reporters.

Activity

Make your own local newspaper

Work in groups of four. Your task is to write the front page of a local newspaper and an editorial (see below) to go inside. The page should be the size of A3 paper. Appoint one of your group to each of these jobs: editor, two sub-editors and a designer. You might be able to get help from a local journalist.

1. Look at a page from one of your local newspapers and discuss how the stories have news value (see list on page 166). Do you think there are different rules for what gives stories news value in a local newspaper?
2. For your front page you need to select up to four stories from 1–7 opposite. Choose the stories that you think would have the most local news value. The whole team can discuss the stories, but the editor will have the final say.
3. Decide on your main story and the order of the remaining stories. The sub-editors will need to edit and rewrite them, using a computer.
4. The editor should write a front page headline for the main story and smaller headlines for the others. He/she should also write an editorial (a short opinion column) on one of the stories.
5. The designer should think of a name for the paper and design the title. He/she should also design the layout of the page, using IT with appropriate software, if possible.
6. Display your page in class and prepare a presentation on why you chose those stories.

Story 1

Press release from the local council

PRESS RELEASE

LOCAL COUNCIL

The council has decided to demolish the old swimming baths and sell the land for the development of luxury housing. This will bring much-needed cash to the council coffers and enable essential work to be carried out on the recreation ground. New swings will be provided, and the tennis courts will receive new nets and fencing. Some funding will go to additional parking at the recreation ground.

The swimming baths have been closed for five years and have been a magnet for vandals. They have become dangerous and costly to secure against break-ins. Although some local people lobbied for the baths to be refurbished, it has not been possible to raise the funds.

Story 2

Press release from the football supporters' club

PRESS RELEASE PRESS RELEASE PRESS RELEASE

BOGSWORTH ROVERS SUPPORTERS' CLUB

An emergency meeting will be held with management next week to discuss ways of helping Bogsworth Rovers out of their financial plight. The Bogsworth Supporters' Club has asked the club to allow its representatives to attend the discussions. The supporters also wish to oppose the owner's plans to vacate Bog Park, the much-loved football ground. The club owner plans to sell the site for development and move the club 50 kilometres away, in order to raise funds. Supporters fear that the move will be the death of the club, since the journey to the new ground is difficult and expensive on public transport. Bogsworth Rovers have been sited in the town for the last 54 years.

Story 3

From the local branch of the Royal Society for the Protection of Birds

RSPB press release

Birdwatchers at the reservoir witnessed the appearance of one of the country's rarest birds last week, when three bitterns landed at the nature reserve surrounding the reservoir. A spokesman for the nature reserve said, 'Although occasional bitterns were recorded over-wintering on the outskirts of cities, it is very rare to see three together so close to the centre.' Recent reports put the number of male bitterns at 20 to 25 individuals in the whole of Britain (a quarter of the 1950s bittern population) because their reed bed habitats have been lost and destroyed through development.

Story 4

From the local reporter

Vandalism and graffiti continue to increase in the borough. Despite a crackdown by the police and rewards of £100 offered for information, figures show that graffiti increased in the vicinity of the railway station last month. Local shopkeepers have been requested not to sell spray cans of paint to under-18 year olds, and estate managers have been asked to remove graffiti as soon as it occurs. However, young people cannot be dissuaded from this unsightly and depressing activity. Two recent arrests have led to the imposition of fines and community service orders.

Story 5

Phoned in report

A restaurant in the town centre was partly demolished last night when a car swerved into the frontage and ended up inside the restaurant. Luckily the accident happened after the restaurant closed and no one was hurt. However, a large amount of damage was done and the restaurant owner is distraught because he opened the restaurant only a month ago. The police have charged a 26-year-old man with driving without insurance or a driving licence and also driving without due care and attention.

Story 6

Phoned in from a local group – ANTIMOB – opposing mobile phone masts

More mobile phone masts are to be erected locally, but they will look like lamp posts in order to preserve the look of the town. A telecommunications company has applied for planning permission to erect eight-metre-high phone masts in Dover Close and Rotherham Street. There is local concern about the safety of phone masts. Some mothers are mounting a campaign to stop them, since they will be close to Dover Primary School, and they are worried about the health of their children. Evidence is mixed about the impact of mobile phone masts, but some research suggests that the rays are harmful to the brains of young children.

Story 7

From another local newspaper

TEENAGER MUGGED AT KNIFEPOINT BY GANG ON TOP OF 63E BUS

A 16-year-old boy from the borough was robbed and threatened with a knife by a group of youths on the top of a 63E bus bound for the town centre. The teenager was travelling on the top deck of the bus at 9.00p.m. last Sunday. A gang of five youths boarded the bus and sat near him. One of the gang drew out a knife and pointed it at the boy's face. The group ordered the teenager to empty his pockets and took £20 and his mobile phone from him. Anyone who has any information about this incident should contact DC Keith Ryan at the local police station.

6.4 Could you be a programme scheduler?

Today, television is probably the most important form of mass media to most people. They cannot imagine life without a television set, and in many homes it is on all the time.

In the very early days there was only one station (BBC), and there was no commercial television, so there were no breaks for advertisements. Now there are lots of television channels – most of which are funded by advertising. The television company has to show programmes that people want to watch so that they can sell the advertising slots within and between programmes. So each television station is concerned about its ratings – the number of people who tune in to each programme. Commercial stations can charge advertisers more for slots near programmes that are very popular and that attract large numbers of viewers.

The BBC is funded through a licence fee paid by everyone who has a television set, so it does not depend on advertising income. Even so, it is very concerned about ratings. It wants more people to watch its programmes and its programme makers are judged by whether their programmes attract big audiences. A big audience justifies spending a lot of money on a programme, which means that the BBC also tries to broadcast popular programmes.

So there is sharp competition between the television channels – they all want to increase their viewing figures. Every week researchers reveal what has been popular that week. An example is given below.

Position	Programme	Channel	Viewers (millions)
1	EastEnders (Tues/Sun)	BBC1	15.90
2	EastEnders (Fri/Sun)	BBC1	15.05
3	EastEnders (Thurs/Sun)	BBC1	14.76
4	EastEnders (Mon/Sun)	BBC1	14.40
5	Coronation Street (Mon)	ITV	13.62
6	Coronation Street (Sun)	ITV	12.42
7	Coronation Street (Fri)	ITV	12.25
8	Coronation Street (Wed)	ITV	11.90
9	Heartbeat	ITV	10.64
10	Emmerdale (Mon)	ITV	10.35
11	Emmerdale (Tues)	ITV	9.64
12	Walking with Dinosaurs	BBC1	9.48

You can see from this table how important 'soaps' are to each channel. However, while soaps may be the most popular programmes, television provides us with a great variety of other programmes.

Some people say that the need to get more people watching popular programmes has led to a 'dumbing down' of the quality of programmes on offer. You are going to have a go at scheduling six hours of Friday evening television.

Education or entertainment?
John Reith was the founding father of the BBC. He wanted to see an independent British broadcasting organisation, which would **educate, inform and entertain** the whole nation, without pressure from politicians or business interests. So does television educate, inform and entertain? Or does it just entertain?

Activity

1 Work in groups of about five. Each group should take on the role of the schedulers on one of the four television channels shown on page 172.

a) It is your job to decide which programmes to schedule on your channel for a typical Friday evening from 6.00 p.m. until midnight (six hours).

b) You have to consider the aims of your channel very carefully but you are also competing with the other channels for viewers.

c) Commercial and satellite channels must allow ten minutes in each hour for adverts.

d) You can choose from the list of programme types below. You are allowed to decide what these might be, for example what sort of drama programme.

e) You can also invent a new programme of your own. This has to attract viewers by its new-style format or exciting/bizarre content.

2 a) Design your schedule as if from a page of the *Radio* or *TV Times*, in which each programme is given a short description. Example:

The Estate – a soap about the people who live on a West Midlands housing estate. Greta discovers she is pregnant, Tommy stabs his step-father, a gas main explodes.

Wildnurse – female vets go to Africa to look after wild animals

b) Make one programme 'choice of the day' and say more about it.

3 When you have completed your schedule, choose one person from the group to describe your channel's Friday evening to the other groups/channels. Say why you think it is the best evening's viewing and would encourage people to stay tuned in.

- **News bulletins (15 minutes)**
- **Weather reports (5 minutes)**
- **Documentaries (30 minutes)**
- **Soaps (30 minutes)**
- **Drama (1 hour)**
- **Quizzes and game shows (30 minutes)**
- **Situation comedies (30 minutes)**
- **Current affairs discussions (30 minutes)**
- **Films (2 hours)**
- **Cartoons (30 minutes)**
- **Costume drama (45 minutes)**
- **Reality TV (30 minutes)**
- **Chat shows (30 minutes)**
- **Docu-soaps, for example fly-on-the-wall programmes (30 minutes)**
- **Make-over programmes, home, garden, people (30 minutes)**
- **Travel/holiday programmes (30 minutes)**
- **Science fiction (30 minutes)**
- **Crime – factual (45 minutes)**
- **Dating/meeting other people (30 minutes)**

Discuss

1 How similar were the schedules for the different channels?

2 How did the aims of the channels affect the choice of programme types?

3 What purposes did the new-format programmes serve? Were they educational, informative or entertaining?

4 Did the funding of the channel (how it gets its money) influence programme scheduling?

5 What do you think should be the main purpose of television channels?

channel W This is the main terrestrial channel. It is funded from the licence fees paid by the public. The licence fee is compulsory and the amount is decided by the government. The channel has a set of rules – a 'charter' – which lays down how it should operate. It must provide a certain number of news bulletins and discussions. It has to educate as well as entertain its viewers who range from three to a hundred years old. It has to include informative programmes in its schedules, including documentaries, discussion programmes and political coverage. It is not allowed to be biased in its coverage of politics. All the same it needs to attract large numbers of viewers to some of its programmes, particularly soaps and drama series.

CHANNEL X This is a new satellite channel aimed at young people aged from 15 to 25. It is paid for by subscription and advertisers. This means that it has to attract lots of people who will pay a £5 per month subscription, in order for the channel to make money by selling advertising slots. It is run by a very adventurous young businessman who has made millions in the film industry. He wants every young person in the country to want to watch Channel X. He can put on what he likes – he does not have to have any news programmes, political programmes or documentaries but he knows he needs a variety of different shows or people will become bored.

Channel Y **This is an independent terrestrial television company. It depends entirely on income from advertising. It sells time during the commercial breaks in programmes. It can charge very large sums of money for time during, before and after the most popular programmes. For this reason, it needs to put on programmes that are popular with the viewers. However, it also wants to have a reputation as a channel which competes with Channel W to provide high quality programmes. It also has an obligation to provide two nightly news bulletins and to produce a range of factual programmes aimed at informing the public.**

Channel Z This is a terrestrial channel. It is paid for by various agencies: the government gives the channel most of its money, but commercial television channels and film companies have to contribute a share. It does not have advertisements. This is a channel for minorities. The idea is that it produces very high quality programmes which are likely to be of interest to a smaller number of viewers. These would include:

- arts programmes, on subjects such as classical music, opera, ballet, painting
- debate and discussion on current issues and politics
- education programmes
- programmes specifically designed for minority ethnic groups
- films which would not get shown on the other channels or in the cinema.

Discuss

In the UK, BBC television is funded by licence fees, paid by everyone who owns a television set. Some people think this should be stopped, while others think it is very important that it carries on. Hold a debate in class: 'Should the BBC continue to be funded by licence payers?' Some of the arguments for both sides are presented here. Sort out the arguments for and against and then add your own ideas.

A No one should be forced to pay a TV licence of over £100.

B The BBC produces high-quality programmes which inform and educate people as well as entertain them.

C Not everybody watches the BBC and they still have to pay.

D If the BBC were not funded by licence fees it would have to have advertisements and one of the best things about it is that programmes are not interrupted by advertisements.

E Powerful people could get control of large sections of the media which means that only certain views would be put to people.

F The BBC and what it broadcasts on the news is trusted throughout the world as being truthful.

G The programmes on commercial channels are the programmes that most people want to see.

H Commercial channels can produce high-quality programmes.

I The BBC produces programmes for minorities, such as cultural and arts programmes or programmes for minority ethnic groups, which would not be produced on commercial channels because the audience is not big enough.

J The BBC is independent from government and commercial (business) control. It can just focus on making good programmes.

K Commercial funding provides a wide choice of a huge number of channels which are specialised, for example a sports channel, history channel or children's channel.

L Television would be dumbed down without the BBC to set a standard.

Discuss

In a democracy, how important is television in keeping people informed and educated?

6.5 Why is freedom of the press important?

'Press freedom' is an essential part of a free and democratic society. Most people agree that a democracy relies on press and broadcasting freedom. The system of government in the UK allows press freedom. This means that the government does not tell the newspapers what they are allowed to print. It is important that we can hear a variety of opinions on political issues. Otherwise, the government could present only its side of an argument and could withhold important information that we need to know.

Information is a great source of power. We therefore aim to keep our media protected and free, as described in this panel.

Some people believe that these measures work and that our media do an excellent job exposing the truth. In the UK undemocratic and illegal actions of powerful people are frequently exposed by the media. Others say that it is wrong to believe what you read and hear in the media. They claim that the media are controlled by people in big business and politics and that alternative points of view never get heard or broadcast.

Press and broadcasting freedom

- The media should be free to report on things which the public needs to know.
- A society should allow all views to be published or heard, unless they incite violence or racial hatred.
- The media should be owned by a variety of people in order to give a range of views.
- The people who work in the media should not be influenced by the government or by the people who own the media.
- People should be able to complain if the media have told lies about them.

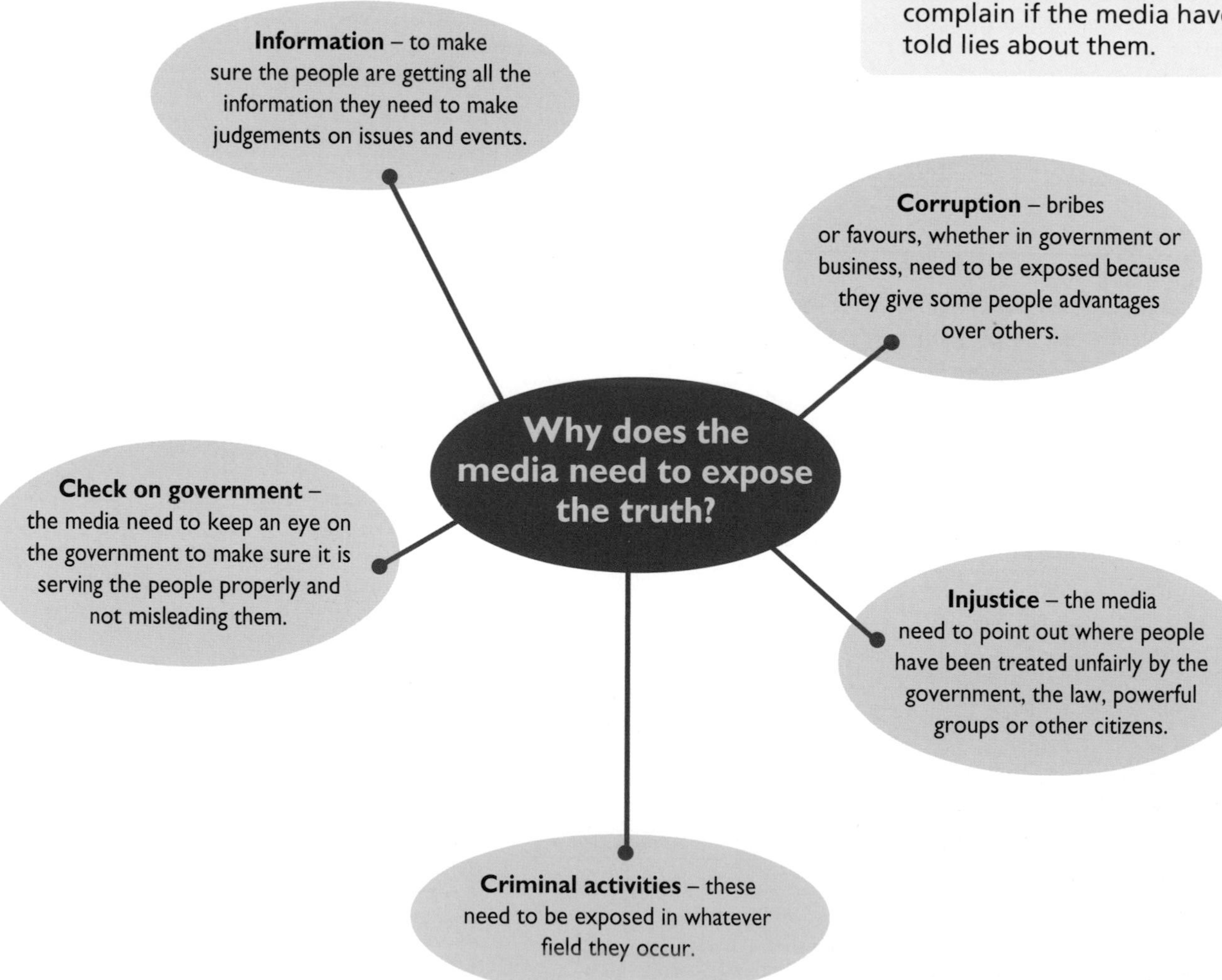

Why does the media need to expose the truth?
Information – to make sure the people are getting all the information they need to make judgements on issues and events.
Corruption – bribes or favours, whether in government or business, need to be exposed because they give some people advantages over others.
Check on government – the media need to keep an eye on the government to make sure it is serving the people properly and not misleading them.
Injustice – the media need to point out where people have been treated unfairly by the government, the law, powerful groups or other citizens.
Criminal activities – these need to be exposed in whatever field they occur.

Who influences what we learn from the media?

Censorship – some governments censor the press, not allowing people to learn things that they do not want them to know. This can be on a large scale, for example in an authoritarian state, where the media are controlled by the government and people are told only what the government wants them to hear. But it can also occur in a democracy where the government does not want the general public to know things about matters of national security.

Media owners – some powerful people own newspapers, magazines, radio and TV channels. This gives them a lot of influence because they ensure that the media they own puts across their personal views. Some media moguls own newspapers, TV channels and satellite TV channels throughout the world, giving them the ability to influence millions of people.

Advertising and sponsorship – newspapers and commercial television channels earn most of their money from advertising and sponsorship. Sponsors pay a lot of money to have their name at the front of a programme or soap opera, particularly if it is very popular. Commercial media are less likely to say unpleasant things about companies that support them.

Political spin – politicians often want to appear in the best possible light. They employ people to get good stories about them into the news and to make bad stories sound much better than they are. This is called 'spinning' the news and the people who do it are called 'spin doctors'.

Activity

1 If you were an editor, would you:
   a) print a bad news story about the leader of a government in your country if the government were known to have put journalists into prison for writing negative things about it?
   b) run a news item on TV which showed the most important sponsor of your television channel as a company that had been involved in corruption
   c) print an editorial which directly contradicted the strongly held views of the owner of your newspaper?

2 Why do you think it is important that media ownership is spread around and not dominated by a few individuals?

3 Think of an example for two of the points in the diagram opposite about why the media needs to expose the truth.

4 Give an example from the past or the present where censorship was/is used to control people's knowledge, thoughts and beliefs.

Discuss

Hold a class debate on the following topic: 'This house believes that, with all its problems, we do have a free press in the UK.'

6.6 Investigative journalism

Influential people – politicians, important business people, celebrities, clergymen – may want to hide misdemeanours from the public. Sometimes such people make public statements about the way people should live but do not follow these in their private lives.

Some journalists believe that it is their job to uncover secrets and expose lies. They don't want to report a story just as it is told – they want to get behind the story and find out what has not been told. They argue that, without their work, corruption in big businesses or wrong-doing by politicians would never be found out.

Activity

1 Read the examples of investigative journalism below. In each case say what kind of organisation is being investigated and what they are accused of doing.

2 Look through a copy of a daily or a Sunday newspaper to find examples of investigative journalism. How can readers know who to believe – the journalists or the people being investigated? Who do you believe in any story you found?

3 What would you expect to happen if a newspaper published a story that is later found to be untrue?

Tobacco Companies Linked to Criminal Organisations in Cigarette Smuggling

A new report by the International Consortium of Investigative Journalists (ICIJ) indicates that tobacco smuggling is increasingly dominated – often with the knowledge and consent of the tobacco companies – by a handful of criminals who in some cases have links to organised crime.

An Invitation to Launder Money

The collaboration between the political, judicial and banking systems in the Principality of Liechtenstein had allowed criminals from around the world to do business there, an investigation by *Der Spiegel* (a German newspaper) found. Outraged by the news magazine's allegations, Liechtenstein sued *Der Spiegel* – the first time a country had sued a publication in German press history. Liechtenstein lost its case.

A Long Ride on the Thunderbolt

Throughout the 1970s and 1980s, Dr Selwyn Leeks administered unmodified electro-convulsive therapy – shock therapy without anaesthetic or muscle relaxants – to children and young people at psychiatric hospitals in Canada, New Zealand and Australia.

The State of the President's Finances: *Can Estrada Explain His Wealth?*

Philippine President Joseph Estrada says his life is an open book. He does not deny the complications of his private life, that he has several mistresses and that he has sired children by them. The President, however, has not exactly been forthright about the financial aspects of his private life and the complex ethical issues, such as conflicts of interest posed by the many and varied business involvements of his various families.

Prisoners of conscience

In some countries there is little or no freedom of the press, and people can be imprisoned for writing articles critical of the government. Amnesty International campaigns against all kinds of abuses of power, including attacks on journalists. It regularly publicises cases of people imprisoned for their beliefs and it thinks that ordinary people can put pressure on governments by writing letters of complaint to the ministers responsible for the oppression of individuals.

Lucien Messan

Journalist, prisoner of conscience, Togo

Lucien Messan is editor of the Togolese newspaper *Le Combat du Peuple* (The Fight of the People). He is an outspoken critic of the government of Togo and was forced to go into hiding when complaints were made about him by the Minister of Communications about an article he had written. When he was caught, he was convicted of defaming the government and imprisoned in Lomé civil prison.

The government of Togo frequently attacks anyone who tries to expose human rights violations committed by the Togolese security forces. In 2000 the government introduced an amendment to the Code de la Presse et de la Communication that limits press freedom. Amnesty International views this as a measure to silence critics, particularly independent journalists. Some have been imprisoned for 'spreading false information'; others have been forced to flee or hide.

Lucien was sentenced on 5 June 2001 to 18 months' imprisonment. He appealed against his sentence and was eventually released on 28 October 2001. On release, Lucien said that the time he had spent in prison had not changed anything and that he would be going back to work. He also denounced the prison conditions, saying, 'We were 1200 prisoners in a 60-square-metre courtyard. If you don't have any money, you die. It was horrible.' The conditions in the prison were so harsh as to amount to cruel, inhuman and degrading treatment.

Imprisonment of journalists continues in Togo. Alphonse Klu, director of *Le Nouvel Echo* (The New Echo), is also being held in Lomé prison. The police are demanding that he reveal his sources for an article in which he reported that a government official is allegedly hiding 'several billion' francs in his basement.

Activity

Read the case of Lucien Messan and find out more about prisoners of conscience from websites such as Amnesty International or Reporters Sans Frontières. Compose a letter about the treatment of one of the prisoners of conscience you have found out about. In the letter give your reasons why you think journalists should be free to write about problems and difficulties in their home country.

Discuss

Do you think that press freedom is important for freedom and democracy? Why or why not? Use the information and ideas from all of the pages in this section.

6.7 Is there too much press freedom?

Some people say that press freedom in the UK has gone too far. For example, newspapers sometimes invade people's privacy by publishing stories about their private lives. The people affected could be politicians, celebrities or ordinary people caught up in a news story.

The newspapers often justify this intrusion by saying that these stories are in the 'public interest'. This means:

- helping detect or uncover crime
- protecting public security or health
- protecting human rights
- preventing individuals or organisations misleading the public.

Discuss

Decide which of the following stories you think are in the 'public interest' and which might be just 'public curiosity'.

A high court judge has been found to be unfaithful to his wife and is visiting prostitutes.

The mother of a celebrity is dying from a terminal illness and the celebrity has visited her in hospital.

A politician has been accused of taking bribes from rich businessmen to get them meetings with government ministers.

A footballer has been seen getting drunk in night-clubs.

A businessman has recently made a lot of money from selling some shares and it is suspected that he had access to information that the shares were about to lose value.

Activity

1. Do you think that the press goes too far on occasions? Should it have its freedom curtailed?
2. There has been much talk of a new 'privacy' law to protect people's personal lives. What do you think would be the advantages and disadvantages of such a law?
3. Working in groups of three, draw up the main points of a new privacy law to restrict the press.
4. Compare your answer to question 3 with that of another group and discuss the difficulties of applying this law in practice.

Discuss

Which of the following statements do you agree with?

A Sometimes newspapers can affect the outcome of a trial because they print information that could influence a jury.

B Newspapers dig into people's private lives and print things that cause a lot of damage.

C Famous people should expect others to be interested in their private lives. It's the price you pay for fame and fortune.

D We need newspapers to find out the truth, otherwise rich and powerful people could get away with wrongdoing.

E The laws of libel in this country are strong enough to protect people. You can always sue.

F The people have a right to know about matters which affect everyone.

G Newspaper journalists hound people to get stories.

H Newspapers tell lies to sell copies. They don't care if what they say is not true.

I A newspaper can print a lie and people remember it. So even if the newspaper prints an apology it may not restore someone's reputation.

The Press Complaints Commission

Public interest is different from public curiosity. When people feel that the press has gone too far, they can complain to the Press Complaints Commission (PCC). It has been set up to keep an eye on the press and to decide when the press has broken the Code of Conduct.

The PCC uses the following headings, as well as a number of others not listed here, to decide about each complaint:

- **Accuracy** – reports should be accurate and an apology must be published later if they are not.
- **Opportunity to reply** – people must be able to reply to inaccuracies.
- **Privacy** – people have a right to privacy and the use of long-lens photography is not allowed.
- **Harassment** – journalists and photographers must not continue to telephone or question after being asked to leave.
- **Intrusion into grief or shock** – enquiries must be sensitive when people are shocked or grieving.
- **Children** – children under the age of sixteen should not be photographed or interviewed on subjects involving their welfare without an adult present. They should not be approached at school. Children involved in sex cases should not be identified.
- **Reporting of crime** – relatives and friends of people convicted should not be identified, especially children.
- **Victims of sexual assault** – victims must not be identified unless there is justification.
- **Misrepresentation** – journalists cannot use trickery (for example pretending to be somebody else) to get a story unless it can be justified as being in the public interest.
- **Discrimination** – journalists must not use a person's race, colour, religion, sex, sexual orientation or disability to describe him/her unless it is directly relevant to the story.
- **Payment for articles** – payment must not be made to witnesses or to convicted criminals for a story.
- **Listening devices** – no listening devices may be used.
- **Hospitals** – journalists or photographers must make themselves known to the authorities before entering non-public areas.
- **Financial journalism** – journalists must not use any information for their personal gain.
- **Confidential sources** – journalists must respect confidential sources.

Activity

The cases opposite are real cases on which the PCC was asked to rule. However the names of the complainants (persons making the complaints) have been withheld.

Your task is to decide whether the complaint should be **upheld** or **rejected**.

Complaint 1

Mr X complained that an article published in the *Sunday Express* headlined 'Isabella, the blonde tipped to be Prince William's wife' contained inaccuracies. This breached Clause 1 (Accuracy) of the Code of Practice.

The article reported that there had been speculation that the daughter of Mr X might be a possible bride for Prince William. It said that 'royal insiders' had said that the girl had formed a 'close bond' with the Prince and that her friends knew that the pair had met over the last year. Mr X objected to the impression given by the article that his daughter and the Prince were in some way romantically connected. He said that they had never met.

The newspaper said that its reporter had been following up an article in *Tatler* magazine which had said that the girl had been 'tipped to be the future Mrs Prince William'. Ms X had also appeared in a piece in the *Mail on Sunday* which had suggested that she was part of Prince William's social circle. The newspaper said that its article had not stated that the girl and Prince William were a pair and only reported the rumours and the published speculation. The girl twice had the opportunity to deny that she had met Prince William when she was approached by the reporter but instead declined to comment.

Complaint 3

A woman complained that an article published in the *Sunday Sport* contained information obtained through misrepresentation. This breached Clause 11 (Misrepresentation) of the Code of Practice.

The woman complained that a reporter had claimed to be a DSS officer undertaking a phone enquiry in order to obtain private information that was later used in an article.

The newspaper denied that any of its journalists had misrepresented themselves during enquiries into the matter. However, the newspaper was unable to provide reporter's notes, transcripts or interview tapes to show how the specific information was otherwise obtained.

Complaint 2

A famous children's author complained that long-range photographs had been taken of her, her partner and her eight-year-old daughter on a private beach. The author said that she had been trying to protect her daughter's identity and privacy. This breached Clause 3 (the Privacy Clause) of the Code of Practice.

The editor had apologised to the complainant but the editor said that the beach in question was a public one, and that she had wanted to include a 'family shot' as it was in keeping with the accompanying article.

Complaint 4

Ms W (a famous TV personality) complained that an article published in the *Sunday Mail* headlined 'TV star Carol's grief over mum' was an intrusion into her grief. This breached Clause 5 (Intrusion into grief or shock) of the Code of Practice.

The article on the front page and two inside pages reported the funeral of Ms W's mother and was accompanied by pictures taken outside the crematorium. The complainant's solicitors said that the piece was an unjustified intrusion into Ms W's grief, made worse by the front page coverage. Photographers at the church had earlier been asked to leave but the mourners had not seen the photographers at the crematorium who were using long-lens photography.

The newspaper said that the funeral had been announced publicly in a newspaper and that it was not uncommon for newspapers to report on the funerals of prominent individuals and their families. The paper's own photographer left when asked to do so and did not take any photographs. It was a freelance photographer who subsequently offered the photographs that were published. There would have been no sense of intrusion at the time as the presence of the photographer had not been detected.

6.8 Can you trust the internet?

The internet is a new and very different kind of mass medium. All other forms of media involve the selection, editing or even censoring of information by people whose job it is to communicate ideas – writers, journalists, photographers, editors, producers, directors.

The internet provides instant access to a vast amount of information from a great variety of sources, which would have taken months of research in the past.

But this means that anyone can post anything on the internet, and that is what happens. It is possible to find pornography, racism, incitement to violence, instructions on how to make a bomb, information about where to get drugs, advice on cheating in exams and plagiarism of other people's work. There are also hoaxes and misinformation, deliberately intended to start false rumours and deceive people about the truth.

Some people say that the internet is the first really open and democratic source of information. Others think it is dangerous and should be subject to government control.

Activity

1 Which of the two points of view, below, do you hold? Or maybe your view is somewhere in the middle?
2 Work in pairs. Prepare a presentation lasting three minutes giving your view of the internet. You could even use the internet in researching your case.
3 Conduct a brief survey in your class to find out who uses the internet, why they use it, and for how long each week.

Viewpoint 1
The internet is dangerous and allows our children to be corrupted. It is responsible for the rise in sexual perversions and in organisations that want to spread violence (for example violent demonstrations and football hooliganism) and terrorism, providing bomb-making instructions. People can also distort the truth by deliberately placing inaccurate information on the internet. There should be some mechanism for filtering what goes on to the internet and people who post shocking or dangerous material should be prosecuted.

Viewpoint 2
For the first time in history, governments cannot control what their people hear and see. No matter how authoritarian a government is, it cannot stop its people from knowing what others are saying about it. This is true freedom. In the past, those in power tried to stop the printing of books for the same reasons that people now want to censor the internet. Ideas can be dangerous because they encourage people to imagine life being different – even to want to change things themselves. There may be obscene or violent information on the internet, but we need to educate people to be able to make judgements about what they read and see. Life is full of bad things, but we cannot censor them and pretend that they don't exist.

Discuss

A device exists for parents to censor the internet for their children. If you had children between nine and fifteen, which of the following would you censor: violent rap, pornography, chat rooms? What else would you not allow them to see?

Internet hoaxes

You have to be very careful about believing information on the internet. Sometimes information is inaccurate because it has not been properly checked. But more and more people are deliberately posting hoaxes, and it is not always obvious that a site is a hoax.

For example, a very elaborate site was launched back in November 1998. It claimed to display artefacts that were found in underground caves beneath the New Mexico desert by the Advanced Contact Intelligence Organisation (ACIO), a secret branch of the US government's National Security Agency. These artefacts were apparently left there by an alien race known as the WingMakers. It is not clear what the aim of the hoax was.

Some hoaxes are not quite so harmless. They prey on people's emotions and fears. After the terrorist attack in September 2001, when hijacked planes were flown into the Twin Towers of the World Trade Centre in New York, many false rumours began to appear on the internet, including names of people who were said to have died, but had not.

For example, the photo here began circulating through e-mail a few days after the events of 11 September 2001. An accompanying message explained that it came from a camera found in the rubble of the World Trade Centre. It was claimed that the photo had been taken just seconds before disaster struck.

The image received attention from both national and international media because of the horror of the event and because of the seeming ignorance of the man in the picture about what is going to happen.

However, the picture is a hoax. The man is wearing heavy clothing on what was a warm day. Also, the view indicates that he is standing on the deck of the second tower to be attacked. The first tower would therefore have been burning fiercely while he happily posed for this snapshot. The hoaxer has since come forward with proof of the original photo taken months before the terrorist attack. He has been trying to do business deals following his fame.

Discuss

1. For what reasons do you think people would place hoaxes on the internet?
2. What might have been the impact of the photo on someone who had lost a relative in the Twin Towers attack?
3. How can you decide whether or not things you see on the internet are true?
4. Why is it important to be able to verify information (test if it is accurate)?

How much should you know?

In the past in Britain it was difficult to get information held about yourself and about events taking place in government departments. This is changing and already people are able to find out about their personal records. By 2005 the **Freedom of Information Act** will allow people to find out more about the workings of government departments and local authorities. This should help our society be more democratic and allow people to be more involved in the government decisions that affect their lives.

Is there a case for controlling what we are allowed to know?

There is often tension between what the government and other organisations think the public should know, and what the media think the public have a right to know. Some people argue that it is not always a good idea for the media to publish information that the government, for varying reasons, wants to withhold. Look at these three examples.

In 2000, Sarah Payne, aged 8, was murdered by a known sex offender. The *News of the World* decided to publish the names of alleged paedophiles. As a result vigilante groups attacked and forced people out of their homes. They did not always target the right people and as a result innocent members of the public suffered. The *News of the World* eventually stopped its campaign.

In 2002 and 2003, fear of terrorism led the police, Special Branch and the secret services to mount operations to attempt to prevent acts of terrorism at airports and other public places and to arrest people suspected of plotting these acts. The media were not allowed to publish details about these operations because it was thought it would threaten security and possibly aid the terrorists.

In times of war, such as the Falklands war in 1982 and the Gulf War in 1991, the media were strictly controlled because it was thought that information, particularly bad news, could damage the morale of British troops and lessen public support for war.

Activity

Do you agree or disagree with the following statements?

- I should be able to read my school and medical records
- I should be allowed to see other people's personal records
- I should be allowed to see the papers and read the record of discussions of local and national government departments.

Give your reasons for agreeing or disagreeing.

Discuss

1 In the three examples here, do you think the media should tell people:
   - where paedophiles or other types of offenders live
   - more about the methods used to prevent terrorism
   - the details of events in a war?
2 Do you think government departments will disclose everything they do as a result of the new Freedom of Information Act? What sorts of things might they still keep secret?
3 What sorts of information do you think the public should definitely not have access to?

section 7

Living in a global community

Key words

- fair trade
- inequality
- interdependence
- sustainable development
- world debt

We are connected to the rest of thc world in many different ways. We depend on other countries. We are affected by them and can affect them. In this section you will think about these links and what it might mean to be a 'citizen of the world'.

You will learn about:

- global problems and globalisation
- international trade and 'fair trade'
- the effects of poverty
- charities and aid
- world debt
- health and sanitation
- sustainable development
- the work of cross-national organisations.

You will use the following skills:

- researching current global issues, including research from ICT-based sources
- expressing and justifying opinions on global issues
- imagining other people's experiences and explaining views that are not your own
- listening to other people's opinions
- contributing to class discussion.

7.1 A divided world

In some parts of the world people are starving.

Bowl of maize
Calories: 490
Protein: 11.60 g
Fat: 2.49 g
Fibre: 10.00g
Ingredients: maize and water.
Average daily adult intake of calories in South Africa: 490
(2 100 recommended)

In the USA, overweight people are suing fast food chains for making them fat.

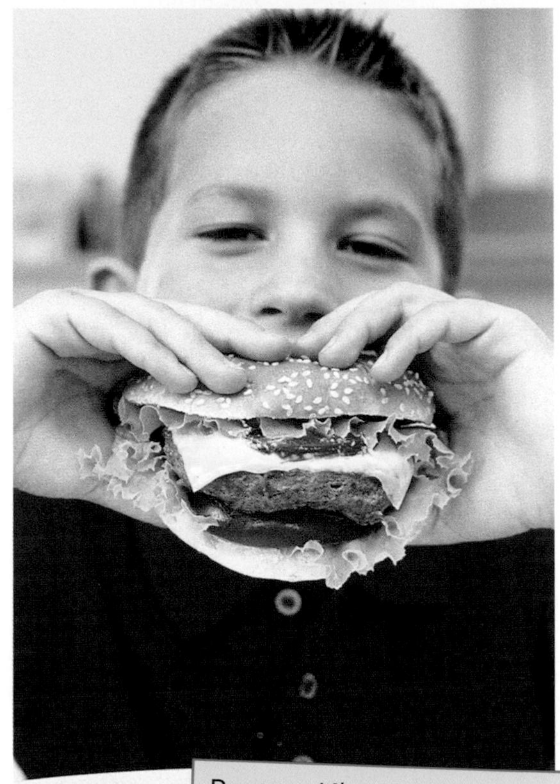

Burger King Whopper
Calories: 646
Protein: 30.60 g
Fat: 37.90 g
Fibre: 3.60 g
Average daily adult intake of calories in the USA: 2 455
(2 400 in the UK)

Poor/rich factfile . . .

- Of the world's 6 billion people around 2.8 billion live on less than $2 a day and 1.2 billion on less than $1 a day.
- The world's richest country, Switzerland, has an income per head of its population 80 times higher than the poorest region, south Asia.
- Each person in the north consumes, on average, ten times more petrol, gas and coal than a person in the south.
- Eight out of every 100 infants in the south do not live to see their fifth birthday.
- Nine out of every 100 boys and 14 of every 100 girls who reach school age in the south do not attend school.

Activity

1 a) What is the difference between the daily calorie intake of an adult in South Africa and in the USA?

b) The bowl of maize and the burger are quite similar in calories. What proportion of a person's daily intake in each country do they represent?

2 What is your opinion of the people who are suing the fast food companies?

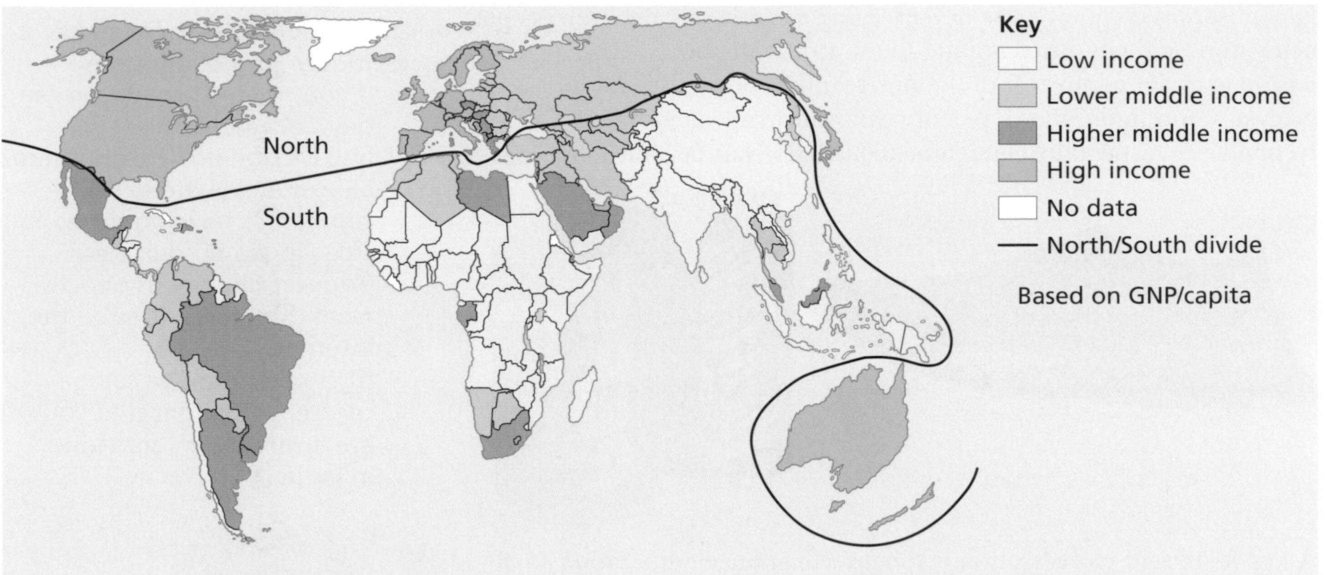

Some countries are much richer and more economically developed than others. One-fifth of the world's population owns 83% of the world's wealth, and almost all of this wealth is concentrated in the richer countries. In the poorer countries, there are huge numbers of people living in poverty. Different names are used to describe the richer and poorer countries:

Poor	Rich
Developing or Underdeveloped	Developed
Third World or Majority World	First World
South	North
Less Economically Developed Country (LEDC)	More Economically Developed Country (MEDC)

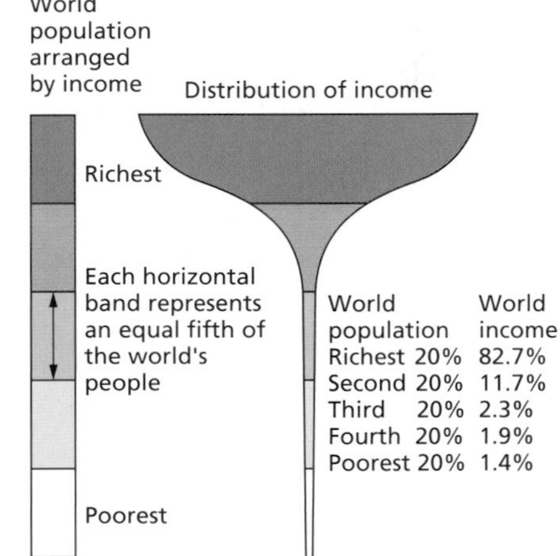

The 'champagne glass' shows how world income is distributed with a fifth of the population receiving nearly 83% of the world's wealth.

3 Draw a different diagram to represent the gap between the wealth of the richest and poorest countries.

4 The gap between richer and poorer countries has been growing rather than decreasing over the last few decades. What reasons can you suggest for this?

5 Which of these statements do you agree with?

a) It is just the way of the world. Some people are richer than others. It will always be like this. There's not much we can do.

b) It's not fair that some people should suffer in abject poverty when others have so much. The people in richer countries should be prepared to give up some of their wealth and change their lifestyle so that poorer countries can be better off.

At the end of this section you can see if you've changed your mind.

7.2 What is globalisation?

Globalisation is the process of increasing connections between people, companies and countries around the world. Trade between countries has gone on for centuries: in the nineteenth century, Britain was at the heart of world trade. But in recent years, due to advances in new technologies, especially communications, trade has become much easier.

How you might come across evidence of globalisation

- If you travel abroad, you can buy Coca-Cola, Nike shoes and McDonald's hamburgers almost everywhere. Big companies have branches in cities in many countries.
- You can buy goods directly from other countries on the internet.
- If you telephone a call centre, you might find you are answered by someone in India.

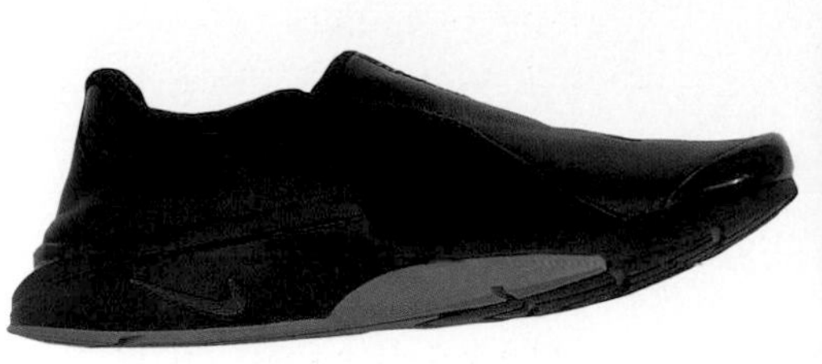

A key feature of globalisation is the growth of huge corporations that dominate world markets. Rapid developments in Information Technology (IT) have enabled these companies to operate across the world much more easily. The emergence of global brands such as Nike and McDonald's has led to a global culture among young people – they all recognise the same brands and slogans. You probably think that is a good thing, but there are some disadvantages.

Multinational companies
The combined income of four top US companies – General Motors, Wal-Mart, Exxon Mobil and Daimlar Chrysler – is greater than the combined national income of the world's 48 poorest countries. Of the world's top 100 economic players, 49 are countries and 51 are multinational companies. These companies have branches and agents in most of the countries across the world. They are so wealthy and powerful that they can persuade small countries to give them favourable conditions in which to operate.

The big international companies make large profits by keeping their costs low. They do this by manufacturing their goods where labour is cheapest. So they might close factories in one country, such as the UK, to go to countries in the developing world, for example the Philippines, where labour is much cheaper. They are so powerful that they can:

- pay low wages because workers often can't find jobs elsewhere
- refuse to deal with trade unions, so workers may work long hours in poor conditions
- force down the price of raw materials because their suppliers don't want to lose their custom
- cause damage to the environment.

Some people argue that these huge companies make big profits by exploiting workers, destroying local businesses in the developing world and by damaging the environment. These concerns have led to anti-globalisation protests at the meetings of world leaders.

Activity

1 Name ten of the world's most famous brands. Use the logos on the flag on page 188 to help you.
2 Can you think of examples of globalisation that you might come into contact with?
3 Discuss in pairs what you think are the disadvantages of large and powerful companies operating all over the world.
4 What are your views on the anti-globalisation protests that have taken place in some cities? Do you think they have an impact or is globalisation unstoppable?

Clothing

The garment (clothing) industry provides a good example of globalisation. More than half of the £23 billion worth of clothes sold in Britain every year is imported. A large proportion comes from Asia, and China is the largest exporter. Cut-throat competition between companies has created a 'race to the bottom'. The countries that win pay the lowest wages, have the longest hours and the worst treatment of their workers. The British rag trade is among the most competitive and shop prices have risen little in the past ten years. This pressure on price has forced British retailers to look for cheaper suppliers.

Do you wear blue jeans?

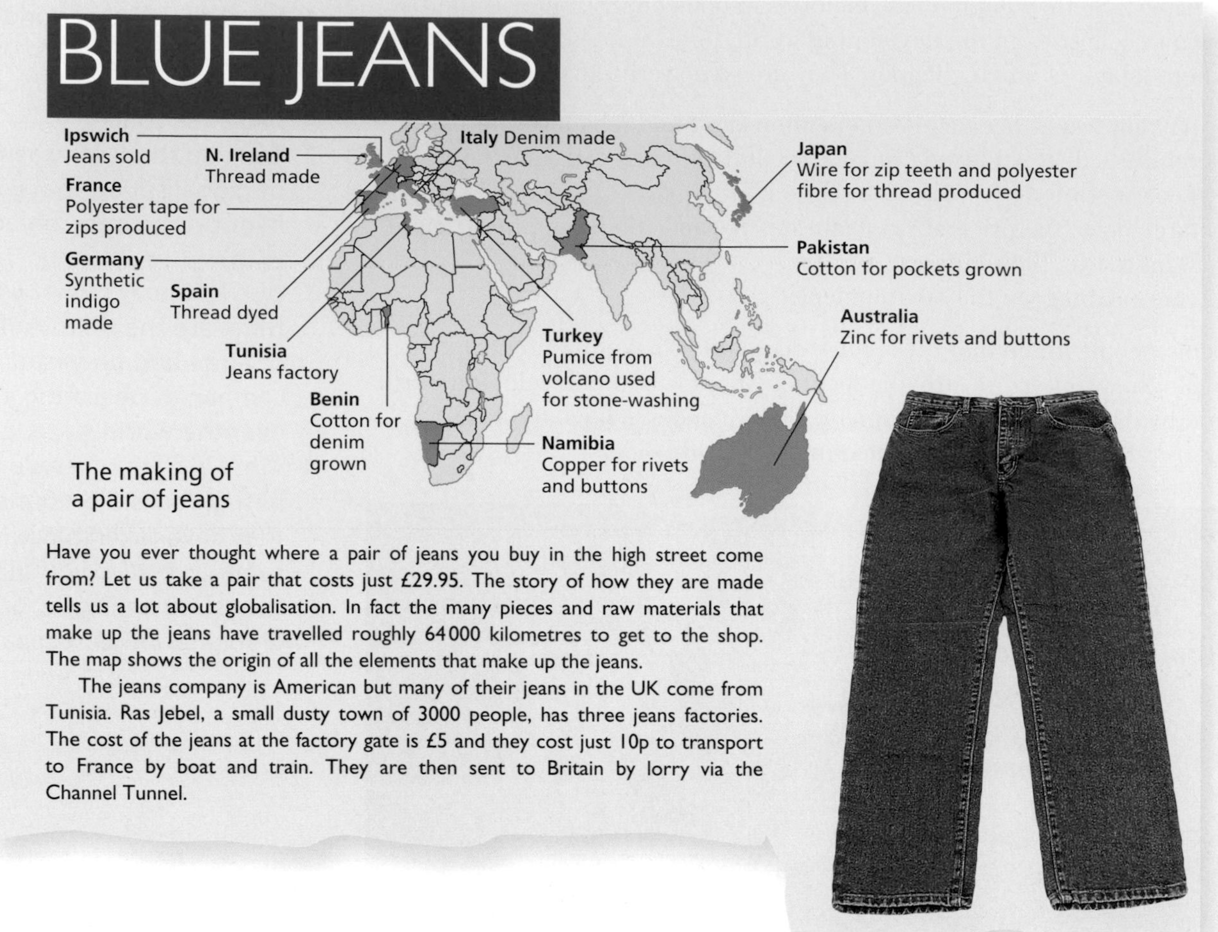

Have you ever thought where a pair of jeans you buy in the high street come from? Let us take a pair that costs just £29.95. The story of how they are made tells us a lot about globalisation. In fact the many pieces and raw materials that make up the jeans have travelled roughly 64 000 kilometres to get to the shop. The map shows the origin of all the elements that make up the jeans.

The jeans company is American but many of their jeans in the UK come from Tunisia. Ras Jebel, a small dusty town of 3000 people, has three jeans factories. The cost of the jeans at the factory gate is £5 and they cost just 10p to transport to France by boat and train. They are then sent to Britain by lorry via the Channel Tunnel.

Activity

1 Read the accounts on page 191 of picking cotton in Benin and making jeans in Tunisia. What is the impact of making jeans on: **a)** people and **b)** the environment?

2 Who said what? Below is a list of people involved in the making and selling of the jeans. Alongside is a list of questions. Match the people to the questions.

People

a) Benin cotton farmer
b) Benin child labourer
c) Ras Jebel resident
d) Tunisian trade unionist
e) Tunisian child
f) Jeans company finance manager
g) Jeans company shareholder
h) British customer

Questions

1 Why isn't mummy home?
2 Why can't you pay me more for my cotton?
3 Why am I sick?
4 Can you increase the bonus?
5 Why are all the fish dead in the stream?
6 Why can't I go to school like the other kids?
7 Why can't a greater share of the price of the jeans go to the people who make them?
8 Why do the jeans cost me £30 when they cost only £5 to make?
9 How can we reduce the costs of making the jeans?
10 How can we increase profits and dividends?
11 Why don't we move production to the Far East where labour costs are lower?

Tunisian jeans factory

In the Ras Jebel factory 500 trained women machinists take home 220 dinars a month – about £110, or 58p per hour. This is above the legal minimum wage of 47p per hour. If they meet their monthly targets, they can make another 30 dinars (£15) per month. Eight production lines of around 60 people each produce 2000 garments a day. They work from 7.15 a.m. until noon, 1 p.m. until 5.45 p.m., with an hour for lunch, and at most two 15-minute toilet breaks. There are no safety guards on the machines and people work fast to try to make the bonus. Most of the factory's 900 workers are members of the trade union, The Federation of Textile Workers. Stonewashing the denim material in huge washers to make it soft takes out some of the indigo dye. In itself this is not harmful, but it cuts out the light in local streams and kills plants and fish.

Benin cotton plantation

The cotton used in the factory is woven in Milan, but it comes from Benin. Benin is one of several West African countries that depends on cotton as a cash crop. Nestor Zinkponon farms three hectares of land in the village of Saklo Agoume in central Benin. At the busiest times of the season 48 people work the fields for about 60p per day. Between the cotton crops are coconut and orange trees, and plots of groundnuts and cassava. The pesticide endosulfin is used to protect the cotton, but also affects the other plants. Last year in Benin 100 people died from endosulfin poisoning. Last year early rains blew away Nestor's fertiliser so he made only £15 profit from his one and a half tonnes of cotton. The only way to make money is to have lots of family members working for free. Consequently Benin has a high drop-out rate from school as the children are needed in the fields.

The Ethical Trade Initiative (ETI) aims to improve conditions for people working in factories supplying goods to western multinational companies.

The ETI Code

1. Workers should work of their own free will; no prison or forced labour should be used.
2. Workers should have freedom of association and to bargain over pay with their employers.
3. Working conditions should be safe and hygienic.
4. Child labour should not be used.
5. Living wages should be paid; enough to meet basic needs and to provide some extra income.
6. Working hours should not be excessive with at least one day off every seven days. Overtime should be voluntary and should not exceed twelve hours a week.
7. There should be no discrimination against women or minorities.
8. Work should be regular not casual.
9. There should be no inhumane or harsh treatment.
10. The code should be monitored by independent inspectors.

Activity

Read the case studies again, and look at the ETI Code.

1. In what ways do you think both the factory and the plantation are in breach of the Ethical Trade Initiative?
2. If you were an independent inspector what would you say to the jeans company, on page 190, to bring their practices into line with the Code of Practice?

Can globalisation be beneficial?

Some aspects of globalisation, such as multinational companies, cheap air travel, global tourism, cheaply manufactured goods, and the sourcing of goods from all over the world, are probably here to stay. And it's not all bad news, as you can see below. People in many countries would like to take advantage of what globalisation offers. This includes people in poorer countries who also want cheaper and more varied consumer goods, although not at the expense of their health, well being and culture. The big question is: how can we make sure that everyone benefits from global interdependence?

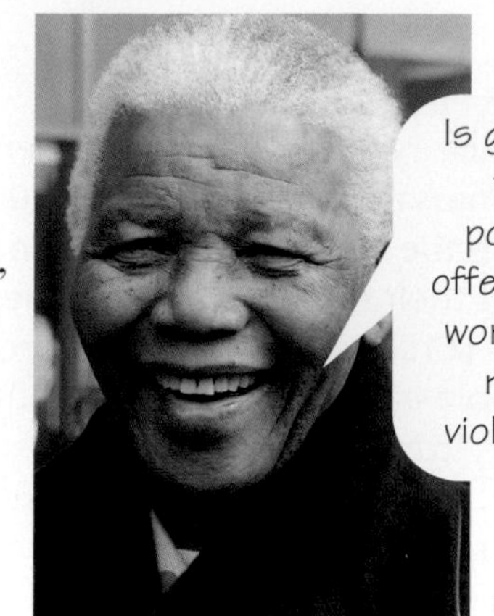

Is globalisation only to benefit the powerful? Does it offer nothing to men, women and children ravaged by the violence of poverty?

Nelson Mandela

Advantages of globalisation

- The increase in world trade has allowed some poorer countries to grow and develop.
- Many poorer countries welcome in international companies wanting to build factories and offices. They bring money into the country, employ lots of people and stimulate the economy by building firms, places to stay, restaurants.
- Not all international companies act badly. Some, like Superdrug and Cadbury Schweppes, follow the Ethical Trade Initiative shown on page 191. Some, like British Airways and Marks and Spencer, have their own code of ethics and consider the impact of their business on the local community. Others, like Bodyshop, set up schools and training facilities. Many are concerned about the environment and pay for projects to protect it.
- The prices of goods for consumers are cheaper because they are produced more cheaply.
- Consumers have a wide choice because they can buy goods from a variety of sources.

BRITISH AIRWAYS

We will:

- Aim to uphold and support human rights wherever we operate
- Trade and compete fairly, working in partnership with our suppliers and business partners to improve social, ethical, environmental and economic performance
- Not tolerate bribery or corruption
- Consider and respect the environment
- Seek opportunities for positive impact on society and the environment, promoting sustainable development
- Work with local communities to develop skills and increase employment through education, training and shared knowledge
- Respect local cultural and religious needs.

Extracts from the British Airways Code of Conduct

Activity

Find some more examples of companies' ethical policies on the internet. In groups make presentations about different policies to the whole class. You could write to some of the companies and ask for more information, or invite a local store manager to the class to explain how the policies work in practice.

Fair trade

Another way of making globalisation less damaging is to set up trading schemes like Fairtrade. In the global free trade market, big companies have forced down the prices paid to small producers for food products such as coffee beans and bananas. As a result farmers and their families cannot afford decent housing, essential medicines or education.

Guarantees a better deal for Third World producers

Fair trade means paying farmers in the developing world a fair price for what they produce so that they can have more control over their lives, and improve their standard of living.

The Fairtrade Foundation awards a Fairtrade Mark to products that meet the following criteria:

1. **The price paid for the product covers the cost of production**
2. **Workers on plantations have decent wages, housing, and health and safety standards**
3. **No child labour or forced labour is allowed**
4. **A percentage of the money they earn is used by the producers to improve their living and working conditions**
5. **Producers are treating the environment in a sustainable way**
6. **Small-scale farmers, and workers on plantations, can join organisations that will help and support them, such as co-operatives or trade unions**
7. **Contracts make sure there is long-term planning for sustainable development**
8. **Advanced payment is given so that smaller producers won't fall into debt.**

Discuss

Do you think that ethical policies will be enough to overcome the problems of globalisation for poorer countries? What else might need to be done by governments and international organisations like the United Nations and the European Union?

Activity

1. Do you think consumers in richer countries should be willing to pay more for fair trade goods if they know the producers are getting a fairer price?
2. Would you or your family buy fair trade products?
3. Draw up a five-point charter which would make globalisation work for poorer countries rather than against them.

Global concerns

Global concerns

The world is becoming increasingly interdependent. What happens in one part of the world affects people in other parts. The countries of the world have to act together to tackle the global concerns shown on this page because it is in everyone's interests. Concerns like global warming, pollution and the use of resources can only be tackled by countries working together. The richer countries need to help poorer countries not only because it is the right thing to do but also because a fairer world would make it a less dangerous place.

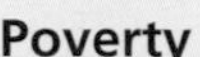

Poverty

More than 1000 million people still live in poverty, a tenth of them in the industrialised world. One in four of the world's people still live in severe poverty. This means that millions of people do not have adequate housing or enough food to eat. At the United Nations Millennium Summit in 2000, world leaders set themselves the target of halving global poverty by 2015, but they are already falling behind.

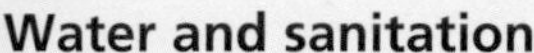

Water and sanitation

Some 1.2 billion people have no access to clean water. Of the 4400 million people in the developing world, nearly 60% lack basic sanitation. This breeds disease and illness. Up to 3 million people die each year of easily preventable waterborne diseases. In many areas of the world there is a looming water shortage.

Health

HIV/AIDS, tuberculosis (TB) and malaria cause more than 5 million deaths and 300 million illnesses every year. Around 40 million people are infected with AIDS, 25 million of them in sub-Saharan Africa. In South Africa 5 million people, 20% of the adult population, have AIDS.

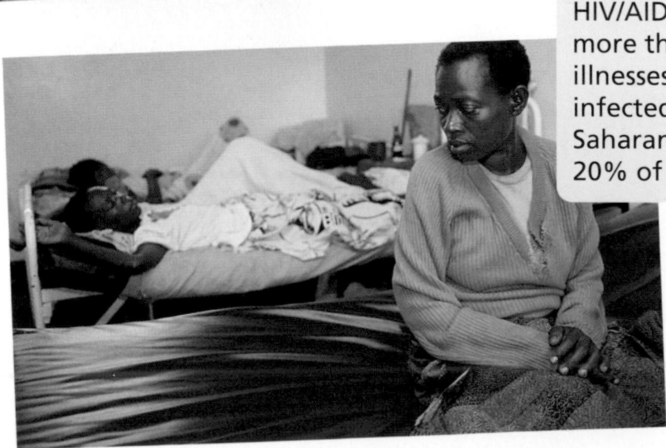

Trade
World trade is heavily weighted in favour of the richer western nations who control it. The producers of commodities like coffee and cotton get very little for their products. The poorest countries, where 40% of the world's population live, produce just 3% of the world's exports. When poorer countries export to the west they face tariffs four times higher than western countries impose on each other.

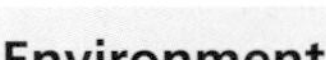

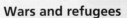

Environment
Economic activity and development is using up the world's resources and polluting the environment. The greenhouse gases generated by the use of fossil fuels appear to be creating a process of global warming. This could lead to melting ice-caps, rising sea levels and desertification, with disastrous effects on people and animals. Development and over-use of resources, causing deforestation, is also destroying habitats and threatening biodiversity (the range of species that live on the Earth). Development needs to take place in a sustainable way so that resources will be available for future generations and the planet Earth is a fit place to live on.

Wars and refugees
Since 1945 there have been over 200 wars, many of them civil wars. These have caused suffering, hardship and poverty as well as a huge number of deaths. The estimate of the number of refugees in the world, largely the result of conflict, is put at 22 million.

Activity

As you work through this section:

a) write five key points about the following topics: globalisation and trade, poverty, health, sustainable development and refugees. You should be able to write your key points on globalisation and trade now.

b) choose one photograph that illustrates a key point in each topic and explain what it shows and why you chose it.

7.3 A poor world?

The effects of poverty

At the beginning of this section, on page 186, you were given some data on poverty in different parts of the world. The pictures below show what this means for people in their everyday lives.

Activity

1 Make a list of all the reasons why some countries are poor.
2 Write a short newspaper article describing the effects of poverty, as shown in the pictures. Select one of the pictures to illustrate your article. You could research more information about poverty throughout the world on the internet.

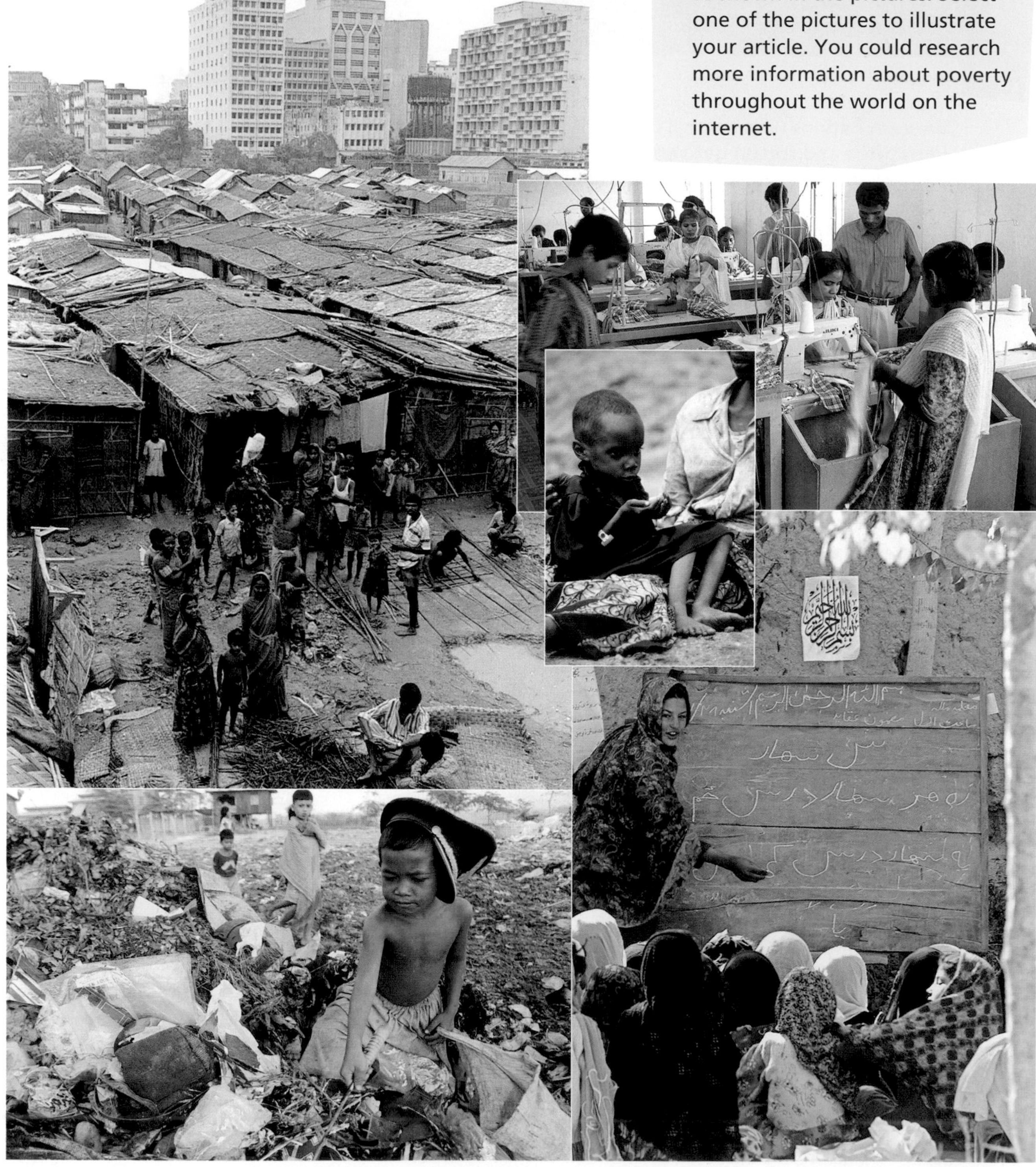

Why are some countries poor?

History and economic development
Some countries are poor today because in the past, powerful European nations took them over as colonies and exploited their natural resources (for example gold and diamonds). Even though these events happened a long time ago, they can still cause problems today. The countries were slower to develop their own economies and have never caught up with the richer countries. This is because the richer countries control the world market for all sorts of goods. So poorer countries have been at a trading disadvantage.

War
Poverty today is often caused by war. Countries at war spend much of their money on weapons and armies, leaving little for healthcare and education. People are forced from their homes by fighting, so they cannot produce food.

Debt
Countries trying to develop their economies borrow money from the richer countries, and then have to pay interest on the loan. They can end up millions of pounds in debt. Many people in the richer countries now think that the world debt itself is the main cause of poverty in poorer countries.

Natural disasters
Sometimes the situation is worsened by natural disasters such as droughts or earthquakes. People become dependent on help from outside of the country.

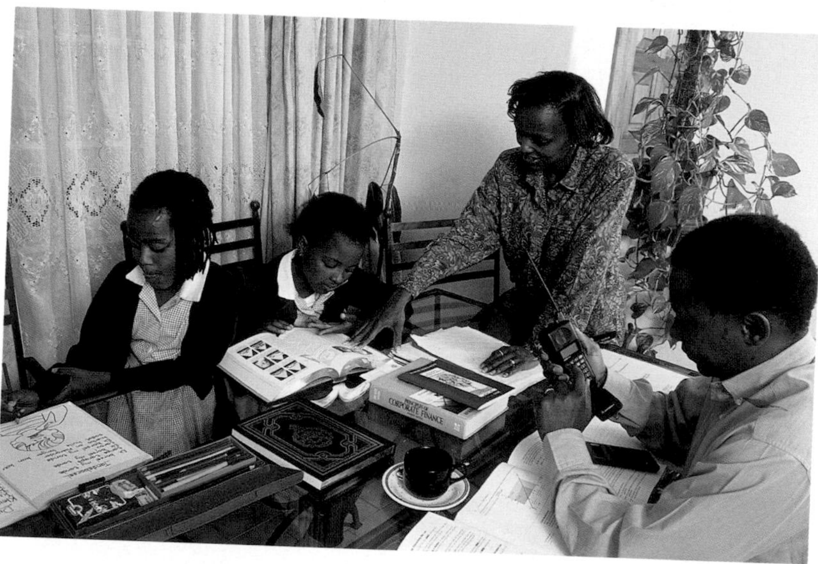

A question of image

There are many reasons for some countries being poorer, or less economically developed, than others. Some of the reasons are historical, some are geographical, and others are political. It is important to understand poverty because it is at the root of many of the world's problems. The world's more economically developed countries, which may have played a part in causing some of this poverty need to play a role in helping to reduce it.

But there is a danger that people who live in rich western countries only ever see very negative images of developing countries, and so form stereotyped impressions of the people who live there. They are often seen as victims, backward or old-fashioned and unable to sort out their own problems. One of the reasons for this is that in the media we only tend to see images like the ones on page 196.

These images are misleading. Not everybody is poor in developing countries. It is often the case that whilst one part of a country may be poor, there is relative prosperity in another part. It is a mixed picture. The people who live in poorer countries work just as hard as those in richer countries – in fact they often work harder, just to survive. They often have similar ambitions for themselves and their children. Education, for example, can bring a better standard of life, and that is why many families in poor countries make sacrifices so that their children can receive a good education. Also people may not be so materially well off but they may have a rich cultural and family life. You have to be careful about making assumptions and judgements.

Discuss

1 Why do you think we usually see negative images – of poverty, hunger, floods – in the media?
2 Why don't we see many images of prosperity and achievement?

What can richer countries do to help?

Governments can help by providing overseas aid and by helping poorer countries with their debt problem (see page 200). But non-governmental organisations (NGOs) like charities play an important part. They raise money so that individual citizens can help people in other countries. Some charities are more political in their approach, seeking to criticise the actions of companies and governments which, they think, are damaging the lives of people in less economically developed countries.

Charities tend to work in three main ways:

1 Helping the victims of natural disasters like floods and earthquakes.
2 Development work – helping to develop the skills, knowledge and technology that will make people independent and in control of their own affairs.
3 Campaigns to persuade people, companies or governments to undertake certain actions, for example buy fair trade goods or cancel debt.

Work charities do

- supplying tents and medicines
- teaching people computer skills
- working with the local community to dig wells
- teaching literacy
- supplying seeds and tools
- providing food and blankets
- building schools and hospitals.

Activity

1 How would you categorise the things mentioned in the 'Work charities do' box – emergency aid or development work?
2 Read the extracts here from three charities. How are they similar and how do they differ? What do you think is the main emphasis of their work, thinking of the three ways of working mentioned above?
3 Assume you win a competition which gives you £1000 to donate to one charity working in the developing world. Which charity would you give it to out of the three described? What are the reasons for your choice?

War on Want

War on Want exists because in the developing world there is a need. The need is for solidarity not charity. For a hand-up not a hand-out. For an end to the root causes of poverty not just its symptoms...

We help people find their own solutions and campaign against the root causes of poverty. In the struggle to end exploitation and oppression War on Want is on the front line, challenging the powerful and helping the dispossessed fight back. We are not afraid to take risks. Our campaigns against baby milk, drug companies and high street banks . . . and our part in fighting apartheid were all highly controversial at the time. We've made it easier for others to be radical.

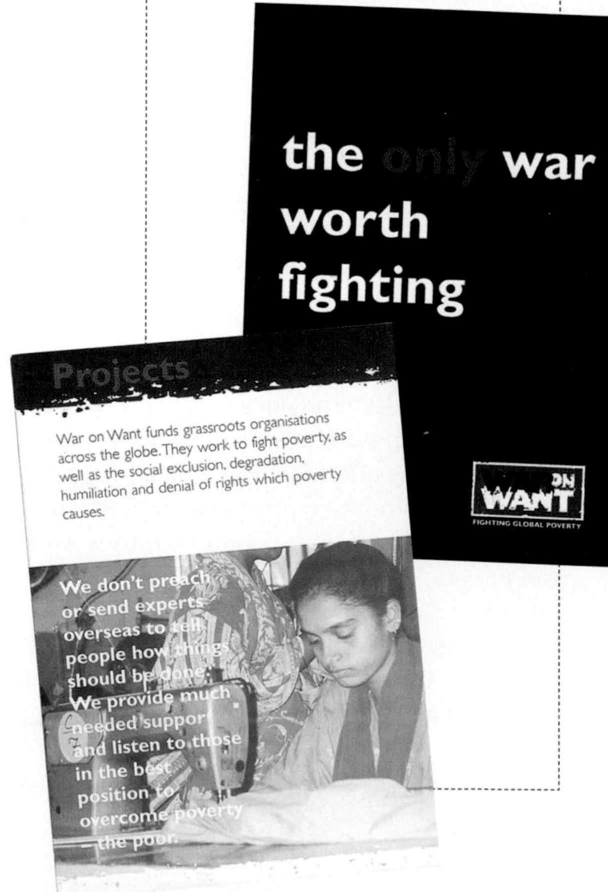

the only war
worth
fighting
ON WANT
FIGHTING GLOBAL POVERTY
Projects
War on Want funds grassroots organisations across the globe. They work to fight poverty, as well as the social exclusion, degradation, humiliation and denial of rights which poverty causes.
We don't preach or send experts overseas to tell people how things should be done. We provide much needed support and listen to those in the best position to overcome poverty – the poor.

"I've never been to school, but I'd like to. My mother can't afford it. She can't buy me the uniform and exercise books. Poverty is a big problem here."
16-YEAR-OLD JABIR FROM TANZANIA
Save the Children is improving the lives of thousands of children like Jabir in around 70 countries across the world through practical projects such as making education more affordable and relevant to their lives. We also tackle the underlying problem – poverty – by lobbying and campaigning for increased international aid and fairer trade rules.
A COMPANY REGISTERED IN LONDON (NO. 178159)
AND LIMITED BY GUARANTEE
REGISTERED CHARITY NO. 213890
17 GROVE LANE, LONDON SE5 8RD, UK
Order code 150220
Save the Children
17 Grove Lane
London SE5 8RD
Telephone (+44) 020 7703 5400
Fax (+44) 020 7703 2278

Save the Children believes all children have a right to a happy, healthy and secure start in life. But that's far from the experience of millions of children around the world. Instead, their childhoods are marred by poverty, ill-health, war, violence and discrimination. And not just in poorer parts of the globe – far too often children in the UK grow up in circumstances that deny their potential.

We start listening to children – learning about their lives, their hopes and views. We support practical projects which involve children and their families in improving their day-to-day lives. We also use our global experience and research to lobby for changes that will benefit all children, including future generations.

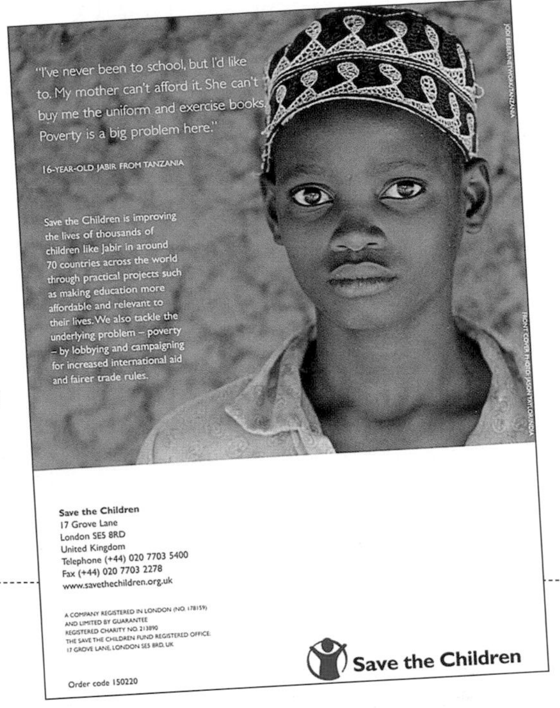

Oxfam

Oxfam's aim is a simple one: to work with others to find lasting solutions to poverty and suffering . . . Our world has enough food and other resources for everyone. If these were shared out more fairly, there would be no need for much of the suffering we see or hear about today.

How do we tackle these issues?

In many different ways, and with help from many different people:

- We have programmes in more than 70 countries. We work with local people to improve their lives. Together we might, for example, train health workers, set up schools or safeguard water supplies.
- We respond to emergencies, providing food and shelter for people driven from their homes by floods, hurricanes and war.
- We speak up on behalf of poor people to governments and powerful organisations. We encourage people to speak up for themselves and change their lives for the better.

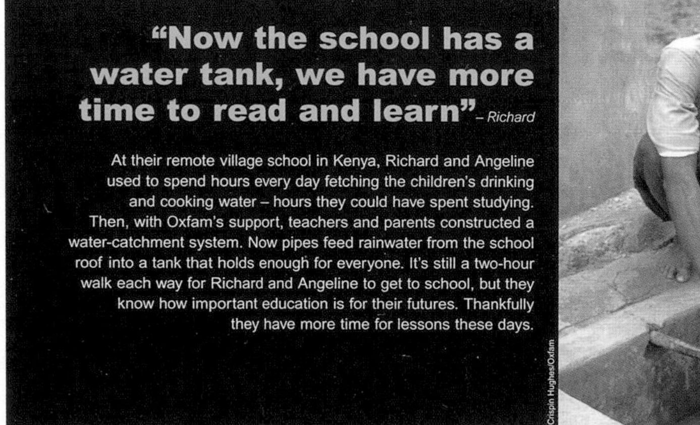

"Now the school has a water tank, we have more time to read and learn" – Richard
At their remote village school in Kenya, Richard and Angeline used to spend hours every day fetching the children's drinking and cooking water – hours they could have spent studying. Then, with Oxfam's support, teachers and parents constructed a water-catchment system. Now pipes feed rainwater from the school roof into a tank that holds enough for everyone. It's still a two-hour walk each way for Richard and Angeline to get to school, but they know how important education is for their futures. Thankfully they have more time for lessons these days.
Crispin Hughes/Oxfam

Should we cancel the debt?

One of the biggest problems facing poor countries is the debt they owe to rich countries. Protests that support the cancellation of the debts have hit the headlines in recent years. The campaigns have been led by the major charities.

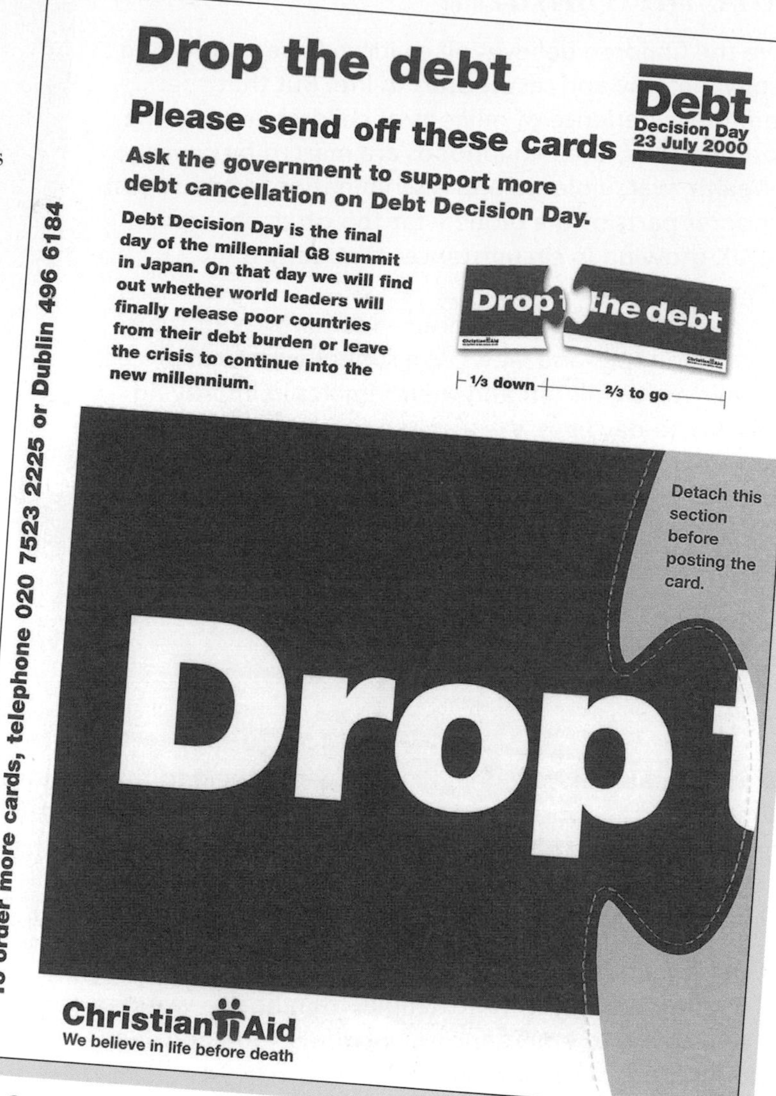

Currently the total debt of the world's 50 poorest nations stands at about $400 billion. The debt is the result of loans made by banks in individual countries and by international bodies – the World Bank and the International Monetary Fund (IMF). Many richer countries are considering whether or not to cancel the debts of very poor countries.

Where did all the debt come from?

In the 1970s the price of oil went up rapidly. The oil-rich countries invested all the money they made in western banks. The banks in turn loaned the money to many newly independent, poorer countries. Interest rates were low and the money was needed for large projects like roads, dams, airports and hospitals. In the 1980s the world economy worsened and interest rates rose so the poor countries had to find more money to pay back to the banks. Sometimes the interest they had to pay back was greater than the amount the country was earning, so they got further and further into debt.

In some countries the money was wasted. It wasn't spent on projects to help the poor or develop the country. Undemocratic governments used the money for themselves and their supporters. It was spent on weapons to fight wars or to build palaces and houses and to buy cars. It was siphoned off by corrupt officials who made themselves rich at the expense of their fellow countrymen.

Debt factfile . . .

- **Every year developing nations pay nine times more in debt repayments than they receive in aid from developed nations.**
- **Sub-Saharan Africa, which includes some of the world's poorest countries, owes around $200 billion, which is four-fifths of its total annual income.**
- **For most poor countries their debt repayments are greater than their spending on education or healthcare. African nations spend four times more on debt than health.**
- **The Jubilee 2000 movement was formed in 1990. It is supported by the Pope and aims for a one-off forgiveness of all debts for the poorest nations.**
- **The World Bank and the IMF often agree to allow countries to pay off their loans over a longer period or to loan more. In return countries often have to cut government spending and open up their market to multinational companies.**

Debt cancellation – yes . . .

- Debt costs lives as poor countries cut back on health and programmes to benefit their poorest people.
- Debt reduces education opportunities – one African country has introduced school fees to raise money.
- Poor countries have to produce 'cash crops' such as coffee that can earn dollars on the world market. This is so they can earn dollars to pay their debt and the coffee is produced instead of food. Poor people cannot afford to buy imported food, which is more expensive than the food that could be grown in their own country.
- Debt punishes the people for the actions of past leaders who were often to blame for the debts.
- Debt is preventing poor countries from investing in education and their future development. While the debt stays, the gap between rich and poor will go on widening.
- Many of the banks were to blame during the 1970s because they made loans on uncertain projects that never made a profit.
- Poor countries can never pay off these debts – they can only hope to pay the interest. Western banks are little better than loan sharks.

Debt cancellation – no . . .

- There are many reasons for problems in the poorer countries. Often they spend huge amounts of money on arms to fight local wars.
- Many poor countries are led by corrupt, undemocratic governments. Debt could be repaid at the same time as investing in schools and hospitals, but the money is being wasted (for example, on palaces).
- Starvation is usually caused by weather conditions or war not debt repayments.
- Cash crops generate valuable foreign currency that can be used to boost the economy. Specialising in products you can sell is the basis of all trade.
- If every government decided that it did not have to honour commitments made by the previous government the world would be in a mess. This would mean that no bank would ever loan money to the poorer countries.
- Poor countries still need money to invest in their infrastructure (roads and railways, etc.) if they are to develop. Cancelling debts would mean that people would not invest in the future.

Activity

In this activity you will take on a role at a meeting called to debate the cancellation of the Republic of Monlia's debt. You should work in a group of six and each person should take on one of the six roles shown opposite.

1 a) Read the scenario below which gives the background to the activity.

b) Study the debt factfile on the previous page which gives some of the facts about world debt.

c) There are also a number of arguments for and against debt cancellation that you may want to use.

d) Make up your mind whether you are for or against cancelling all or some of the debt. Write down your arguments and use them when it is your turn to speak.

2 The First Secretary should chair the meeting and decide who speaks first. Each person should be allowed a couple of minutes to voice their opinions. The options are:

- cancel all the debt
- cancel a proportion of the debt
- postpone interest payments for an agreed period
- leave things as they are.

There might also be some conditions that you would want Monlia to meet if all or part of the debt were cancelled.

The First Secretary should encourage discussion and the group should try to agree on which option to take.

Scenario

Monlia is a poor African country, one of the world's 30 poorest countries. Since independence 30 years ago there have been several governments and two civil wars. Debt was built up during the 1970s, when much of the money was borrowed from the London International Bank (LIB) and the World Bank. The current government is democratic but it is struggling with several problems:

- the price of agricultural cash crops is low on world markets – so income is inadequate
- in the elections promises were made to improve the economy and public services
- there is an AIDS epidemic
- 50% of the population are illiterate.

The debt to the LIB is £500 million and the World Bank £2 billion. It is estimated that the annual interest payments are £125 million. The Monlian government wishes to borrow more money from the World Bank to fulfil the election promises. The Bank is insisting that Monlia honours its debt repayments and cuts public spending. There has been some political unrest in Monlia Town, the capital, organised by people who oppose the government.

Roles

HM Treasury – First Secretary

You have called the meeting to discuss how the debts of Monlia could be reduced or cancelled. Your job is to chair the meeting and to try to apply pressure on the LIB and the World Bank. You believe that the richer countries need to behave more responsibly towards the poorer countries if they are to aid their development.

Chief Executive – London International Bank

The debt, and the interest on the debt, is money which the Bank expects to receive. If the loan were cancelled this would mean a massive loss to the Bank and its shareholders. The Bank and other banks would never again loan money to poor countries.

Secretary of State for International Development

You are responsible for the UK's aid programme to developing countries. Your goal is to help Monlia and similar countries to develop and prosper with help from the UK. You genuinely want to help the people but you don't want to antagonise the banks.

Director of World Bank

Your bank is responsible for making loans to many poorer countries. You believe it is important that countries use loans properly. They have to cut wasteful public spending. They have to introduce free trade and allow international companies access to their economies. Cancelling all the debts of poorer countries would undermine the world system.

Jubilee 2000

You represent a group of development organisations that wants the rich countries to cancel all the debts of poorer countries. You think that it is appalling that health services and education are being cut to make interest payments to rich banks. You are also worried about international companies being allowed in. You know that where this has happened in the past, these big companies wipe out locally controlled businesses and get control of the country's resources – for instance timber, minerals, gold and crops like coffee and sugar – and there tends to be an overemphasis on cash crops.

Monlian Minister of Finance

You represent the government of Monlia and are aware that, although the debt is crippling, you will want to borrow more money in future. Cancelling or postponing debt repayments would be popular in the country. This would help stop opposition protests. However, if you let foreign companies in to your economy, they will probably take over your existing companies and dominate your economy. They will provide employment but your country will not benefit from the money each company earns.

Discuss

1. Was the group able to agree? If not, what were the main things that stopped agreement?
2. Has taking part in the role play made you more or less in favour of cancelling the debt of poor countries?
3. What do you think would be the best solution for the UK? Do you think we should persuade other countries to cancel debts?
4. If we cancel debts what should be asked in return?
5. Do you think the British taxpayer should compensate banks that have lost money through cancelled debts?
6. Would you support cancelling the debts of poor countries?

A healthy world?

Switzerland 78.99

UK 77.37

US 76.23

India 63.40

Africa 45.89

Average time that people live

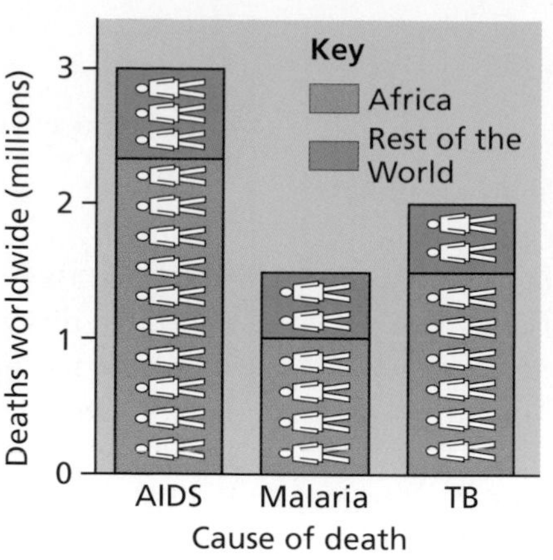

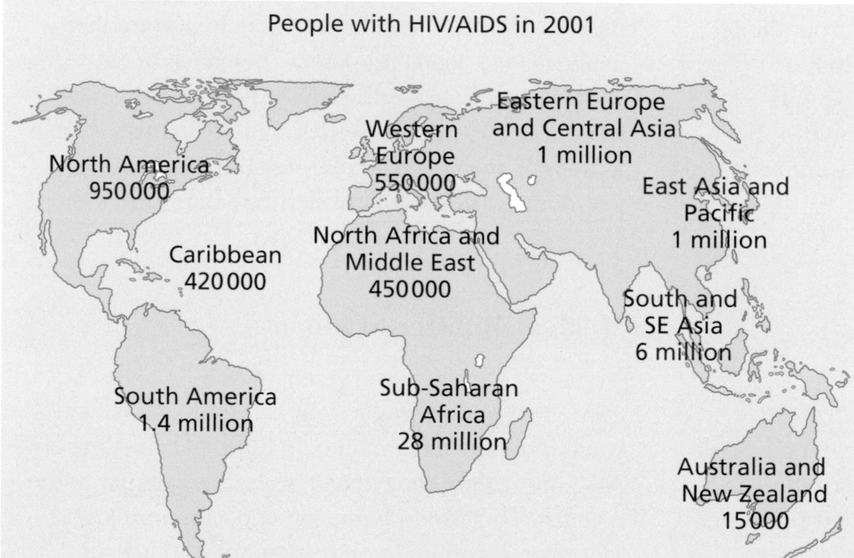

Activity

1 Which part of the world has:
   a) the highest rate of deaths from AIDS, TB and malaria?
   b) the most people infected with HIV/AIDS?
2 How much longer, on average, do people in western countries live than African people?
3 What reasons can you suggest for these huge differences?

Malaria

Malaria is transmitted by the bite of the mosquito. 90% of deaths from malaria occur in sub-Saharan Africa where medicines are scarce and becoming ineffective. However, providing insecticide-impregnated nets to prevent children being bitten during the night could cut deaths by 20%.

George Osiga, 28, who lives in western Kenya, describes the impact of malaria on his village, Nina:
'Everyone has malaria. Recently we have buried ten people from this disease, including my aunt . . . Everyone knows mosquitoes are the danger, but the problem is the people are poor. Even if you tell them about bed-nets, they are thinking about how they will eat . . . I am worried about my wife and my second-born, Marcy. They are always complaining of malaria. I have taken them to hospital, and they have taken different medicines, but still they have headaches . . . and now my youngest boy is also starting . . . For myself, it comes and goes. Last year, I was affected almost all year with malaria, so I could not work well.'

AIDS

Every day there are 15 000 new HIV infections. Of these, 95% are in developing countries. Nelson Mandela has warned: 'AIDS today in Africa is claiming more lives than the sum total of all wars, famines and floods, and the ravages of such deadly diseases as malaria. It is devastating families and communities.' Millions of children have been left orphaned. Families without their breadwinners spiral into poverty and hunger.

The rapid spread of AIDS is connected to poverty. It spreads in a poor environment where sex workers infect young men migrating to cities for work who then pass on the disease. Also, a lack of good nutrition and medical treatment for minor infections means that people with HIV cannot resist and die quickly. HIV forms a deadly partnership with TB, which strikes people with weakened immune systems.

Sibongile Shabane

'I am 37 years old, a single parent of two children. My fiancé died in 1994. On the death certificate it was clearly stated that he died of AIDS. I was tested for AIDS; it was a terrible shock when the doctor told me that I had HIV and there was no cure for it – and I needed to go home and wait for death. I was confused and overwhelmed with shock, scared of death and thinking of my children . . . I cried alone. I never felt so alone in my life . . . no one talked to me.'

When Sibongile went home she was supported by her mother and later became a field worker for an AIDS awareness project in her own community. She received death threats because of her work.

'It was very difficult, because not only my life was in danger, my family too was affected. My mother, who was a church leader, suffered isolation . . . I was not welcomed in my church because I was HIV positive and open about my status. I remember my son telling me how the children isolated him at school. This was very painful for me, but there was never a day when I thought about quitting the work on HIV/AIDS activism . . .'

Sibongile won an award for her work.

'I wish God could give me two more years to do more work, so that I can proudly reflect on my ten years living with HIV. I want my life to be a living testimony that people with HIV/AIDS can make a difference in life . . . and [to be remembered] as someone who lived and worked for the betterment of the people with AIDS and their children.'

Activity

1. Make a list of the ways diseases like AIDS and malaria 'devastate communities' in poor countries. Think of the impact on families, friends, education of children, skilled workers, people to do jobs on land, etc.
2. What do you think are the biggest obstacles to stopping the spread of AIDS and cutting deaths from malaria?

Tackling AIDS

Lack of health education in many developing countries means that many people still do not understand the risk they face or how to protect themselves. Handing out condoms is not a simple answer because some men won't use them with their wives. Education is not always straightforward. But also poor countries can't afford the drugs and medical facilities needed to test for and treat AIDS.

The drugs issue

Anti-retroviral drugs are available that can keep people with HIV alive and able to work and function in society. But the big drug companies charge very high prices for these – up to $10 000 dollars a year. South Africa found it could import cheap copies of the drugs which brought the price down to nearer $450. But the copies were illegal. The drug companies took the South African government to court to try to stop South Africa importing the drugs. There was an international outcry against the drugs companies who finally dropped the case.

The drugs companies

Some of the big drugs companies have bigger turnovers than the gross national incomes of the countries they sell to. For example:

Drug company	Turnover	Country	Gross national income
GlaxoSmithKline	$31.6 billion	Kenya	$10.7 billion
Roche	$15.5 billion	Zimbabwe	$ 6.3 billion

Poor countries like South Africa and Brazil say that it is immoral for the hugely rich and powerful drug companies to deny drugs to desperate people.

UNAIDS

The United Nations set up UNAIDS in 1996 to help governments. It tries to develop awareness of AIDS in ways that get through to people, especially young people who are most likely to become infected. It has:

- worked with MTV, the music channel, aimed at young people
- sponsored a TV soap in Nigeria
- worked with local and church groups in Africa.

A group of African women declared at a recent gathering on HIV in Kampala: 'We are the real experts in our communities about how HIV affects individuals and their families.'

Activity

1 You are an AIDS educator in a developing country. Draw up an outline for a campaign on two fronts.
  a) In the developing country, to make people aware of the risks of AIDS and ways of protecting themselves. You can use TV, radio, clinic or leaflets (see the UNAIDS box for ideas).
  b) In the UK to persuade the government and people (through charities) to provide money for clinics and drugs.

2 Do you think the drugs companies have a legitimate case? Here is what they say…

We spend millions on research and development.

It's unfair that other companies make similar drugs and sell them cheaper because they've learnt from our research.

If this happens a lot, then companies will not be prepared to spend millions to develop drugs, so there will be no progress.

Water

Some 1.2 billion people in developing countries do not have clean drinking water; over twice that number don't have access to proper sanitation. Humans need about 11.5 litres of water per day for healthy living (you use 10 litres of water each time you flush the toilet) but in many countries of the world this is hard to get. The result is that poor people spend a lot of their income on water, women and children spend a large part of their day collecting it and people suffer ill health. Up to 3 million people die each year of water-borne diseases.

Children in particular suffer serious health problems as a result of unclean and scarce water. Dirty water often leads to diarrhoea. This leads to malnourishment and makes them more likely to get infections which may kill them. In developing countries, thousands of children die of diarrhoea, dysentery and dehydration. Lack of water makes it difficult to wash and this can lead to skin diseases such as scabies and eye diseases such as trachoma.

It is women who often take the burden of water collection, walking up to eight kilometres or more in parts of Africa, carrying heavy loads which may cause spinal or pelvic damage. It also takes up a great deal of time, which could be spent on agriculture or other paid employment.

How much does a day's water cost?

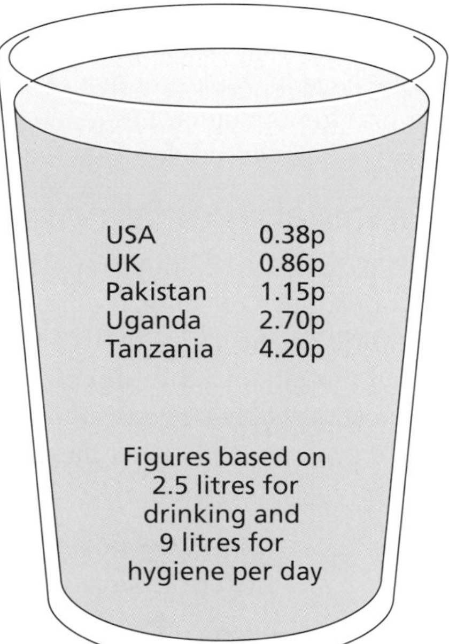

USA 0.38p
UK 0.86p
Pakistan 1.15p
Uganda 2.70p
Tanzania 4.20p
Figures based on 2.5 litres for drinking and 9 litres for hygiene per day

Case study: *Elmas Kassa*

Thirteen-year-old Elmas Kassa lives in Addis Ababa, Ethiopia. Her father is a labourer and her mother a washerwoman.

'I collect water four times a day in a 20-litre clay jar. It's hard work! . . . I've never been to school as I have to help my mother so we can earn enough money. Our house doesn't have a bathroom. I wash myself in the kitchen once a week. When I need the toilet I have to go down to the river in the gully behind my house. We're only supposed to go after dark when people can't see us. If I could alter my life, I would like to go to school and have more clothes.'

At the Johannesburg world conference in 2002, the nations represented committed themselves to halving the number of people without access to clean water and adequate sanitation by 2015.

Activity

1 In pairs, go through one day and list your use of water.
2 What daily jobs in the home would be difficult without lots of water?
3 Use all the information here to draw up a webpage for a charity informing people of the impact of not having clean water in developing countries.

Research

Look at www.wateraid.org for more information about water and how local communities can help solve their own problems.

7.4 A better world for everyone

Ending world debt, reducing inequality, helping countries to help themselves and develop their economies – these are all ways in which people are trying to make the world better for everyone. However, economic development has often had bad effects on the environment.

We have to think, not just of ourselves, but of future generations – our children, grandchildren and great grandchildren. What kind of world will we have left for them to live in?

Sustainable development

In 1987 a United Nations report called 'Our Common Future' stressed the importance of countries developing in a way that did not use up all the world's natural resources or harm the environment. The report called this **sustainable development**, and defined it as 'development that meets people's needs in the present, and maintains the ability of future generations to meet their own needs'.

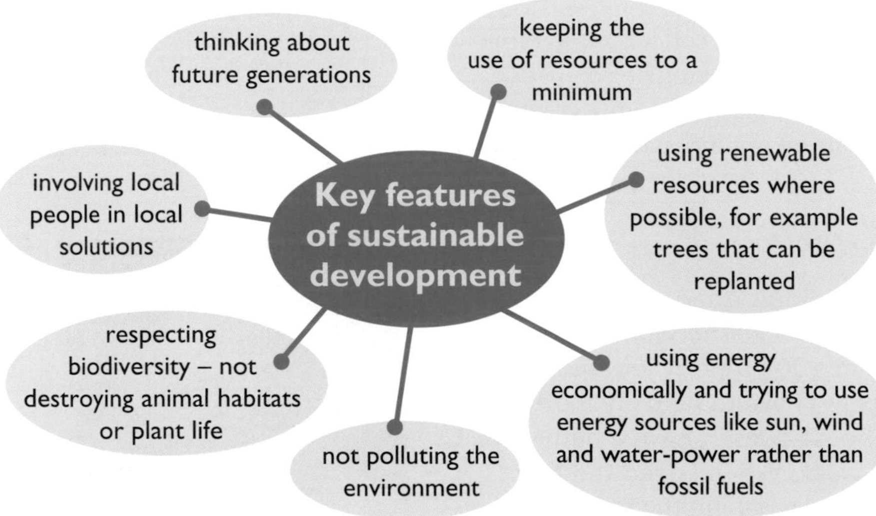

Key features of sustainable development
thinking about future generations
keeping the use of resources to a minimum
using renewable resources where possible, for example trees that can be replanted
using energy economically and trying to use energy sources like sun, wind and water-power rather than fossil fuels
not polluting the environment
respecting biodiversity – not destroying animal habitats or plant life
involving local people in local solutions

All societies want to improve the standard of living of their people. This means that they all want to develop their economy, have better living conditions, earn more money and have better education and health care. Development can affect the environment, however, through things like air pollution, deforestation, energy consumption and the production of waste.

What is the impact of development?

You can examine any proposed development – local or global – by looking at its likely impact on four different things:

- the economy
- the environment
- social factors
- politics.

Development often has economic advantages, such as jobs and profits for the developer, but it also has an impact on the environment and people's way of life. Decisions are made by local politicians but people can have their say if they don't like a planned development.

Activity

An example of development is the building of new houses on open countryside, called 'green-field' sites.

1 Work in pairs. Decide which of the following are arguments for green-field house building and which are against.
2 Choose the three arguments that you most agree with.

A

People like to live in new houses because they are clean, modern and convenient.

B

Many solid, well-built, old houses have been left empty and could be renovated and used.

C

Building new houses usually means loss of open countryside, which people and animals need.

D

Because people all want to live in nice homes, we must build many new houses.

E

Housing development generates jobs and wealth.

F

If land is used for house building, it cannot be used in food production and farming.

G

Houses are needed near to areas where there is work. If there are not enough houses in these areas, more must be built.

H

If houses are not built where they are needed, the prices of houses already there rise and people cannot afford to buy them.

I

Some people own more than one house. If they were not allowed to, there would be more houses to go round.

J

More houses mean more roads and therefore more traffic and pollution.

Activity

1 Analyse the impact of housing development on the countryside or greenbelt near your area by answering the questions written in the chart below. Copy the chart and write in your answers.

2 Discuss as a class the impact that house building might have on the economy, the environment and people's way of life.

3 Discuss who makes decisions in your area and how local people get their views heard.

4 Since we need new homes, how can house building be made more sustainable? Can we go on building new houses on open countryside?

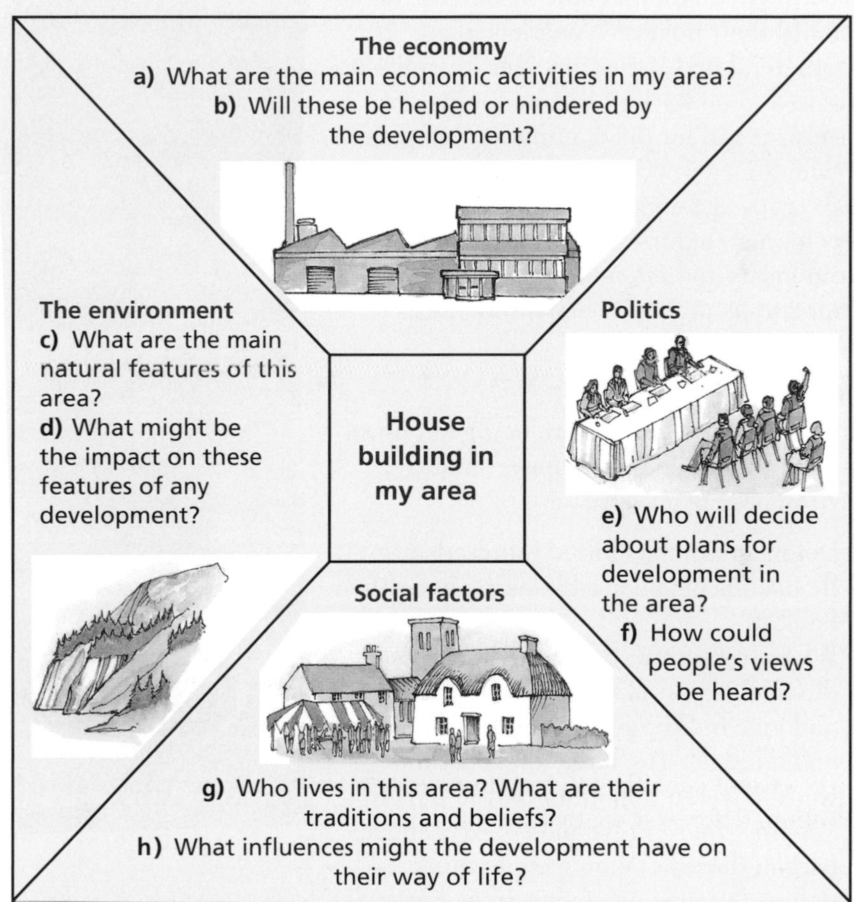

The economy
a) What are the main economic activities in my area?
b) Will these be helped or hindered by the development?
The environment
c) What are the main natural features of this area?
d) What might be the impact on these features of any development?
House building in my area
Politics
e) Who will decide about plans for development in the area?
f) How could people's views be heard?
Social factors
g) Who lives in this area? What are their traditions and beliefs?
h) What influences might the development have on their way of life?

Extra activity

You could use the same chart and questions to discuss the likely impacts on your area of:

- a new road
- an out-of-town development, such as a supermarket
- a new factory
- a leisure complex providing sports facilities.

A sustainable world?

We have looked at an example of local development – house building. But development is not just a local issue. Some kinds of development can cause pollution and waste of natural resources, and this can, eventually, affect everyone in the world. Building of any kind uses resources, one of the most important of which is wood.

Deforestation

Deforestation happens when many trees are cleared from a large area and not replanted. People cut down trees because wood is essential for humans. For some people, wood provides fuel. People also need timber to build their homes. Wood has many commercial and industrial uses as well – it is sold abroad for building materials, for furniture, and for the manufacture of paper.

Sometimes wooded land is cleared to grow cash crops or for cattle ranching. In developing countries, land is needed to build towns and cities. Here are two photographs of forest before and after deforestation.

The Amazon rainforest

Effects of clearing and burning the forest for farming, Brazil

Effects of deforestation

All over the world trees are being cut down and not replanted. The impact on the environment is massive.

- Deforestation has killed hundreds of thousands of species by taking away their habitat.
- When trees grow, they take in carbon dioxide as part of their growth process, and give out oxygen, needed by humans and animals. The large forests of the world have an important part to play in keeping the right balance of oxygen and carbon dioxide. Many people think deforestation is one factor in global warming because there are fewer trees to do this important job. Also, when trees decompose or are burned after they have been cut down, they release carbon dioxide back into the atmosphere.
- Deforestation causes soil erosion because when trees are cut down, their roots can no longer hold soil in place and the hard rain washes away the soil. Soil erosion then causes the silting-up of lakes and rivers. Without soil and water, the land becomes desert, and nothing can be grown.

People who live in forest areas say they have the right to cut down their trees in order to develop their economy, just as people in Europe did hundreds of years ago. But some poorer people suffer from the loss of forests. Their food supplies of nuts, berries and animals disappear. They can no longer collect rubber from the trees or make medicines from woodland plants. The soil erosion prevents them from growing food to eat.

Activity

1 Work in pairs. Draw up a chart with two columns like this:

Reasons for deforestation	Impact of deforestation

2 Write all the reasons in the first column and the impacts in the second column.
3 Discuss what could be done to try to prevent deforestation. Think up solutions to the problem using the following headings: recycling, boycotting, replanting, land management.
4 Read the case study below describing how one small area saved its forest. List all the actions that the people had to take to make the project a success.

Discuss

1 How do our economic activities affect developing countries?
2 How do their economic activities affect us?
3 What can people in this country do to promote a sustainable world?

Case study: *Deforestation*

Keshapur is a village in the Indian state of Orissa. It is close to a big hill – Binjagari Hill. Fifty years ago, Binjagari Hill was covered in woodland and was home to an enormous range of wildlife. The forest provided the local people with almost everything they needed to live – wood for fires, grass and scrub for the animals, mangoes, dates, nuts, bananas, guava and aubergines to eat. People built their homes from wood and used the leaves, berries and roots as natural medicines. They had picnics in the forest and paddled in the streams.

Then a new law was passed by the government, lifting restrictions on the use of the forest. People came from far and near to take the fruit, chop down the trees, and sell the wood to factories. Over the next 30 years, the forest began to vanish. Where the trees had been, there were open spaces. The rains fell straight onto the soil and washed it away. The sun baked the ground hard and food could not be grown. The forest was turning into a desert.

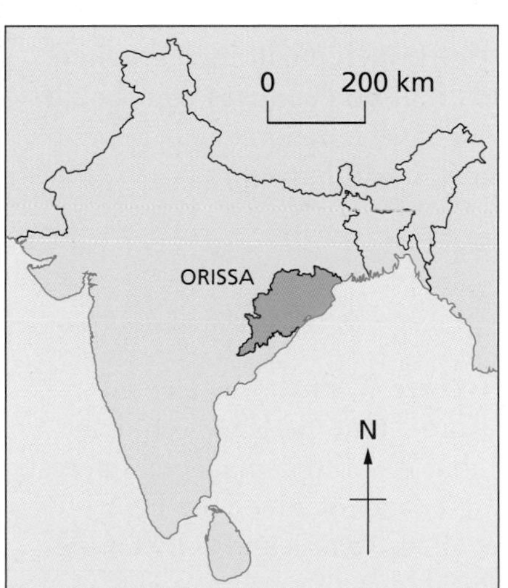

Eventually, people who remembered the forest as it had been, began to talk about replanting the forest and restoring it to its former state. However, by this time, almost everyone kept goats. They needed the milk and the meat that goats provided, and they were relying almost entirely on their goats as a source of food. But goats eat anything, including young green shoots, so it would be impossible to plant trees where goats grazed. Everyone had to be convinced of the need to sell the goats, protect the young trees and allow the forest to grow back. This was very hard and the group of people from Keshapur had to persuade everyone to stick together, share their rice and put up with some hard times.

They gathered seeds and cuttings from the few trees that were left and everyone worked at tending the young trees until they were ready to replant on the hill. They visited other villages around the hill and explained what they were doing, asking for help. Others joined them and, gradually, the forest grew back.

Global warming

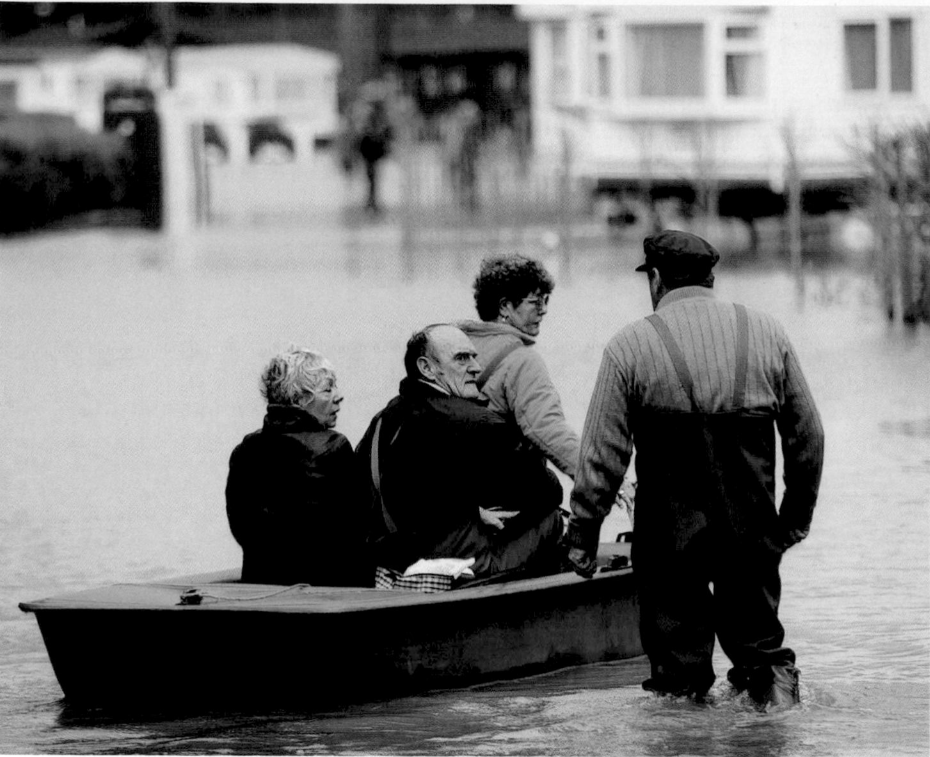

Some people believe that increased flooding in the UK is the result of global warming.

Global warming is a topic you will probably have studied in geography or science. It refers to the concerns of some scientists that the Earth's temperature is gradually rising. It is thought that heat is trapped in the Earth's atmosphere by gases, mainly carbon dioxide. This is called the 'greenhouse effect'. The gases are produced by:

- the burning of fossil fuels (coal, oil, gas)
- the use of man-made chemicals
- deforestation, which prevents carbon dioxide being absorbed.

These scientists believe increases in temperature could dramatically change the world's climate. The polar ice caps will melt, changing the temperature of the sea and raising sea levels. Some areas will become wetter, while some will become drier.

However, other scientists dismiss the theory and say that it is natural for the Earth's temperature to change over time. They say there is not enough evidence to prove that there is a permanent change taking place.

The Kyoto conference on climate change in 1997 proposed that developed countries should be set targets for the reduction of emissions that might lead to global warming. Many developing nations blamed the richer countries for most of the existing environmental damage. They want to be able to develop their countries (which might increase their emissions) and say it is the richer industrialised countries that should cut back. There is still disagreement about what action needs to be taken. If a country is to reduce emissions, it will have to:

- reduce energy use and burn less fossil fuel
- recycle and reuse more waste
- manage natural resources.

In 2001, in the USA, the Republican George W Bush was elected President and very soon afterwards declared that the USA would not stick to the Kyoto agreement. He said that it would damage the interests of American companies and hurt the US economy. Since the USA is responsible for 25% of the world's greenhouse gases and is by far the world's greatest polluter, this was a mortal blow to world attempts to restrain global warming.

Activity

Either on your own or working as a pair read through the questionnaire on page 213. Each part of the questionnaire has three statements. Decide on which statement you agree with – you can choose only one. Keep a note of the letter you choose for each question. When you have completed the questionnaire calculate your score.

Global environment: where do you stand?

Do you:

- always take a strong environmental line
- think that the evidence for global warming is unclear and exaggerated
- think that growth and development in poorer countries is more important than rich countries' worries about the environment?

Questionnaire

1 Global warming

A The greenhouse effect will lead to environmental disaster in this century with ice-caps melting, coastal floods and disaster.

B The world's temperature has always changed over the years – it could just as easily fall as rise in this century.

C Sensible reductions in the use of fossil fuels will help prevent global warming.

2 Greenhouse gases

A They are the main cause of global warming and rich countries need to take the lead in action to reduce the emissions of carbon dioxide and other harmful gases.

B Action to reduce harmful gases will damage industry and employment in both the developed and developing worlds. We need to be careful that we do not endanger the world economy.

C It is not enough for rich countries to reduce pollution – the poor countries also need targets to reduce harmful gases.

3 Industrial pollution

A Industries that cause a lot of pollution are being moved to poor countries to escape from tough environmental laws at home.

B There is no evidence that multinationals are damaging the environment by relocating to poor countries – to behave badly would harm their reputations.

C The world needs one standard for industries to protect the environment wherever they are located.

4 Deforestation

A It is essential to stop the rainforests being destroyed in order to preserve species and to prevent global warming.

B Countries with rainforest have a right to cut them down for farmland and to attract trade and investment.

C We need to balance reductions in the rainforest with the planting of trees in other parts of the world.

5 Green technology

A We need to switch urgently to renewable sources of energy such as solar, wind and water power.

B Alternative energy sources are inefficient and need a massive investment of money – nuclear power and fossil fuels provide the best available options.

C We need to find cheap ways of transferring new technologies to poorer countries so that they can reduce pollution and produce energy at a lower cost.

Scoring

Score +10 for every statement **A** you agreed with.
Score −10 for every statement **B** you agreed with.
Score +5 for every statement **C** you agreed with.

+25 to +50	You are very concerned about the environment and the future of the planet. You are a Green.
+10 to +24	You are concerned about the planet, but are realistic about what can be achieved. You also think that the world economy and economic growth for rich and poor countries is important.
+10 to −10	You are probably a bit confused or have not made up your mind one way or the other.
−10 to −50	You are not a Green. Trade, growth and development are much more important for you. You think that the concerns of the environmentalists have been exaggerated.

Migrants and refugees

Poverty, wars, disasters and oppression can all lead people to leave the countries where they were born to find safety and security in another country. People have moved around the world for hundreds of years. Many people have left the UK to live in places such as South Africa, Australia, Canada and the USA – seeing a better life there with more opportunities for their children. When people leave their homeland to find a better life elsewhere, they are called 'economic migrants'.

Migrants arriving in the USA at the beginning of the twentieth century.

When people are forced to leave their country, they are called refugees. The United Nations High Commission on Refugees (UNHCR) has defined refugees as '*people who flee their country because of a well-founded fear of persecution for reasons of race, religion, nationality, political opinion, or membership of a particular social group. A refugee either cannot return home or is afraid to do so.*'

Refugees are often fleeing civil war. The wars may be caused by disagreements between different ethnic groups. The groups may be racist towards each other and there may have been attempts at genocide – the killing of a whole ethnic group.

The two case studies on page 215 describe some recent ethnic conflicts, which have forced people to flee and become refugees.

Activity

Some things encourage people to leave their homeland, and some things make them want to go somewhere else. These reasons for migrating are called 'push' factors, (say, persecution), or 'pull' factors (say, better jobs).

In two columns make a list of as many 'push' and 'pull' factors as you can.

Activity

1 Read the two case studies and the statements by the refugees on page 215.
2 Write a short magazine article or a wall display entitled 'Why there are refugees'. Use quotes and photos. You could carry out further research on the topic using the internet.
3 Contact a refugee organisation to invite a refugee speaker to come and talk to your class. You could add what you learn from the speaker to your article or display.
4 Look at the information on human rights on page 16. Which of these rights are refugees seeking?

Case study 1: *Yugoslavia*

Yugoslavia, created in 1918, contained people of different ethnic groups: Serbs, Croats, Slovenes, Bosnians, Montenegrins, Albanians, Hungarians and Macedonians. They all had different cultures, histories and religions. After 1945, under Communist control, Yugoslavia was formed into six separate republics, each of which contained a majority of one ethnic group although there were also fairly large minorities of other groups.

After the collapse of Communism in 1989, Yugoslavia began to disintegrate. Some areas declared themselves independent. Slovenia and Croatia were recognised by the rest of the world as independent countries. Serbia, the strongest of the republics, under Slobodan Milosevic, tried to seize large parts of other republics, particularly Bosnia and Kosovo. Fighting in all these areas led to terrible crimes during the 1990s as the Serbs attempted literally to wipe out other ethnic groups. In 1999, the stream of refugees became a flood, as 800 000 people fled in terror to the rest of Europe. Serbia withdrew from Kosovo when NATO air strikes hit Serbia. Bitter hostility remains in the region.

A Kosovan man who has had his home destroyed

Nysret, a 45-year-old man from Studime said he had watched as Serb gunmen executed his 35-year-old brother. 'They said absolutely nothing. They just took him from the tractor and shot him in the face with an automatic rifle. When he fell to the ground they shot him again,' he said. He went on to list the names of seven other relatives he had seen killed in the same way that day, before asking that the names not be used to protect other relatives left behind. 'Alongside the road to Vushtri I have seen at least fifty dead bodies . . . If you want a witness to these murders, I would like to be called,' he said.

Case study 2: *Rwanda*

In the African country of Rwanda, there are two different ethnic groups – the Hutus and the Tutsis. In 1959, the majority ethnic group, the Hutus, overthrew the ruling Tutsi king. Over the next few years, thousands of Tutsis were killed, and 150 000 were driven into exile in neighbouring countries. The children of these exiles later formed a rebel group and a civil war began in 1990. In April 1994, the extremist Hutus went on a murderous rampage, killing roughly 800 000 Tutsis and some moderate Hutus.

The Tutsi rebels defeated the Hutu regime and ended the genocide in July 1994, but approximately 2 million Hutu refugees – many fearing Tutsi retribution – fled to the neighbouring countries. Since then most of the refugees have returned. Rwanda continues to struggle to recover and foster reconciliation between the two groups.

Young boys forced to become soldiers

Charlotte Mupfasoni tells her story:

'In the city of Gitarama, they stopped me and while they were hitting me, a young woman came and took pity on me. She didn't know me. When they finished beating me, she took me with her. She was Hutu. When we came across a barrier and they stopped us, she would tell them, 'This is my child'. They would let us continue. When we arrived at the Pentecostal Church of Nyabisindu, I saw that there were many refugees there. But our numbers diminished quickly because they would come regularly to select young boys and young girls to kill. Whenever they came, I put myself next to the Hutu girl and she'd say I was her younger sister.'

Seeking asylum

asy'lum *n*: a sanctuary; a place of safety and refuge

When people flee from persecution in their own country, they try to find safety for themselves and their families in another country. An asylum seeker is a person who has fled his or her own country and is asking for refugee status in another country.

The numerous wars raging today in the world mean that thousands of people are trying to find safety. Although it is difficult to give accurate figures, the United Nations estimates that there are now over 20 million refugees worldwide. The vast majority of these remain in developing countries, near to the countries they have fled from, hoping to return to their homes when the danger is over. People don't want to leave their homes, their possessions, their families, and become refugees. The best way to reduce the number of refugees is for politicians to try to help sort out the wars and conflicts that cause mass migrations.

However, until all conflicts can be resolved, refugees need to be helped. But how?

No country can allow unlimited numbers of people to enter. There has to be a way of deciding who is genuinely in danger of human rights abuses if they return home. The problem for democratic governments is that they have many individual cases to deal with, and this takes time.

Activity

1 What problems do asylum seekers face who have just entered the UK?
2 Read the article opposite on proposals for asylum centres. Write down the arguments for and against the building of these centres.
3 Find an article on asylum seekers in a newspaper or on the internet. What view does the article take on asylum seekers? Do you agree with it or not?

The UK government says

'The United Kingdom has a proud tradition of providing a safe haven for genuine refugees. The UK government is determined to ensure that genuine refugees are properly protected and that there is no incentive for people who wish to migrate for other reasons to misuse asylum procedures.

'The government is committed to delivering a fairer, faster and firmer immigration and asylum system . . .'

The main features of the UK asylum system are as follows:

- All claims for asylum receive a fair hearing
- All claimants have the responsibility to:
  - tell the truth about their circumstances
  - obey the law
  - keep in regular contact with the authorities
  - leave the country if their claim is ultimately rejected
- Support is provided to asylum seekers who are destitute
- Accommodation is provided on a 'no choice' basis
- Asylum seekers can appeal if their applications are refused
- Those recognised as refugees will be granted immediate settlement in the UK and helped to build a new life.

The government is setting up special centres for asylum seekers because it is easier to:

- deal with applications more quickly
- supply services such as health and education
- stop asylum seekers absconding and disappearing.

Asylum centre plans spark protests

Campaigners oppose Home Office choice of remote rural locations

Thousands of asylum seekers are to be housed at eight centres throughout rural parts of Britain – thus doubling the population of some areas.

Plans to create 'asylum villages' in the countryside, part of Home Office moves to reform the asylum system, have provoked outrage among local residents, rural campaigners and asylum groups, who believe that the centres would be more suited to urban locations.

In Worcestershire, local council officials believe a self-contained centre for 750 people will be built between a landfill site for refuse and a burial site for more than 100 000 animals destroyed during the foot-and-mouth crisis. The site, more than 10 miles from the nearest town, is owned by the Ministry of Defence and is used for testing laser technology.

Government plans seen by the *Observer* show that the European-style accommodation centres will include shops, catering, sports facilities and a playground around a village green. Interpreting, legal and educational services will be provided on site, and asylum seekers will be free to come and go.

At a packed meeting on Friday at the nearby village of Bishampton (population 500), Mid-Worcestershire MP Peter Luff told villagers he welcomed the proposals for the accommodation centres in principle, but added: 'I have a deep philosophical objection to siting these centres in remote rural locations. We've been dumped on enough around here.'

Others in the area said they had concerns about the law and order implications of the new asylum centre. The local postmaster and owner of Bishampton's general store, said: 'If 70 blokes from the centre came walking down the street, I'd want to shut up shop. I can't afford to lose £10 worth of stock, let alone more.'

Another local man said he was concerned that a single police constable patrolled the four villages surrounding the site: 'These people will be young, poor and dispossessed. If they were to turn to crime, or if they were to gang up, what do we have to protect us?'

Asylum charities last night joined in condemning the plans: 'Placing people in such isolated rural communities is at odds with the Government's policy of integration and inclusion,' said a spokeswoman for Refugee Action.

Nick Hardwick, chief executive of the Refugee Council, said: 'The experience of similar centres on the continent which are away from urban centres and where everything is provided on site is that the asylum-seekers become very isolated and institutionalised and those who are allowed to stay have huge problems integrating.'

From the *Observer*, 10 February 2002

A day in the life . . .

Refugees at the centres will be free to come and go, but food and other benefits will be dependent on their returning to the centre every night.

Residents will be split into male, female, mixed and family blocks.

9–10 a.m.: Breakfast (all meals provided full-board at the centre)

11 a.m.: English classes and careers advice

Lessons for children of school age

1–2 p.m.: Lunch

2–5 p.m.: Legal advice and medical check-ups. Lessons for children of school age.

Sporting activities and workshops for adults

6–7 p.m.: Evening meal followed by roll call

7.00 p.m.–midnight: Free time

7.5 World organisations

The Commonwealth

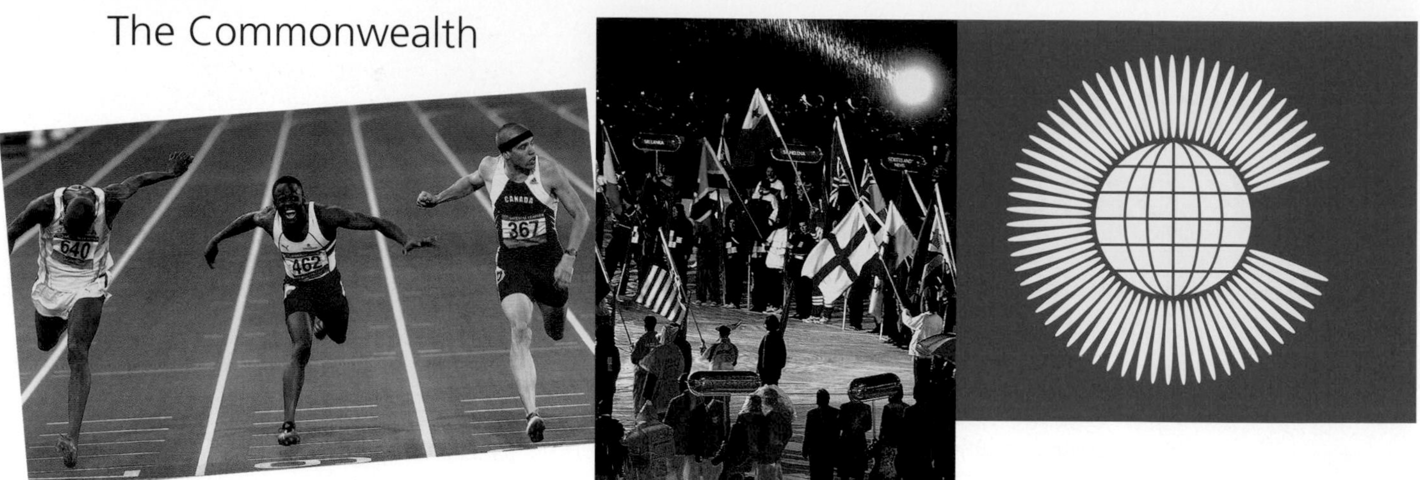

In the summer of 2002, the Commonwealth Games were held in Manchester. The games are often referred to as the 'friendly games' because of the goodwill between the athletes and countries taking part. The Commonwealth Games are held every four years.

What is the Commonwealth?

- It is a voluntary organisation of 54 states representing 1.7 billion people.
- It is a multiracial association of equal, sovereign states.
- The king or queen of the UK is head of the Commonwealth.
- The Commonwealth heads of government meet every two years to make decisions about issues such as trade, democratic progress and requests for help.
- It is guided by the Harare Declaration of 1991 that set out the main principles of the Commonwealth, which is committed to:
  - human rights and equality, opposing all forms of racial oppression
  - the rule of law
  - the right to participate by means of free and democratic political processes.

Discuss

1 What is the value of the Commonwealth Games for the athletes and countries that participate?

2 What do you think are the advantages of belonging to the Commonwealth?

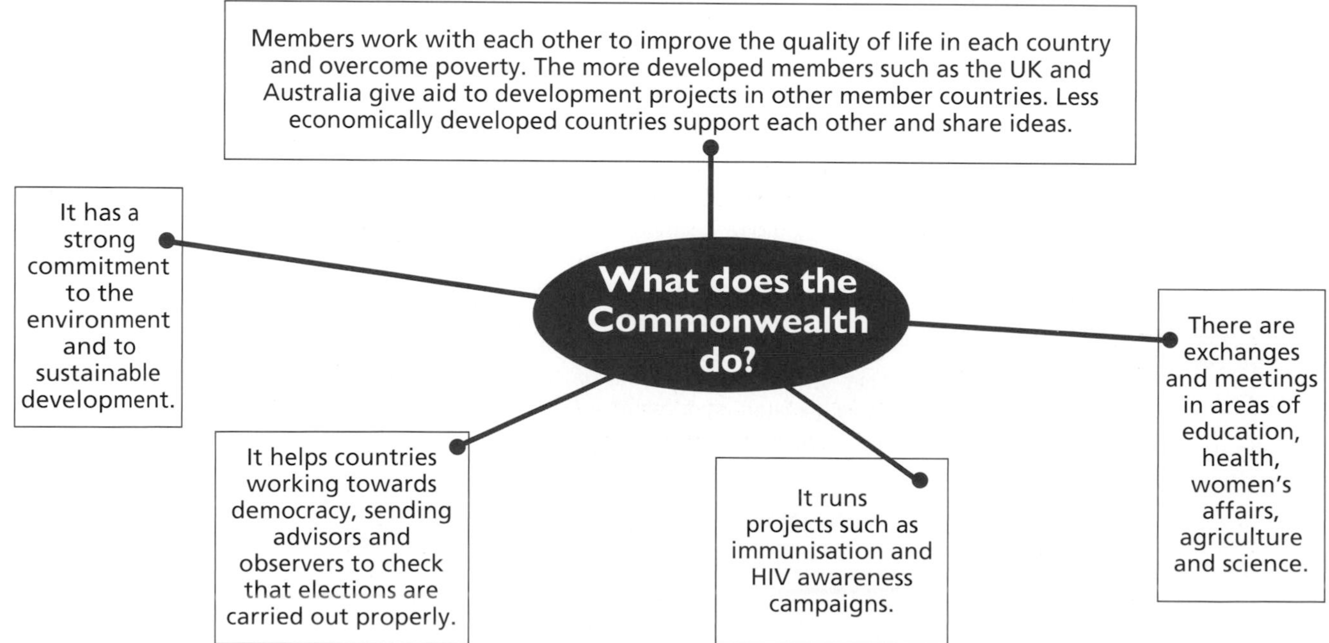

Members work with each other to improve the quality of life in each country and overcome poverty. The more developed members such as the UK and Australia give aid to development projects in other member countries. Less economically developed countries support each other and share ideas.
It has a strong commitment to the environment and to sustainable development.
What does the Commonwealth do?
There are exchanges and meetings in areas of education, health, women's affairs, agriculture and science.
It helps countries working towards democracy, sending advisors and observers to check that elections are carried out properly.
It runs projects such as immunisation and HIV awareness campaigns.

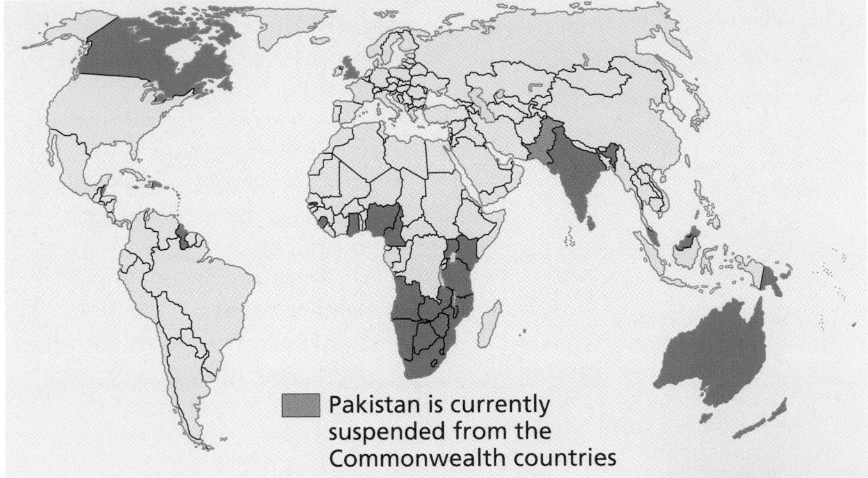
Pakistan is currently suspended from the Commonwealth countries

Issues

The Commonwealth (countries shown in blue, above) is committed to promoting democracy and good government. When a military government took over in Nigeria in 1995, Nigeria was suspended from the Commonwealth for four years. Pakistan was also suspended in 1999.

In 2002, Zimbabwe posed a major problem. The President, Robert Mugabe, was accused of:

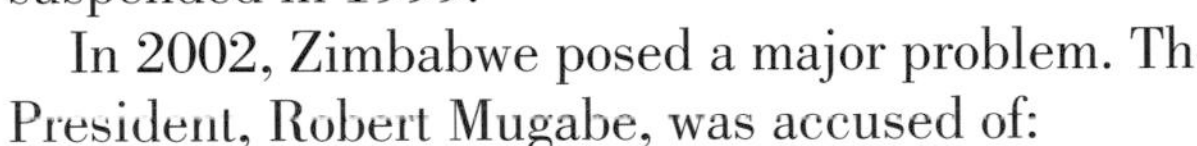

- creating an atmosphere of violence in his country leading up to elections
- not providing enough polling booths and closing them early even though queues of people were waiting to vote
- passing a law controlling the media
- arresting opposition politicians
- encouraging black Zimbabweans to seize the land of white farmers who owned most of the land in the country.

This was a difficult issue for the Commonwealth because it raised its colonial past. It was mainly white countries, particularly Britain, the old colonial master, that were objecting to Mugabe's regime. But many black African leaders thought that the Commonwealth should not interfere in the internal affairs of an African state. There seemed to be a white/black divide in the Commonwealth organisation.

In March 2002, the Commonwealth suspended Zimbabwe because of the violence and intimidation that accompanied the re-election of Mugabe as president. But the Commonwealth's action was largely symbolic and had little real impact on Mugabe's government. The suspension was renewed in March 2003 although some African leaders wanted Zimbabwe to be readmitted.

Discuss

Why do you think that countries that used to be controlled by the UK want to be part of the Commonwealth with the Queen as its head?

Origins

In the nineteenth century Britain had a huge empire stretching right around the world. Britain controlled a large number of 'colonies'. In these, English became the official language and British systems of law, public administration and education were imported.

During the twentieth century, particularly after the Second World War, Britain's former colonies gained their independence. Sometimes this was the result of a long and bitter struggle with the British, but often it was achieved through a process of negotiation and agreement. Many of the countries felt they could benefit from forming an association in which they would support each other and, in particular, help the development of smaller countries. Also, they shared a language and similar systems of law and education.

Activity

Decide which of these two statements you agree with and give two reasons for your choice.

1

The Commonwealth is outdated and ineffective. On issues that really count, such as defending democracy, it has little influence and is reluctant to take action.

2

The Commonwealth promotes friendship and goodwill, and does some useful work.

How effective is the United Nations?

You would think that the way to solve the world's problems is through a world organisation which co-ordinates the actions of countries of the world and prevents wars between them. The world has such an organisation – the United Nations (UN). But the problems persist. So how effective is the UN?

Aims of the UN

- to prevent wars wherever possible
- to develop friendly relations between countries
- to solve problems, such as refugees, by international co-operation
- to promote respect for human rights
- to achieve freedoms for all whatever their race, sex, language or religion

How the United Nations works

General Assembly
All member states send representatives to the General Assembly. It meets at intervals to discuss world issues. Each country has one vote. A majority of two-thirds is needed for important decisions or to pass a UN resolution. But the UN can only make recommendations – its decisions are not binding on members. The Assembly has little real power.

The Security Council
This consists of five powerful permanent member countries – the USA, Russia, China, Britain and France – and ten other countries who join it for shorter periods. It is really the Security Council that makes key decisions, for instance, when the UN is to get involved in peacekeeping operations. Each permanent member has a 'veto' on important decisions. This means that they all have to agree.

Secretary General
The Secretary General is the figurehead and spokesperson of the United Nations, who heads the administration of the UN, called the Secretariat.

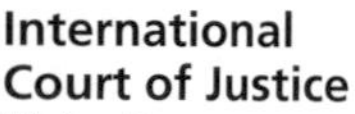

International Court of Justice
This sits at The Hague in the Netherlands. It settles legal disputes between countries. It also runs the War Crimes Commission which has recently put Slobodan Milosovic on trial for war crimes in Bosnia.

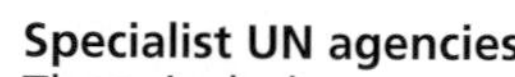

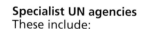

Specialist UN agencies
These include:

- the World Health Organisation (WHO) which tries to improve the health of people in all countries and fight diseases by vaccination programmes
- the United Nations High Commission for Refugees (UNHCR) which leads and co-ordinates international action to safeguard the rights and well-being of refugees
- the International Labour Organisation (ILO) which works to improve the rights of workers around the world and improve their conditions
- UNAIDS which supports the 33 million currently infected with the HIV virus (see page 206)
- the United Nations Children's Fund (UNICEF).

How did it begin?

The United Nations was set up in 1945 in San Francisco at the end of the Second World War when 51 nations signed the UN Charter (its rules). The horrors of the war and the problems it created made the leaders of the world realise that there had to be a better way of settling arguments between countries. In 1948 the United Nations approved the Universal Declaration of Human Rights, which you can see on pages 224–25. This was written against the backdrop of the suffering caused by the Holocaust, the millions dead and the millions made homeless by the war. In 2002 the UN had 189 member countries.

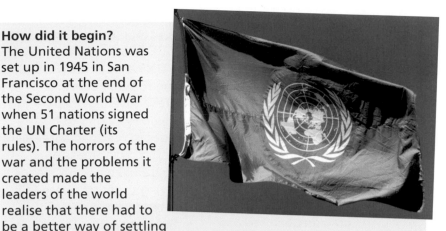

Activity

1 Draw a spider diagram to show the different organisations of the UN.
2 Use the internet to find out about the work of one of the UN agencies, such as UNICEF in the case study below. Present a short paper on it to your class.

Case study: *UNICEF*

UNICEF, the United Nations Children's Fund, was created in 1946 to provide food, clothing, health care and school supplies for children in Europe after the Second World War. It was thought it would last for only a couple of years but over 50 years later UNICEF is the largest organisation working for children worldwide. UNICEF works with governments to ensure that the most needy children are immunised, have health care, have clean water and nutritious food and go to school. UNICEF helps families with children in times of conflict or disaster, keeping families together and making 'child friendly' spaces for children in refugee camps.

UNICEF helps countries reach the standards for children's lives laid down in the United Nations Conventions on the Rights of the Child. Every country except two – Somalia and the USA – has agreed to meet these standards, which state that children have a right to survive, develop, be protected and to participate in decision-making on important aspects of their lives. These rights belong to all children under eighteen years whatever their race, culture or religion. UNICEF gets the money it needs to pay for its work from governments, businesses and individual people who make donations.

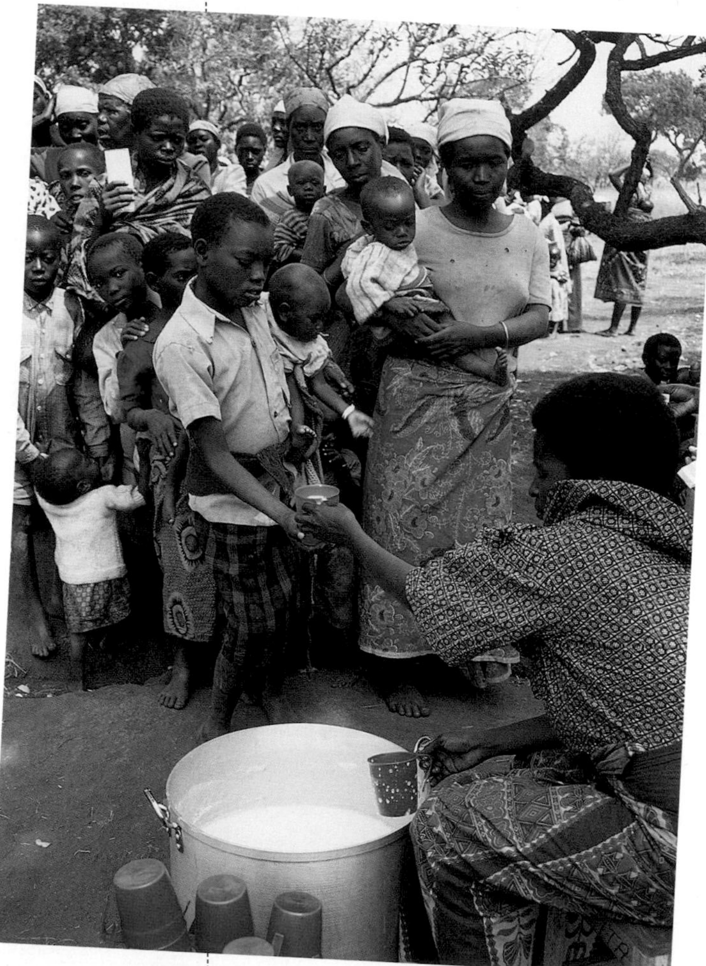

International peacekeeping

Since the end of the Second World War, there have been over 200 wars in the world. We tend to think of wars as armed conflict between countries, but many of the wars have been within a country, that is civil wars. The United Nations has an important role in peacekeeping. The Security Council must agree all peacekeeping operations. Since 1948 there have been over 54 peacekeeping operations, 41 in the last twelve years. Although UN peacekeeping cost about $2.6 billion in 2000, governments spent $750 billion on arms. The costs of peacekeeping are small relative to the costs of the death and destruction caused by wars.

Activity

The UN has four main ways of trying to bring peace:

- Preventive diplomacy – this involves talking to both sides to reach an agreement before war breaks out
- Peacemaking – this means trying to set up peace talks after a war has begun
- Peacekeeping – the use of soldiers, police and civilians to maintain peace
- Peacebuilding – taking action to put democracy and rules in place so that war in the future is less likely.

Look at the photographs. Decide which way of bringing peace and security the UN is using in each case.

1 UN inspectors check the destruction of chemical weapons in Iraq

2 British soldier on patrol in Croatia, 1992

3 Kofi Annan holds talks with Pakistani representatives, over Afghanistan, 2001

4 UN observation post in Macedonia, 1994

5 UN staff explain voting procedures in Namibia, 1999

6 UN Security Council meets to discuss the situation in Iraq, 2003

The UN in action

The United Nations has fought wars to stop invasions in the Korean War (1950–55) and the Gulf War (1990–91). It has also played a useful role in arranging ceasefires when two countries are ready to end a war, for example in the Iran–Iraq War in 1988.

But the UN has had great difficulty in trying to make peace when two countries or groups within a country are determined to fight each other. It has failed to stop the Arab–Israeli conflict although it has passed resolutions requiring the Israelis to withdraw from the Arab land they have settled on and to stop their occupation of Palestinian territory. The Israelis have simply ignored the UN.

The UN found the civil wars in the former Yugoslavia very hard to deal with in the 1990s. In the Bosnian conflict it sent in troops to divide the Bosnian Serbs and Muslims. But the troops proved ineffective because they were not instructed to fight or take tough action. The Serbs carried on with their policy of 'ethnic cleansing', killing Muslim men and raping Muslim women. In Srebrenica a Dutch peacekeeping force had to stand by, allowing the Serbs to massacre thousands of Muslims. Later in the conflict, in Kosovo, the Americans and British bombed Belgrade (the Serbian capital) to force the Serb army out of Kosovo, then UN forces moved in to separate and protect Serbs and Albanians living there. Many people were unhappy that civilians had been killed in the bombing but supporters of tough action pointed to how the Serbs had ignored and abused UN forces in Bosnia.

Activity

Look at the statements below and the other material in this section.

1. What do you think are the main strengths and weaknesses of the UN? Make two lists.
2. List the UN's achievements throughout the world.
3. Divide the class in half and debate the motion: 'This house believes the UN has outlived its usefulness and has become irrelevant.'
4. What do you think could be done to make the UN stronger and more effective?

Strengths and weaknesses of the UN

A The UN is the only organisation in the world that has the moral authority to speak for the world. It can condemn the worst atrocities and bring lots of countries together because of the values it represents.

B The UN does valuable work in its agencies but that could be done by other non-governmental organisations like the big charities.

C The UN does not have its own money and cannot borrow money from banks. It depends on member countries who sometimes won't pay up.

D The permanent members of the Security Council have the right of veto. So one of these can prevent the UN from taking action. And it is often very difficult to get them to agree.

E The UN does tremendous work all over the world and has saved millions of lives. It is because it is the UN that it gets a lot of support and is not seen to be taking sides.

F The UN has failed in its main aim to keep peace. If countries want to ignore it, they do.

G The UN has no army. It relies on governments to supply troops for peacekeeping operations. Sometimes they are unwilling to do this and sometimes the soldiers have not been properly trained.

On December 10, 1948, the General Assembly of the United Nations adopted and proclaimed the Universal Declaration of Human Rights, the full text of which appears on this wallchart. Following this historic act the Assembly called upon all Member countries to publicise the text of the Declaration and "to cause it to be disseminated, displayed, read and expounded principally in schools and other educational institutions, without distinction based on the political status of countries or territories."

UNIVERSAL DECLARATION OF HUMAN RIGHTS

The world is a very different place than it was in 1948, but the words of the Declaration still ring true. Let us in the 21st century restate our commitment, as individuals, communities and governments, to the principles by which we would like our world to be shaped in the future.

The CO-OPERATIVE BANK

UNIVERSAL DECLA

THE UNIVERSAL DECLARATION OF HUMAN RIGHTS AS A COMMON STANDARD OF ACHIEV
THIS DECLARATION CONSTANTLY IN MIND, SHALL STRIVE BY TEACHING AND EDUCATION T
TO SECURE THEIR UNIVERSAL AND EFFECTIVE RECOGNITION AND OBSERVANCE, BOTH AM

ALL HUMAN BEINGS ARE BORN FREE AND EQUAL IN DIGNITY AND RIGHTS. THEY ARE ENDOWED WITH REASON AND CONSCIENCE AND SHOULD ACT TOWARDS ONE ANOTHER IN A SPIRIT OF BROTHERHOOD. ARTICLE 1

ARTICLE 2

Everyone is entitled to all the rights and freedoms set forth in this Declaration, without distinction of any kind, such as race, colour, sex, language, religion, political or other opinion, national or social origin, property, birth or other status.
Furthermore, no distinction shall be made on the basis of the political, jurisdictional or international status of the country or territory to which a person belongs, whether it be independent, trust, non-self-governing or under any other limitation of sovereignty.

EVERYO
RIGHT
LIBER
SECU
OF PERS

ARTICLE 7 ALL ARE EQUAL BEFORE THE LAW AND ARE ENTITLED WITHOUT ANY DISCRIMINATION TO EQUAL PROTECTION OF THE LAW. ALL ARE ENTITLED TO EQUAL PROTECTION AGAINST ANY DISCRIMINATION IN VIOLATION OF THIS DECLARATION AND AGAINST ANY INCITEMENT TO SUCH DISCRIMINATION.

Article 8

Everyone has the right to an effective remedy by the competent national tribunals for acts violating the fundamental rights granted them by the constitution or by law.

Article 9
No one shall be subjected t
detention or

preamble

whereas recognition of the inherent dignity and of the equal and inalienable rights of all members of the human family is the foundation of freedom, justice and peace in the world. *whereas* disregard and contempt for human rights have resulted in barbarous acts which have outraged the conscience of humankind, and the advent of a world in which human beings shall enjoy freedom of speech and belief and freedom from fear and want has been proclaimed as the highest aspiration of the common people. *whereas* it is essential, if human beings are not to be compelled to have recourse, as a last resort, to rebellion against tyranny and oppression, that human rights should be protected by the rule of law. *whereas* it is essential to promote the development of friendly relations between nations. *whereas* the peoples of the United Nations have in the Charter reaffirmed their faith in fundamental human rights, in the dignity and worth of the human person and in the equal rights of men and women and have determined to promote social progress and better standards of life in larger freedom. *whereas* Member States have pledged themselves to achieve, in co-operation with the United Nations, the promotion of universal respect for an observance of human rights and fundamental freedoms. *whereas* a common understanding of these rights and freedoms is of the greatest importance for the full realization of this pledge.

This poster is published by the New Internationalist magazine which provides a unique perspective on issues of world development, social justice and the environment. Each month the magazine focuses on a different theme, such as Democracy or Fair Trade, Cuba or Climate Change.
Visit our website on http://www.newint.org/ ISBN 1-869847-54-7

For subscription rates and information please ring: Aotearoa/New Zealand +64 33 656 153, Australia and PNG (08) 8232 1563, Canada (905) 946-0407, United States (800) 661 8700, UK/Rest of World (0044) or (0) 1858 438896

For further information on The Co-operative Bank products and services call 0800 90 50 90 or contact our website on http://www.co-op.co.uk

References to man have been changed to include women.

Article 13.

1. Everyone has the right to *freedom of movement* and residence within the borders of each state.

2. Everyone has the *right to leave any country,* including their own, and to return to their country.

ARTICLE 14

1 *Everyone has the right to seek and enjoy in other countries asylum from persecution.*

2 This right may not be invoked in the case of prosecutions genuinely arising from non-political crimes or from acts contrary to the purposes and principles of the United Nations.

2. NO ONE SHALL
DEPRIVED OF THE
NOR DENIED T
CHANGE THEIR

Article 19

Everyone has the right to freedom of opinions and expression; this right includes freedom to hold opinions without interference and to seek, receive and impart information and ideas through any media and regardless of frontiers.

Article 20

(1) Everyone has the right to freedom of peaceful assembly and association.

(2) No one may be compelled to belong to an association.

ARTICLE

(1) EVERYONE HAS TH
PART IN THE GOVERN
COUNTRY, DIRECTLY OR
CHOSEN REPRE
(2) EVERYONE HAS
EQUAL ACCESS TO P
THEIR COU

(3) THE WILL OF THE PE
BASIS OF THE AUTHORI
THIS WILL SHALL BE EXP
AND GENUINE ELECTI
BE UNIVERSAL AND
AND SHALL BE HELD BY
EQUIVALENT FREE VOT

Article 25. (1) Everyone has the right to a standard of living adequate for the health and well-being of themselves and their family, including food, clothing, housing and medical care and necessary social services, and the right to security in the event of unemployment, sickness, disability, widowhood, old age or other lack of livelihood in circumstances beyond their control. (2) Motherhood and childhood are entitled to special care and assistance. All children, whether born in or out of wedlock, shall enjoy the same social protection.

ARTICLE 26.

(1) Everyone has the right to education. Education shall be free, at least in the elementary and fundamental stages. Elementary education shall be compulsory. Technical and professional education shall be made generally available and higher education shall be equally accessible to all on the basis of merit.

(2) Education shall be directed to the full development of the human personality and to the strengthening of respect for human rights and fundamental freedoms. It shall promote understanding, tolerance and friendship among all nations, racial or religious groups, and shall further the activities of the United Nations for the maintenance of peace.

(3) Parents have a prior right to choose the kind of education that shall be given to their children.

Article 27.

**(1) Everyone has the righ
in the cultural life of the
the arts and to share in s
and its benefits.
(2) Everyone has the righ
of the moral and materia
from any scientific, liter
production of which they**

TION OF HUMAN RIGHTS

NERAL ASSEMBLY *proclaims*

L PEOPLES AND ALL NATIONS, TO THE END THAT EVERY INDIVIDUAL AND EVERY ORGAN OF SOCIETY, KEEPING
SPECT FOR THESE RIGHTS AND FREEDOMS AND BY PROGRESSIVE MEASURES, NATIONAL AND INTERNATIONAL,
LES OF MEMBER STATES THEMSELVES AND AMONG THE PEOPLES OF TERRITORIES UNDER THEIR JURISDICTION.

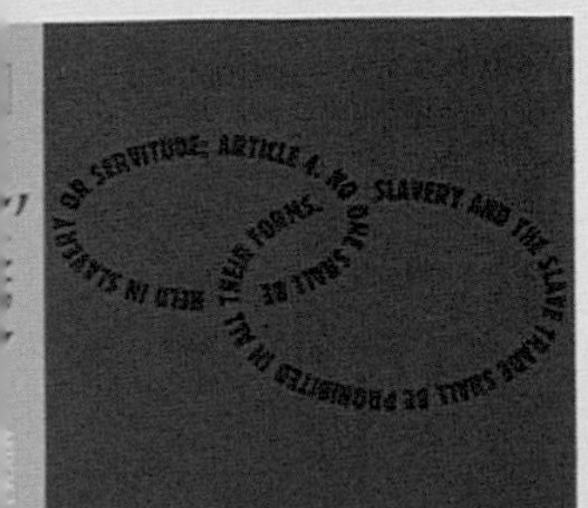

ARTICLE 4. NO ONE SHALL BE HELD IN SLAVERY OR SERVITUDE; SLAVERY AND THE SLAVE TRADE SHALL BE PROHIBITED IN ALL THEIR FORMS.

Article 5.
No one shall be subjected to torture or to cruel, inhuman or degrading treatment or punishment.

ARTICLE 6
Everyone has the right to recognition everywhere as a person before the law.

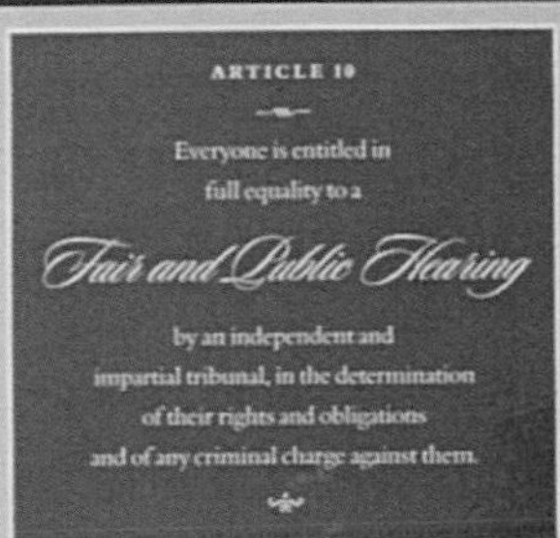

ARTICLE 10

ARTICLE ELEVEN (1) Everyone charged with a penal offence has the right to be presumed innocent until proved guilty according to the law in a public trial at which they have had all the guarantees necessary for their defence. (2) No one shall be held guilty of any penal offence on account of any act or omission which did not constitute a penal offence, under national or international law, at a time when it was committed. Nor shall a heavier penalty be imposed than the one that was applicable at the time the penal offence was committed

ARTICLE 12.
NO ONE SHALL BE SUBJECTED TO ARBITRARY INTERFERENCE WITH THEIR PRIVACY FAMILY HOME OR CORRESPONDENCE NOR TO ATTACKS UPON THEIR HONOUR AND REPUTATION
EVERYONE HAS THE RIGHT TO THE PROTECTION OF THE LAW AGAINST SUCH INTERFERENCE OR ATTACKS.

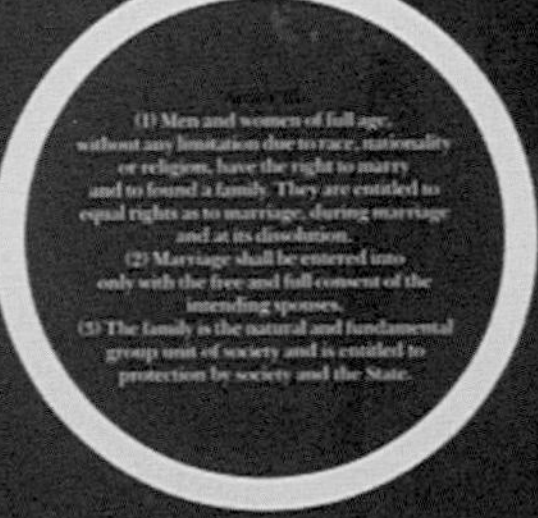

(1) Men and women of full age, without any limitation due to race, nationality or religion, have the right to marry and to found a family. They are entitled to equal rights as to marriage, during marriage and at its dissolution.
(2) Marriage shall be entered into only with the free and full consent of the intending spouses.
(3) The family is the natural and fundamental group unit of society and is entitled to protection by society and the State.

ARTICLE 17. (1) EVERYONE HAS THE RIGHT TO OWN PROPERTY ALONE AS WELL AS IN ASSOCIATION WITH OTHERS. (2) NO ONE SHALL BE ARBITRARILY DEPRIVED OF THEIR PROPERTY.

EVERYONE HAS THE RIGHT TO FREEDOM OF THOUGHT, CONSCIENCE AND RELIGION; THIS RIGHT INCLUDES FREEDOM TO CHANGE THEIR RELIGION OR BELIEF AND FREEDOM, EITHER ALONE OR IN COMMUNITY WITH OTHERS AND IN PUBLIC OR IN PRIVATE, TO MANIFEST THEIR RELIGION OR BELIEF IN TEACHING, PRACTICE, WORSHIP AND OBSERVANCE.

ARTICLE 22.
EVERYONE, AS A MEMBER OF SOCIETY, HAS THE RIGHT TO SOCIAL SECURITY AND IS ENTITLED TO REALIZATION, THROUGH NATIONAL EFFORT AND INTERNATIONAL CO-OPERATION AND IN ACCORDANCE WITH THE ORGANIZATION AND RESOURCES OF EACH STATE, OF THE ECONOMIC, SOCIAL AND CULTURAL RIGHTS INDISPENSABLE FOR THEIR DIGNITY AND THE FREE DEVELOPMENT OF THEIR PERSONALITY.

Article 23
(1) Everyone has the right to work, to free choice of employment, to just and favourable conditions of work and to protection against unemployment.
(2) Everyone, without any discrimination, has the right to equal pay for equal work.
(3) Everyone who works has the right to just and favourable remuneration ensuring for themselves and their family an existence worthy of human dignity, and supplemented, if necessary, by other means of social protection.
(4) Everyone has the right to form and to join trade unions for the protection of their interests.

ARTICLE 24. EVERYONE HAS THE RIGHT TO REST AND LEISURE, INCLUDING REASONABLE LIMITATION OF WORKING HOURS AND PERIODIC HOLIDAYS WITH PAY.

ARTICLE 28. EVERYONE IS ENTITLED TO A SOCIAL AND INTERNATIONAL ORDER IN WHICH THE RIGHTS AND FREEDOMS SET FORTH IN THIS DECLARATION CAN BE FULLY REALIZED.

Article 29. (1) Everyone has duties to the community in which alone the free and full development of their personality is possible.
(2) In the exercise of their rights and freedoms, everyone shall be subject to such limitations as are determined by law solely for the purpose of securing due recognition and respect for the rights and freedoms of others and of meeting the just requirements of morality, public order and the general welfare in a democratic society.
(3) These rights and freedoms may in no case be exercised contrary to the purposes and principles of the United Nations.

ARTICLE 30
Nothing in this Declaration may be interpreted as implying for any State, group or person any right to engage in any activity or to perform any act aimed at the destruction of any of the rights and freedoms set forth herein.

Key words

appeals the process by which decisions and judgments made by courts can be reviewed, especially if new evidence is available

Cabinet a group of MPs who are the heads of major government departments. They meet regularly, usually once a week, with the Prime Minister to discuss government policy and make decisions about how it will be carried out

censorship banning or changing information or material in newspapers, books, films, TV programmes, photographs, etc., to prevent its being seen by the public

citizenship (1) the legal status attached to being regarded as a citizen of a country, which carries certain rights and duties; (2) the rights, responsibilities and obligations that people have in their local community and country, and in respect of those living in other countries

civil law covers disputes between people and is often about rights, such as consumer rights, issues about marriage and divorce, accidents at work, contracts

community (1) a group of people who live in a particular geographical locality; (2) a group whose members share common interests and values

consumer rights the legal rights consumers have to seek redress if the goods and services they purchase are not up to standard

credit (1) the financial standing of a person, how much money and wealth they have; (2) the amount of money you can borrow through credit cards and loans

criminal law covers actions that are regarded as crimes against the whole society, such as theft, murder, speeding and damage to property

democracy a system of government where people regularly elect their leaders and have a say in the way a country is governed

devolution passing authority and some decision-making from central to regional government

the economy all the organisations that provide goods and services and all the individuals and organisations that buy them

electoral system the system by which people vote to choose the people who govern them, for example, the first-past-the-post system used in most local and national elections in the UK

employment rights the rights that workers have by law to protect them in the workplace

fair trade giving producers in the developing world a fair price for their goods

freedom of information allowing the public to get access to information about their own lives, such as medical records, and to the working of local and government bodies

freedom of the press the ability of the press to write and broadcast what they like

human rights rights that are held to belong to any person. The United Nations Universal Declaration of Human Rights, 1948, sets out a full list of the rights that all people should have. These include the right to life, liberty, education, freedom of movement and equality before the law

identity who somebody is; the view people have of themselves which often includes the group(s) to which they belong, such as an ethnic or religious group

image the way a person or a country, a place or an event is represented, for example, by a picture, a diagram or a description

inequality where wealth is not fairly distributed between countries or within countries; some countries and some people have much more than others

interdependence the way countries depend on each other, through trade, for their survival and economic well-being

low pay wages which are considerably below those of other workers

market the place where goods and services are bought and sold

media the newspapers, TV, films, radio, books and magazines, advertising, the internet – ways of communicating with large numbers of people

misinformation giving wrong information or misleading people

monarchy a system of government in which a king or queen plays an important part in running a country

National Minimum Wage the minimum amount of money that an employer can pay workers. In October 2003 it was fixed at £4.50 per hour

naturalisation the legal process a person has to go through to become a citizen of a country

neighbourhood the area in which a group of people live in close contact

Parliament the place where MPs meet to discuss important issues, make laws, and question the government about the way it is running the country

political party an organised group of people who share a particular set of values, views and objectives and who put people forward to stand in elections

pressure group an organisation which has strong opinions on a particular issue and attempts to influence the people who make decisions

price the amount charged for a product

prisons secure buildings where convicted criminals are deprived of their freedom and kept away from the public

proportional representation an electoral system in which the number of seats a party gets is in proportion to the number of votes it receives

regeneration the renewal of an area which usually involves new buildings, the renovation of old buildings, new shops and businesses

republic a system of government where the people or their elected representatives hold power rather than a monarch. Usually, the head of state is called the president

sentencing punishment given to a person who has been found guilty in court

sustainable development development which meets the needs of people today without damaging the ability of future generations to meet their needs

trade union an organisation that looks after and protects its members, and provides them with a range of services

voluntary organisations groups of people who work together to promote a cause, raise awareness of a specific issue, raise money, and/or support people in the local community or overseas

volunteering giving up time to work locally or internationally, usually for the benefit of others

workfare a scheme designed to make people who have been unemployed for some time work on government-approved projects or risk losing their benefits

world debt the money owed by poorer countries in the developing world to richer countries

Index

V

W

Y

Z

Acknowledgements

The authors are particularly grateful to Oona King for allowing us to use her experiences as an MP in Section 4.

Photographs and logos reproduced by kind permission of:
Cover ImageState/Michael Denora; **p.1** Collections/Michael George; **p.2** John Townson/Creation; **p.3** *t* Impact Photos/Peter Arkell, *b* Popperfoto; **p.4** School Councils UK; **p.7** *t* Rex Features, *c* Image State, *b* Camera Press; **p.8** Image State/Pictor; **p.9** John Townson/Creation; **p.10** Popperfoto; **p.15** Per Bang-Jensen/Loung Ung; **p.18** *t* PA News Photos, *l* and *r* Topham Picturepoint; **p.19** *t* London Features International Ltd, *b* Kobal Collection; **p.22** *all* John Townson/Creation; **p.26** Topham Picturepoint; **p.29** Popperfoto; **pp.30–31** Topham Picturepoint; **p.32** Lincolnshire Police (www.lincs.police.uk); **p.33** Topham Picturepoint; **p.50** PA News Photos; **p.54** Topham Picturepoint; **p.57** *t* BBC, *c* Topham Picturepoint, *b* Life File; **p.60** Popperfoto; **p.62** *both* © The Celebration Company; **p.63** *b* Mark Pearson, North News & Pictures; **p.66–67** *both* Changemakers Foundation Ltd.; **p.83** © Lancashire County Council; **p.85** PA News Photos; **p.86** Kobal Collection; **p.94** *l* Topham Picturepoint *r* and **pp.95–96** *all* Oona King, MP; **p.98** *tl* Topham Picturepoint, *others* © Scottish National Party, © Scottish Conservative and Unionist Party, © Democratic Unionist Party, © Social Democratic and Labour Party, © Plaid Cymru, © Scottish Liberal Democrats, help given by the Liberal Democrat Party, © Labour Party, © Ulster Unionist Party, © Conservative Party, © Green Party of England and Wales, © UK Independence Party, © ProLife Alliance, © Third Way 1990, PO Box 1243, London SW7 3PB. All rights reserved, Monster Raving Loony Party/with thanks to Alan Howling Lord Hope and Cat Mandu; **p.102** PA News Photos; **p.106** © Telegraph Group Limited (2002); **p.108** *br* Topham Picturepoint *others* ® RSPCA, © National Union of Teachers, © Campaign for Nuclear Disarmament, © Nacro, © British Medical Association, © NSPCC, © Amnesty International Publications, 1 Easton Street, London WC1X 0DW, United Kingdom http://www.amnesty.org, © Help the Aged, © Road Haulage Association Ltd; **p.109** *t* Impact Photos/Peter Arkell, *c* Popperfoto, *b* Rex Features; **p.110** Popperfoto; **p.112** RSPCA/RTL Photo library; **p.113** Topham Picturepoint; **p.118** Robert Harding Picture Library; **p.120** *t* and *cr* Popperfoto, *br* Topham Picturepoint, *bl* PA News Photos; **p.121** *tl* and *tr* PA News Photos, *cl* BBC, *cr* by kind permission of The Queen's Awards Office, *ca* and *cb* John Townson/Creation, *bra* and *bl* Topham Picturepoint, *br* Katz/Frank Spooner Pictures; **p.122** Robert Harding Picture Library; **pp.127–28** John Townson/Creation; **p.129** Panos/Veronica Garbutt; **p.130** John Townson/ Creation; **p.133** Robert Harding Picture Library/Andy Williams; **p.134** Sally & Richard Greenhill; **p.147** *tl* Photos For Books, *tr* A1 Pix, *b* Robert Harding Picture Library; **p.148** *tl* Collections/Sophia Skyers, *tr* Popperfoto, *b* Collections/Penny Tweedie; **p.149** *tl* Collections/Brian Shuel, *tr* Topham Picturepoint, *b* Collections/Penny Tweedie; **p.150** Topham Picturepoint; **p.156** Jeff Moore (jeff@jmal.co.uk); **p.158** Photos For Books; **p.159** PA News Photos; **p.162** *t* Topham Picturepoint, *c* Panos Pictures/Chris Stowers, *br* Popperfoto; **p.163** *tl* Impact Photos/Mohamed Ansar, *bl* Link/Greg English, *r* John Townson/Creation; **p.164** *t* Advertising Archive, *c* Gucci Group, *b* Topham Picturepoint; **p.165** *both* Advertising Archive; **p.169** *l* Topham Picturepoint, *r* John Townson/Creation; **p.177** ©Amnesty International Publications, 1 Easton Street, London WC1X 0DW, United Kingdom http://www.amnesty.org; **p.183** (www.museumofhoaxes.com/photos/wtcphoto.html); **p.185** Popperfoto; **p.186** *l* Popperfoto, *r* Image State; **p.188** *all* John Townson/Creation; **p.189** *t* Topham Picturepoint, *b* Robert Harding Picture Library; **p.190** John Townson/Creation; **p.191** *t* AFP/Feth Belaid, *b* Financial Times/Sarah Murray; **p.192** *t* London Features International Ltd, *c* British Airways, *b* Panos Pictures; **p.193** *all* John Townson/Creation; **p.194** *tr* PA News Photos, *cl* Panos Pictures/Eric Miller, *r* Popperfoto, *b* Panos Pictures; **p.195** *tl* and *tr* Image State, *b* Ricardo Mazalan/Associated Press; **p.196** *tl, bl* and *br* Popperfoto, *tra* Hutchison Library, *trb* Robert Harding Picture Library; **p.197** Panos Pictures/Giséle Wulfsohn; **p.198** www.waronwant.org; **p.199** *t* reproduced with the permission of Save the Children, www.savethechildren.org.uk, *b* reproduced with the permission of Oxfam GB, 274 Banbury Road, Oxford, OX2 7DZ, www.oxfam.org.uk; **p.200** reproduced with permission of Christian Aid; **p.203** Popperfoto; **p.204** © James Astill/*Guardian* Newspaper; **p.205** Panos Pictures; **p.210** *t* Bruce Coleman Collection, *b* Popperfoto; **p.212** Popperfoto; **p.214** Peter Newark's Pictures; **p.215** *t* Panos Pictures, *b* Hutchison Library; **p.218** *l* and *c* PA News Photos; **p.219** Topham Picturepoint; **p.221** *t* Topham Picturepoint, *b* Robert Harding Picture Library; **p.222** *t, cl, cr* and *bl* UN Photo Unit Department of Public Information, Room S-805-0, UN, New York, NY 10017 Fax: 212 963 1658 (www.un.org/depts/dpko/photos), *c* and *br* Popperfoto; **pp.224–25** *New Internationalist*.

t = top, *b* = bottom, *l* = left, *r* = right, *a* = above

Text extracts reproduced by kind permission of:
p.14 NINETEEN EIGHTY FOUR by George Orwell (Copyright © George Orwell, 1949) by permission of Bill Hamilton as the Literary Executor of the Estate of the Late Sonia Brownell Orwell and Secker & Warburg Ltd.; **p.15** © Andy Brouwer; **p.17** *Woman Loses Right to Die*, © *The Independent*, 29 November, 2001; *Christian Schools Ask for Right to Hit Pupils*, Tania Branigan, © *Guardian*, 3 November, 2001; *Cox to Sue Sunday People*, Jessica Hodgson, © *Guardian*, 29 October, 2001; **p.19** © Commission for Racial Equality; *Social Trends 2002, Office for National Statistics*, Crown Copyright material is reproduced under Class Licence Number C02P000060 with the permission of the Controller of HMSO; **p.26** Extract from *BBC News Online bbc.co.uk/news reproduced by permission of the BBC*; **p.28** *Police Research Series*, Crown Copyright material is reproduced under Class Licence Number C02P000060 with the permission of the Controller of HMSO; **p.29** *Home Office*, Crown Copyright material is reproduced under Class Licence Number C02P000060 with the permission of the Controller of HMSO; **p.31** Extract from *BBC News Online bbc.co.uk/news reproduced by permission of the BBC*; **p.32** © Lincolnshire Police; **p.46** *Justice in the Round*, © Rosemary Hartill. Originally appeared in the *Guardian* 9 May, 2001; **p.50** *One Woman's Experience Inside Prison*, Steven Morris, © *Guardian*, 27 November, 2001; **p.51** *Inside*, John Hoskisson, John Murray (Publishers) Limited (1998); **p.52** *British Crime Survey (2000)* Crown Copyright material is reproduced under Class Licence Number C02P000060 with the permission of the Controller of HMSO; **p.53** *British Crime Survey (2001)* Crown Copyright material is reproduced under Class Licence Number C02P000060 with the permission of the Controller of HMSO; **p.60** *Ignorance, Misunderstanding and Fear*, David Ward © *Guardian*, 12 December, 2001; **p.61** *Mean Streets in a Divided Town*, Angelique Chrisafis © *Guardian*, 12 December, 2001; **p.63** *Laager Toffs*, © Chris Arnot. Originally published in the *Guardian* 30 January 2002; **p.67** © Times Educational Supplement, 7 March, 2003; **p.83** © Lancashire County Council; **pp.86–7** *Monty Python and the Holy Grail*, Graham Chapman, John Cleese, Terry Gilliam, Eric Idle, Terry Jones, Michael Palin, © Methuen Publishing Limited (2002); **pp.88–9** John Townson/Creation; **p.106** *Committee on Standards in Public Life*, Crown Copyright material is reproduced under Class Licence Number C02P000060 with the permission of the Controller of HMSO; **p.150** © Times Newspapers Limited, London (2002); **p.151** *In the Red*, © Fran Abrams. Originally published in the *Guardian*, 29 January, 2002; **p.153** From *A Better Way to Work*, TUC, 2000; **p.176** *Tobacco Companies Linked to Criminal Organisations in Cigarette Smuggling* This report was produced by the International Consortium of Investigative Journalists, a project of the Center for Public Integrity in Washington, D.C. All rights reserved; *An Invitation to Launder Money*, © Der Spiegel, November 8, 1999; *A Long Ride on the Thunderbolt*, © The Age, March 13 1999; *The State of the President's Finances*, Philippine Center of Investigative Journalism, July 23, 2000; **p.177** *West African Human Rights Defenders Under Attack. Togo: imprisonment and ill-treatment of an independent journalist*, 3 August 2001, AI INDEX: AFR 57/013/2001.©Amnesty International Publications, 1 Easton Street, London WC1X 0DW, United Kingdom http://www.amnesty.org; **p.192** © British Airways; **p.193** © Fairtrade; **p.204** *Living with Malaria*, James Astill, © *Guardian*, 22 August, 2002; **p.205** Sibongile's story, Interviewed by Bongi Zengele-Nzimande Co-ordinator for Job Creation Project of the Worker Ministry (13/10/2001) © CAFOD; **p.207** © WaterAid; **p.215** Charlotte Mupfasoni text reproduced with the permission of UNICEF; **p.216** *Home Office* Crown Copyright material is reproduced under Class Licence Number C02P000060 with the permission of the Controller of HMSO; **p.217** *Asylum Centre Plans Spark Protest*, Martin Bright and Paul Harris, *The Observer*, 10 February, 2002.

Every effort has been made to contact copyright holders, but if any have been inadvertently overlooked the publishers will be pleased to make the necessary arrangements at the earliest opportunity.